GAIA ALCHEMY

"Few things are more important today than bringing humane values to the science, technology, and information sectors. It requires a person of vision and imagination. I have known Stephan Harding for many years and have seen firsthand how his genius and big heart help science evolve to the next level. This latest book, *Gaia Alchemy,* is a beautiful blueprint for transforming contemporary knowledge and returning soul to our planet."

THOMAS MOORE, AUTHOR OF #1 NEW YORK TIMES BESTSELLER
CARE OF THE SOUL AND *SOUL THERAPY*

"In this time of global crises and evolutionary opportunities, it's vital that we reclaim our innate human ability to learn *from* our animate Earth using our feeling senses, our imaginations, and our dreams. Western science, in contrast, has specialized in learning *about* our world, using logic, quantification, and the illusion of separation. Harding shows us how to alchemically unite and integrate these two modes of knowing and why it's both necessary and rapturous, and he does so with brilliance, imagination, humor, grace, and, above all, heart. *Gaia Alchemy* is a world-shifting masterwork, an essential read for all twenty-first-century lovers and defenders of life."

BILL PLOTKIN, PH.D.,
FOUNDER OF ANIMAS VALLEY INSTITUTE AND
AUTHOR OF *SOULCRAFT, WILD MIND,* AND
THE JOURNEY OF SOUL INITIATION

"Harding shows how Western empirical science, which is at the root of so much material progress but also the cause of blatant destruction, can find its way back into the heart of subjective living experience. *Gaia Alchemy* points to a new union of calculating and intuiting mind, of measuring and of contemplating beauty, and does so from a firm foundation in Western culture, not by borrowing from Asian or Indigenous cosmologies. Profound, erudite, timely, and immensely necessary, *Gaia Alchemy* builds a bridge between the head and the heart. A landmark work for the Anthropocene."

ANDREAS WEBER, PH.D., PHILOSOPHER, BIOLOGIST,
AND AUTHOR OF *THE BIOLOGY OF WONDER,*
ENLIVENMENT, AND *SHARING LIFE*

"Desperate for a way beyond the reductive mindset of contemporary science, a keenly creative biologist excavates the medieval 'Great Work' of alchemy, the immediate precursor of modern science. This book is a record of Harding's deeply personal quest to bring alchemy's esoteric insights to bear on the catastrophic situation in which our planet now finds itself.

DAVID ABRAM, PH.D., AUTHOR OF
THE SPELL OF THE SENSUOUS AND *BECOMING ANIMAL*

"A brave book that offers a profound celebration of the marriage between science and soul, showing convincingly that there is no conflict between reason and intuition; in fact, they are good companions. A close collaborator of James Lovelock, who proposed Gaia theory, Stephan has been able to develop an original and authentic understanding of relationships between science and psyche. In this compelling book, rooted in rigorous science and poetic imagination, Stephan outlines a new paradigm for a holistic worldview. Read this book and it will inspire you to look at the world and see it whole."

SATISH KUMAR, COFOUNDER OF SCHUMACHER COLLEGE AND
EDITOR EMERITUS OF *RESURGENCE AND ECOLOGIST*

"A remarkable and lively synthesis of leading-edge science and the deep wisdom of the archetypal psyche. Harding's bold and engaging vision works its own alchemical transformation on the reader, guiding us from the lead of the dominant mechanistic and disenchanted worldview to the gold of an experiential understanding of Gaia as the ensouled body in which we live and have our being. This book will prove invaluable to those seeking a more integral approach to Earth System Science, to the psychologically minded who long for deeper connections with the living Earth, and to all who are called to participate in the Great Work of our times."

SEAN KELLY, PH.D., AUTHOR OF
BECOMING GAIA AND *COMING HOME*

"In this bold and extraordinary book Stephan Harding, an eminent ecologist, makes a surprising defense of alchemy as a tool with which to reconnect with the more-than-human world. Pursue the path of alchemy, he says, and we can restore ourselves to ourselves, and, even more importantly, to Gaia, the living soul of the planet. By offering exercises that anyone can try for themselves, Stephan opens doorways so that everyone can experience Gaian consciousness firsthand. At a time when so many are looking to Indigenous cultures for the answers to our ever-mounting ecological ills, it is refreshing to find someone offering homegrown tools, techniques, and methods that stem from the intellectual roots of Western culture. All the tools we need are to be found in the alembic of the unconscious, in the union of opposites between the scientific rational domain of logos and the deep waters of mythos. I can think of no better guide to steer us through this much-needed process."

ANDY LETCHER, PH.D., SENIOR LECTURER
AT SCHUMACHER COLLEGE, PROGRAM LEAD FOR
THE M.A. IN ENGAGED ECOLOGY, AND AUTHOR OF *SHROOM*

"*Gaia Alchemy* arises like a phoenix out of the ashes of our terribly precise but ultimately life-denying sciences of reduction, abstraction, and objectification. Harding's storied and deeply personal account of his imaginal journey into Gaia alchemy is a timely invitation to each of us to cultivate ways of *knowing* and *being* adequate to the great Planet-Being with whom we live."

JONATHAN M. CODE, M.ED., LECTURER IN SUSTAINABLE LAND
MANAGEMENT AT ROYAL AGRICULTURAL UNIVERSITY

"Stephan Harding's teaching is always illuminating. In *Gaia Alchemy,* he shows how, through the relationship between science, alchemy, and depth psychology, we can reach toward an experience of nondual Gaian soul in our lives."

PETER REASON, PH.D., PROFESSOR EMERITUS
AT THE UNIVERSITY OF BATH

"Stephan Harding tells an enthralling new story of Gaia, one where we begin with Gaia rather than ourselves. His unique union of science, myth, and alchemy—invoking both our rational and intuitive ways of thinking and exploring how they may and must come together—brings us into a new vision of a Gaia consciousness. A brilliant book."

JULES CASHFORD, JUNGIAN ANALYST AND
COAUTHOR OF *THE MYTH OF THE GODDESS*

"With the emergence of a Gaian science that restores mind to Earth, we have a new lens through which to divine alchemical meaning in geo-ecological processes. This is the dazzling new vista for the healing of both Earth and ourselves that *Gaia Alchemy* opens up."

FREYA MATHEWS, ADJUNCT PROFESSOR OF
ENVIRONMENTAL PHILOSOPHY AT LA TROBE UNIVERSITY
AND AUTHOR OF *REINHABITING REALITY*

GAIA
ALCHEMY

The Reuniting of Science, Psyche, and Soul

STEPHAN HARDING, PH.D.

Bear & Company
Rochester, Vermont

Bear & Company
One Park Street
Rochester, Vermont 05767
www.BearandCompanyBooks.com

Text stock is SFI certified

Bear & Company is a division of Inner Traditions International

Cataloging-in-Publication Data for this title is available from the Library of Congress

ISBN 978-1-59143-425-2 (print)
ISBN 978-1-59143-426-9 (ebook)

Printed and bound in the United States by Lake Book Manfacturing, Inc.
The text stock is SFI certified. The Sustainable Forestry Initiative® program
promotes sustainable forest management.

10 9 8 7 6 5 4 3 2 1

Text design and layout by Debbie Glogover
This book was typeset in Garamond Premier Pro with Fnord, Futura, Legacy Sans,
and Optima used as display typefaces

To send correspondence to the author of this book, mail a first-class letter to the
author c/o Inner Traditions • Bear & Company, One Park Street, Rochester, VT
05767, and we will forward the communication.

For Julian David, wise elder of Luscombe,
great mentor, and friend.

And for Stephen Harrod Buhner, who so ably
shows the way into deep Gaia connection.

Contents

⚮

Foreword

Stephen Harrod Buhner

Science has made us immensely clever but has not made us wise.

STEPHAN HARDING

I first met Stephan Harding in 2013 when I was invited to teach for a week at Schumacher College in the U.K. at the Dartington Trust Estate. It was to prove a seminal moment for me in my own work and life. At nearly the same time I also met David Abram, who has often taught at Schumacher and is a good friend of Stephan Harding. It was the first time that I had met contemporaries who had spent most of their life, as I have done, focused on developing the capacity for holistic perception and reasoning and then using those capacities to understand Earth from a very different orientation than that of reductive science.

Interestingly, while each of us had begun from significantly different starting points, we'd found our way to an identical destination. Our insights from decades of personal and scientific work were differentiated by that starting location—that is, our descriptions of the territory through which we had traveled were unique—but I found that we were now talking about an identical process of perception and orientation as well as a very similar experience of Earth as a living organism. Thus while David Abram would say, *"You are, therefore I am"* and I would say, *"I feel therefore I am,"* Stephan would (more wordily) say, *"I discover who I am in those moments when my feelings, thoughts, sensings, and intuitions embed me within the rich tapestry of Gaia's living body."* In other words, our identities come from feeling, sensing, and experiencing the existence of living, sentient beings outside ourselves. It is in relationship to the world that we are.

David has his Ph.D. in philosophy while also having extensive training as a magician. Stephan has a degree in zoology from the University of Durham and a later doctorate on the behavioral ecology of the muntjac deer from Oxford. And I? I have avoided advanced degrees like the plague, preferring to become an independent scholar. I have spent most of my time in the transition zone between the village and the wildness of the world. In other words, I'm not generally considered acceptable in polite society. My bachelor's degree is in transcultural epistemology but it was the kind of degree that allowed me to learn from teachers throughout the world, the ones who had created startling innovations in contemporary science and healing and ecology. It didn't happen in a classroom. Hence, my degree is more properly what might be called experiential epistemology, that is the exploration of different states of mind and being and their impacts on sustainable habitation of Earth. Out of that came the construction of a very different way of life and work, one that is incredibly similar to those that David has found and which Stephan has found and talks about in this book.

David has focused much of his work on crafting an intellectual, philosophical structure that could support holistic perceptions of the world as a replacement to the reductive mechanicalism that has been in place the last few centuries. He teaches throughout the world at universities and conferences without having a permanent academic position. Stephan has spent most of his career at Schumacher College teaching students in Schumacher's holistic science master's degree program how to develop holistic perceptions of nature as foundational to a different kind of science.

I, in contrast, spent those same decades teaching outside academic institutions, working primarily with older students who had been touched by the wildness of Earth and wished to deepen an intimate connection with the green world, medicinal plants, and Earth itself. David is a philosopher, Stephan a professor and scientific ecologist, and I am someone far more comfortable in wilderness, barely able to tolerate the academic world or conventional social structures. Because of these differences, it was a wonder to me then that as the three of us talked over our journey through life there was so much similarity to what we had experienced. It was the first time I had ever felt this kind of companionship . . . of intellect, of heart, of purpose. In truth, all three of us served something larger than ourselves, something outside the human: Gaia.

An additional aspect of our common journey was that we had each found that to develop a capacity for holistic perception necessitated a great deal of internal work—both psychological and of the soul. It hasn't always been easy. Stephan is succinct about that when he speaks of his personal struggles in this book. He is moving against the dominant intellectual and philosophical paradigm of the West in which he was trained. In fact, the focus of this book is remaking oneself in order to more fully perceive and interact with the living ecosystems around us. He uses alchemy as a metaphor for that process of personal transformation, hence the title of the book.

This process of personal transformation is crucial to our sustainable habitation of Earth. Nearly all of us in the Western world (and I suspect many in the Eastern) live now in what is essentially a virtual reality. Over the past several centuries, a global civilization has been constructed on top of the ecological world, the movement toward which substantially escalated during the twentieth century. The ecological world is *foundational* to all life here. However, the civilizational structure resting atop it is now so comprehensive that many people take it as foundational rather than virtual. It possesses, as all virtual realities do, a series of assumptions that are used to give that civilizational structure form and definition. Regrettably, those assumptions have little to do with the ecological reality upon which the civilizational structure rests. Instead, they are founded upon our constructed beliefs, presuppositions, and untestable hypotheses, which constitute the mental software of this virtual reality. That is where our problem, and danger, lies.

Over time, human behavior, social identities, and material infra-structures have been dissociated from the ecological realities that underlie them. In consequence, as the civilizational structure extracts more and more ecological capital (as opposed to ecological interest) from the ecological foundations of the planet, planetary health is failing at greater and greater rates. As it does so, the civilizational structure that rests atop it begins to wobble. And it is wobbling now at ever increasing rates.

Another way of saying all this is that the climate of mind *in here*—inside each of us—gives rise to the climate problems *out there*. To get an experiential sense of the climate of mind that lives inside Western peoples, just visit an ecologically devastated landscape. That is the form it takes in the outer world. The climate of mind always comes first. Then, as it expresses itself through behavior, the outward world becomes its mirror.

What David Abram, Stephan Harding, and I have each done in our own way, is to actively work to understand and then alter the climate of mind *inside ourselves,* the one we had taken on as we were schooled, as we absorbed the mental software that is so pervasive now that most people just absorb it into themselves as they do the air they breathe.

One of the more difficult problems for those of us who wish to alter this climate of mind inside us is that a great deal of our mental software is absorbed very early in life. It inhabits layers of the self far deeper than the rational mind can easily go. In consequence, a great deal of our identity rests upon it. Over time, we come to identify ourselves, our boundaries, the world around us, other people, all life forms, even the planet itself, from assumptions embedded within that mental software. As such, it is very difficult to alter it later on. To do so means that we have to engage, at a very deep level, with the foundational structures of the self *then* change them. This takes a great deal of internal contemplation over a long period of time. It is a bit like performing psychological surgery while still living inside the psychological structure that is being cut away. It's not easy. There are moments of severe self-doubt and times of emotional turmoil. As the process goes deeper, there are periods when all that is felt is a pervasive lack of meaning, in both the interior and exterior worlds. This is most pronounced as the foundational structures of the self are taken apart and laboriously restructured so that a more ecologically congruent and holistic form can take its place.

In other words, because the same type of thinking that got us into this mess is not going to get us out, we have to learn an entirely different kind of thinking. That new way of thinking rests upon different assumptions. It also utilizes a different type of perception. It is a thinking intimately interwoven with the feelings and perceptions of the heart, which utilizes a form of nonphysical touching. This is to say that we feel the touch of the world upon us with something other than our skin. (Like when you go into a restaurant with a friend and turn to each other to say, "This place feels weird. Let's leave.") It emerges out of the heart's ability to feel the touch of meaning upon it.

As the heart is rekindled as an integral element of being, we learn to *care* as a habit of living. A primary truth of life is that we tend to be far less careless with things when our heart cares for them. Far more comes from this: a new kind of science emerges as well. As George Washington Carver once put it, "Anything will give up its secrets if you love it enough."

The transformational process, that is, the journey from one paradigm to another, takes years, as Stephan's book makes clear. The reworking of the self takes time. Unexamined beliefs are discovered and examined, discarded if useless or inaccurate to the real world, then replaced with others more conducive to a whole life and a whole self. What you find in my work, in David Abram's, and Stephan Harding's is that process of learning to think, perceive, and live from a different paradigm, a different way of being. From it comes a very different kind of science and a very different kind of rationality.

As Stephan comments, "Every one of us, scientists included, has a psyche that takes part in the wider psyche of nature." He notes that walking away from our isolation, giving up the paradigm where we are merely a mind inhabiting a ball of resources hurtling around the sun and instead choosing to walk deeper into that psyche brings us something important, an experience of meaning that mere intellectualism can never provide. "We find ourselves wonderfully embedded in the life of our planet more and more often in sacred moments of sheer wonder at the miracle of it all."

You can sense here the difficulty involved with this kind of shift in science. It is in direct opposition to the requirement to remain unfeelingly objective, to stand apart as if the scientist is not also embedded within the world they are studying. In that scientific world, they are trained to give up the sacred, as well as the sense of wonder with which we are all born, as guides to their work of understanding the world. Stephan is instead insisting on giving up a dissociated rationality and taking a very different path. And while there are more and more scientists moving toward this different path, there are millions more who are not. In fact, there are massively large and powerful institutions (and a great deal of money) whose existence rests upon dissociated rationality. To take the path that Stephan takes in this book, to speak so plainly in this particular metaphor, and to share his personal struggles and thoughts is very brave.

He begins simply, as anyone exploring a new landscape must do. He walks carefully, actively working to find stable ground upon which he can set his feet. He starts in the most important place of all: reclaiming of the feeling self. "Go outside," he urges, and as you walk, let yourself notice "if a particular locale sparks even the slightest glimmer of gladness in you." It is at this point that the entire structure of personal identity begins to change. What an idea! To walk through the world paying attention to the emergence of gladness in the self at the touch of the green world, then turning to that touch, and finding out what it has to teach you. Such a different kind of science.

As the process continues, it becomes a way of life, encouraging the gladness of the world to emerge within the self. The touch of the outward brings parts of the self, and heart, alive in ways they perhaps have not been for decades. Moving from that new feeling-imbued state into the old dissociated mental state and back again makes plain the impact on the heart and self of that older paradigm. Sooner or later, it forces a decision about just what kind of life is to be lived. As Stephan says, after a while he "abandoned the strict scientific materialism instilled into me by my education once I became aware of its alienating effects."

Stephan goes into some depth on how that form of science and thinking became dominant in the West. It's important that he does so. Those of us who struggle to move from one type of being to another must, to one extent or another, *think* through the subtle dynamics of the old form while constructing the new one that is coming into being. It's crucial to replace the intellectual foundations of both self-identity and world-identity by a system that is more accurate to the ecological world. It forces a reckoning with our intellectual history. We have to think it through, and as we do we have to *feel* the impact of the differences in the new way of being when compared to the old. This is because we are not just *thinking* our way, we are *feeling* our way to a different way of being. Thus, what is constructed becomes far more sophisticated than what it replaces, for it has within it room for the full range of the human, not merely a shorn-off intellect. As Stephan shares, there are truths about the world and self that can only be found by the scientist who feels, who has reclaimed the entirety of their humanity. Of necessity, such scientists train the whole human self to interact with the outward world while at the same time sitting as a student at its feet, allowing Earth itself to teach them of its mystery.

This is the crucial shift that our times are demanding of us. Our civilization now stands upon the edge of an ecological cliff, and it is the dissection of the natural world and the subsequent manipulation of the parts by a reductive science and technology that has brought us there.

As Stephan says:

We've got to bring soul into science. We need to retell [the] scientific account of the rainbow as story, step by step. Everything you know about the rainbow from science must be there, including the maths, all as soul, all as story. Then we merge the two as an alchemical coniunctio. This is a modern coniunctio, which it is our challenge to create, to give birth to right here in our own times.

Coniunctio is an ancient alchemical term, which means "to blend two substances, which often appear to be antithetical to each other, into one unified whole." That whole then possesses the attributes of each, but the union of the two balances out the weaknesses that each possesses alone. The whole that comes into being also possesses capacities that only emerge at the moment they join together, capacities that neither possesses by itself. The whole is far more than the sum of the parts. Stephan works in two realms simultaneously, the inner and the outer. That union necessitates the blending of two ways of being in order that the outer world can be accurately seen and understood. Thus, for the union to occur, an alchemical transformation in both the inner and outer worlds must take place—or perhaps more accurately, the joining of the two is, by its nature, an alchemical process. A very simplistic way of putting it is that it turns lead into gold. More properly, the process of unification takes that which is inferior by itself and refines it into something far more precious.

In a rather remarkable line Stephan says this:

> Gaia alchemy heals the Cartesian split **by making matter and psyche intensely aware of each other** as an unbroken wholeness in the *unus mundus*. . . . As fact and image meld within us, an integrated style of consciousness is born—an epiphany happens that combines our deeply buried Indigenous soulful outlook with a modern mentality informed and shaped by the stunning discoveries of the contemporary sciences of the Earth. [emphasis mine]

What a beautiful line that is: "making matter and psyche intensely aware of each other." It is here he makes plain that there is something surrounding us other than the human, something with which we can make contact, with which we can interact. There is, in fact, intelligence in matter. At this point, the departure from reductive materialism becomes complete and a "deeply ecological style of consciousness" emerges. Out of this consciousness, as James Lovelock (with whom Harding has worked in the past) comments, came the concept of Gaia in a single intuitive flash.

There are many jewels in this book, some of them quite wonderful to the eye, heart, and mind. I will leave you with this one:

A deep knowing then dawned on me that Gaia, too, has been going through her particular alchemical transformations during her four-and-a-half-billion year evolutionary journey. I sensed that Gaia's next and perhaps most important transformation can happen only with the participation of those of us human beings who realize the meaning of our belonging to her soils, to her waters, to her biosphere, to her mountains and atmosphere, to her soul and her spirit. I know now beyond doubt that we are fully alive to Gaia and each other when we engage in the planetary task of healing this aged, richly cultured, widely intelligent, wildly creative creaturely planet of ours to fulfill her own mysterious transformations . . . by loving her as deeply and as wisely as we can.

STEPHEN HARROD BUHNER
THE GILA WILDERNESS,
NEW MEXICO

STEPHEN HARROD BUHNER is an interdisciplinary, independent scholar who is a Fellow of Schumacher College and a researcher for the Foundation for Gaian Studies. He is the author of several books including, with Inner Traditions, *The Secret Teachings of Plants* and *Plant Intelligence and the Imaginal Realm*. He is the winner of a Nautilus Book Award and the BBC Environmental Book of the Year Award for *The Lost Language of Plants*. He says, "I am and always have been interested in the invisibles of life, those meanings and communications that touch us from the heart of Earth and let us know that we are surrounded by more intelligence, mystery, and caring than our American culture admits of; how to reinhabit our interbeing with the world; how to sit in the council of all life as kin rather than dominators; and how to live sustainably on this Earth that I love more than I know how to say." Visit his website for more information: stephenharrodbuhner.com.

Acknowledgments

Although writing a book is a solitary task, it cannot be done without the help and encouragement from family, friends, and colleagues. My first thanks go to my wife, Julia, our son, Oscar, and my stepmother, Lucy, for your patience and support during the two years or so it took to complete this work.

I also give thanks to the great teachers of holistic science with whom I've pondered and studied the hidden depths of nature over many years at Schumacher College: James Lovelock, Brian Goodwin, Lynn Margulis, Margaret Colquhoun, Craig Holdrege, and Henri Bortoft to mention but a few.

Thank you also to those friends who read and commented on all or parts of the manuscript: Julian David, Jeffrey Kiehl, Jules Cashford, Tuck Tyrrel, Stephen Harrod Buhner, Lorna Howarth, Deirdre Hyde, Oliver Tringham, and my daughter, Victoria Bastiansen.

I give thanks to all the staff and students at Schumacher College who have supported me with such kindness and friendship during this long journey. Thanks also to the students of the first ever course on Gaia alchemy that myself, Bia Tadema, and Luiz Vasconcelos held online, hosted by Escola Schumacher Brazil; the work of our little group of explorers continues.

I would like to thank Adam McLean for his invaluable advice on how to source and reproduce alchemical images. Thank you to Julia for your artwork for figures 2.3, 5.3, 13.7, and 15.2, and Oscar for drawing figure 17.3. Thanks also to Richard Bizley for so generously donating his wonderful paintings for figures 12.3 and 12.4 and also to my great friend Deirdre Hyde for allowing me to use her painting of a Costa Rican mangrove for figure 12.5 and also for creating figure 16.3.

Finally I would like to thank Patricia Rydle, Kayla Toher, and Stuart Sudekum at Bear & Co. for your excellent help and support during my final preparations of the manuscript.

Science Meets Alchemy

Our culture has forgotten, for the most part, to pay attention to dreams. Yet, this book would not have been written had I not listened carefully to a certain dream person. She is venerably old, dressed as a Bulgarian peasant with a long stripy skirt almost covering her green shoes. A light blue top tucked into a golden belt circles her ample waist. In the dream I notice her sitting near me on the deck of a large cruise ship, looking out to sea. Nearby, young men jump into the ship's outdoor swimming pool, and there are holidaymakers everywhere. How out of place we both are on this ship. She wants help to walk, and she seems very weak. I offer her my hand. She takes it, and I am amazed by the warmth and gentle strength of her wizened claw.

"You are a scientist," she says, gazing at me with that fierce, almost masculine face of hers. "Just what I need to give me energy and determination." She gathers strength surprisingly quickly as, hand in hand, we walk to where she needs to go.

There is a small but growing band of scientists who have broken through the taboo that forbids us from listening to psyche. There are those of us trained in science who take dreams, symbols, and alchemical images seriously, who work with them consciously. I am one of those, so perhaps that's why, as I hold out my hand to Old Woman,* there is a sense of a new world being born between us, a world of greater Gaian

---

*Inner figures from the unconscious are referred to without a preceding article in Jungian psychology, myths, and stories.

consciousness in which we humans, each one of us in our own way, feels more comfortable in our skin and learns to live in peace and harmony within the vast lustrous biosphere of this ancient planet of ours.

Working with psyche has taught me that it is wise to pay attention to important dreams a little more than to the dictates of logic and reason. Alchemical images come from the part of psyche that sends us our dreams, and so I give these images great credit too when it comes to cultivating a deeper sense of life's meaning. It takes courage and trust to walk this path. If we do so with care and diligence, we find ourselves wonderfully embedded in the life of our planet. A person who does this will experience sacred moments of sheer wonder at the miracle of it all more and more often. The images—dream and alchemical—want to help us heal ourselves and our Earth.

The next day I meet her again.

"I need you to write that book you have been thinking about. I will help you. Your book will help me feel strong and that will help the world."

"I've been thinking of calling it *Gaia Alchemy*," I tell her.

"That's good. I like that," she says. "It makes science and alchemy mutually acceptable to each other." She encourages me to start work right away. I know it would be foolish to refuse the advice of someone from so deep in the psyche.*

Old Woman represents that part of me, that part of our culture, which has lost a living connection with the *anima mundi* of the ancient Greeks, the soul of nature—the soul of the world.

Old Woman is herself the anima mundi. She is Gaia. How strange that Old Woman needs science to make her well again, that she can't survive without the vital energy science can give her. Perhaps to be whole in itself the deep ancient psyche where Old Woman resides needs to assimilate our modern scientific understandings of our slowly spinning, evolving Earth.

---

*You will notice that I use both "the psyche" and "psyche." When I write "the psyche" I refer to a mostly analytical frame from which we are inclined to analyze the products of psyche as external observers. When I use "psyche" I refer to the depths of psyche that we directly perceive with our heart and intuition in a profoundly participatory way.

Science and alchemy: both are ways of knowing that are part of us; part of our brain and body structure; part of our human psyche. Both are needed for our wholeness and our planet's. Every one of us, scientists included, has a psyche that takes part in the much wider psyche of nature, so why not investigate the connections between Gaian science and alchemy? There are delicious fruits here just waiting to be plucked in this marvelous garden of our deeper reality. The litmus test is how much insight we are given into the nature of Gaia—how much we experience our own life richly entangled within her mysterious coevolutionary depths.

I'm going to take you on a journey back to medieval Europe to encounter the discoveries of the best alchemists of those times who searched for the soul of nature in their retorts and alembics. We will also explore some of our recent scientific discoveries about how our planet regulates her surface conditions thanks to feedbacks between all her living beings and her rocks, atmosphere, and waters. We'll be pioneers in discovering a new, contemporary Gaian consciousness by bringing these two aspects of ourselves, science and psyche, together after the tragic 400-year separation inflicted upon us by the scientific revolution. Using story, science, conversation, meditation, craft work, and time spent in nature, we'll discover a new yet also immensely ancient way of living well with Gaia. We'll make moves toward reintegrating ourselves with our living Earth, and we'll experience intimations of our lost wholeness in this huge gigacosmos of swirling galaxies redolent with meaning and purpose.

Let the healing begin.

First Steps

The mystery of life isn't a problem to solve but a reality to experience.

FRANK HERBERT

Modern science demands only half the man not the whole.

C. G. JUNG

I am a scientist—a scientific ecologist to be precise, but just as much drawn to music, art, philosophy, and the psychology of Carl Jung as the scientific ecology in which I was trained. The aim of this book is to meld the ancient wisdom of alchemy with the modern science of Gaia theory.

Gaia theory is a scientific understanding of the Earth as a great planetary organism, as a self-regulating complex system; alchemy is the ancient art of personal transformation and nature connection. My quest has been to discover whether we can experience a Gaia that is more vibrant, full of meaning, and alive by alchemizing science, thereby re-ensouling science and our culture and thus freeing both from their analytical dryness.

I approached this quest by investigating what happens to our ecological awareness when we bring the science of Gaia deep into the realm of alchemical image and vice versa. I have found that uniting these opposites can help us develop a style of consciousness in which we experience

4

ourselves as integral and responsible members of our planet's vast swirling living body. I have found for myself that this union of science and alchemy leads us toward what I refer to as "Gaian consciousness" by deflecting our psychological life away from too much rationality and by plunging us into the deeply living qualities of nature, which we perceive with our feeling, sensing, and intuition. It seems to me and many others that without this kind of "Gaian consciousness" within each of us, it seems unlikely that our complex technological society will survive for very much longer.

If you like the sound of what I am proposing here with Gaia alchemy, then may treasures be revealed for you in these pages. If not, then may the great beauty, inner light, and meaning of nature find you, heal you, and bless you upon some other golden pathway into your own unique wisdom. The alchemical quest is a completely individual one, a process entirely of our own that for me is a calling just as strong as that of being a zoologist and ecologist. If you feel similar callings, then perhaps this book could help you as my Gaian alchemical quest has helped me far beyond what I could have imagined when I began to tread this path.

I'll tell you of my own highly individual journey toward what I sense as my own Philosopher's Stone, which is to say my own hermaphroditic amalgam of Gaian science and alchemy. You won't find a great amount of abstract theory here. Instead, I will mostly present my own personal experience with Gaia alchemy, which I hope will trigger readers to find their own pathway into falling in love with our planet's rocks, atmosphere, living beings, and waters.

I did my first degree in zoology at Durham University and then, with the Animal Ecology Research Group at Oxford University, did my doctoral research on the behavioral ecology of the muntjac deer in southern England. After that I taught conservation biology and ecology at the National University in Costa Rica for nearly three years before spending three months exploring Buddhism while helping out in a Tibetan Buddhist monastery in Nepal. Then I spent another year at Oxford before becoming a founding faculty member at Schumacher College, Dartington, where I had been appointed (in 1990) as the college's resident ecologist. The college is part of the Dartington Hall

Trust in south Devon, founded by Dorothy and Leonard Elmhirst in the 1920s as a rural location for radical experimentation with holistic living and learning inspired by two sages from India: Rabindranath Tagore in the 1920s and Satish Kumar since 1990. I am still on the faculty at Schumacher College and have been teaching and researching here for the last thirty years on the themes of Gaia theory, deep ecology, and holistic science.

Some three months after starting at Schumacher, I met James Ephraim Lovelock, the man who pioneered Gaia theory and who led the very first course at Schumacher College in January 1991. Thus, I first encountered the science of Gaia through its original innovator. I found it astonishing that such a small and (then) wholly unknown college could host such a highly distinguished scientist as its first principal teacher on the theme of Earth as a living organism. Lovelock and I hit it off immediately and thus began many visits to him and his wife, Sandy, in their home-cum-laboratory in the deep countryside of the Devon-Cornwall border during which we would explore Gaia through both science and philosophy. Through these visits, Lovelock and I became firm friends. I grew to know him simply as Jim.

In some way that I could not then fully discern, the image of Gaia held something powerful for which I had been searching during my career as a scientific ecologist: the promise of a deeper sense of wholeness, of a final integration of psyche and matter not just at the quantum level of invisible subatomic particles, atoms, and molecules with which we are vaguely familiar, but also at the ecological level of tangible beings such as rocks, atmosphere, water, and life. Decades later, I sense more and more that the image of Gaia has reappeared in our times to help us heal the tragic split between psyche and matter that is creating our contemporary global crisis. Perhaps we need, dare I say it, an ancient *sacred* global image to heal a contemporary *secular* global crisis.

I became part of a small group of scientists deeply inspired by Jim's visionary, highly original systems-based understanding of our Earth as a vast, self-regulating planetary entity, thanks to the multifarious feedbacks between her living beings and her planet's rocks, atmosphere, and water. We attempted to model this Gaian understanding mathematically on our whirring computers while Jim and I collaborated scientifically for a few years developing ecological extensions to his pioneering Daisyworld model, the first ever mathematical investigation of feedbacks between organisms (in this case, dark and light daisies) and their physical environment: namely, the surface temperature of their planet. Daisyworld has interesting alchemical implications, which we will explore later in the book.

Another most important person for me was the mathematical biologist Brian Goodwin. Brian brought the idea of the M.Sc. in holistic science to Schumacher College, where we taught it together with distinguished guest teachers from its inception in 1998 and thereafter for many years and had students from all over the world. I am deeply indebted to Brian for showing me the immense beauty that emerges from kinds of mathematics that approach the living soul of nature by building in feedback relationships between the actors in any system. I refer here to chaos and complexity theories, in which Brian was a world class expert.

I am also deeply grateful for my friendship with Arne Naess, who taught me so much about deep ecology, both in the classroom and in the mountains.

Another firm friend in Gaia for me was Lynn Margulis, the great American evolutionary biologist who was Jim's earliest collaborator in presenting his Gaia hypothesis to the scientific community. Margulis brought the details of microbial metabolism and ecology into the Gaia hypothesis, showing how bacteria and other microbes greatly modify the waters, rocks, and atmosphere of our planet. She was also a great pioneer and champion of symbiosis rather than of random gene mutation (as in neo-Darwinism) as the great source of innovation in the evolutionary history of our planet. Despite immense opposition, she championed what was once thought improbable but is now accepted as solid science: that mitochondria (those little organelles that produce energy inside cells with nuclei) and chloroplasts (the photosynthetic organelles inside plant and algal cells) are descended from once free living bacteria engulfed by their larger host bacteria thousands of millions of years ago.

Lynn Margulis was the best biology teacher I have ever had. She was brilliantly holistic, deeply dedicated to her science, and immensely passionate about symbiosis as the primary force in the evolution of life. Like Jim, she too taught at Schumacher College with me on several occasions, delighting and informing us with her rich knowledge of the microbial world with which she was so enamored. I am deeply grateful to them both, for thanks to them Gaia continues to blow my socks off. Sometimes I shake with astonishment at the enormous significance of Gaia's reappearance in our culture as a powerful image of the sacred Earth. At other times the science of Gaia amazes me: planet cooling clouds seeded by trees; bacteria in clouds deciding when it rains; tiny marine algae in the surface ocean cooling the planet by seeding clouds and precipitating chalk; fungal tubes linked to roots in the soil transferring food and information among members of the plant community . . . and that's just the start.

Another very important person for me in my quest to write this book on Gaia alchemy is Jeffrey Kiehl. Jeffrey has a Ph.D. in atmospheric science and until recently was head of the Climate Change Research Section in the National Center for Atmospheric Research in Boulder, Colorado. We met online over supervising the master's thesis of one of our students. As well as being a senior climate scientist with many peer-reviewed papers published in several key areas of climate science, Jeffrey is also a highly respected and seasoned Jungian analyst with a strong interest in alchemy. So, as well as being a first-class scientist versed in Gaia theory, ecology, and quantum physics, Jeffrey has deep insights into alchemy's hidden meanings and knows the relevant literature extremely well. As will be discussed shortly, the Jungian ideas that have fascinated Jeffrey also fascinate me and thus feature prominently in this book.

Strangely enough, for some time before we met, Jeffrey had been developing ideas and delivering teaching sessions on what he calls alchemical ecology, which explores very similar terrain to Gaia alchemy by using alchemy to reenvision the science of ecology and the dynamics of ecosystems. It astonished us both to discover that an almost identical inspiration had occurred to each of us independently long before we knew each other. Our sense is that we received these insights from transpersonal realms of psyche, an inspiration that commits us to exploring alchemical ecology and Gaia alchemy together to help wake us up to the wonder and meaning of our living planet and all her beings in this time of crisis.

During our regular online meetings Jeffrey has offered me invaluable orientation and guidance in my search for Gaia alchemy, which I write about here. This book could not have been written without Jeffrey, and I am deeply grateful for his invaluable help and support.

Jeffrey came over to England in the summer of 2019 so that we could deepen our explorations together without needing to interface via a computer. I arranged for him to stay in some wonderful rooms in Jill Goodridge's charming period thatched cottage in the little village of Week just ten minutes' walk westward from our house on the Schumacher College campus at the Old Postern. Jill's wonderfully florescent garden and her little sitting room became our alchemical vessel— our *vas*—in which we devoted ourselves wholeheartedly to healing and transforming our relationship with nature by amalgamating the most up-to-date Gaian, climate, and ecological sciences with alchemical insights handed down to us by our predecessors, those remarkable prescientific alchemical explorers of nature. I digitally recorded these vibrant conversations and will bring you flavors of them at key points in the book.

The common thread between the companions in my quest whom I have introduced to you here is that all of us are scientists who have sensed that our planet is in some way a great self-regulating being, perhaps even alive in the way a living organism is. I am grateful to science for what it has taught us factually about the world, but I have also come to realize that science on its own will not help us make the world a better place, for science develops our thinking to a huge extent but does not deliberately and systematically develop our feelings of love for the whole of nature. The result of this is that we are unable to perceive the immense value and importance of Gaia and all her beings. All this because we scientists have not been educated from early on how to cultivate, refine, and listen to those feelings of love and valuing as part and parcel of our practice of science.

Science has made us immensely clever but has not made us wise. It is wisdom we need now in this time of severe global ecological crisis. We need a new kind of science that values wisdom a little bit more than cleverness. We must become "Gaia-wise" in these very difficult times by putting wisdom and science together. This is what we at Schumacher College call holistic science.

But what is wisdom? A wise person knows how to think, how to value, how to sense, and how to evoke intuitive insights and knows when and how to bring these modalities compassionately to the fore in any given situation. Such a person also pays attention to dreams, knows how to enter deep meditative states, and feels the thrum of living nature in their heart. Obtaining this kind of consciousness may seem almost impossible today. However, by simply intending to do this, somehow it happens more and more.

Wisdom springs from ancient regions of psyche, from our most earthy, down-to-earth feeling for the things and beings around us. Science, quite rightly, seeks new models, new concepts, new ideas, and new experiments. In contrast, wisdom flourishes when we make contact with ways of seeing and understanding that have been with us since the very first glimmerings of human consciousness in humanity's early days of hunting and gathering, when we first wondered at the majesty of the stars and at the immense profusion of living beings around us.

Alchemy is a pathway to wisdom. The great Swiss psychologist Carl Gustav Jung, who I have mentioned as an influence on my fellow Gaian scientist Jeffrey Kiehl, rediscovered how it helps us release the deep nature-connecting powers buried deep in the psyche. Jung is also the founder of depth psychology, the science of the unconscious mind and its relation to our conscious self. As he pointed out, there is no wisdom without the participation of our two-million-year-old Self: the part of us that holds the wisdom and experience of humanity accumulated down the ages (see Stevens 1993).

Alchemy opens up channels into valuing, sensing, intuiting, and thinking that we never knew we had. It makes us more whole, more alive, more earthy. Furthermore, it helps us to realize that thinking is just one of our four major ways of knowing and encourages us to cultivate the poor relation in our personality—the way of knowing we like least and which makes us feel most uncomfortable. Often, for scientists and other thinking types, this "inferior function" (as Jung called it) is feeling. By feeling, I mean our ability to perceive the value of things not with our heads but with our hearts, which are of course connected with love. We need much more of this way of feeling and perceiving the immense of value of nature to help us through these troubled times.

In addition to looking at Jung's ideas, we'll also follow the advice of one of the heirs to Jung's work, James Hillman, by being very careful with language. As Hillman says in his book *Alchemical Psychology,* the ways we speak and write reveal our collective cultural biases, showing us which life-giving forces we fail to actualize and experience in our everyday lives. Without us even noticing it, our Western languages plunge us into a particularly overanalytical bent of mind that leads us to destroy our planetary ecology by turning the world into an "out-there" of dead "things."

This severe one-sidedness is, as Hillman indicates, a cultural neurosis. Hillman's cure for the neurosis of our language is to transform our over-rational way of speaking into an alchemical relationship with the world. We must heal fast before our time runs out as we find ourselves running for cover in the climate emergency, as many already are being forced to do in various parts of the world. Even here in sedate England, many recent unprecedented flooding events have demonstrated the urgency of our situation.

Hillman even detects this analytical cultural bias in depth psychological terms within his own discipline: *anima, unconscious,* and *ego.* We will use these terms as we go about the business of alchemizing the science of Gaia and so must always keep in mind their limitations and their neurotic bias. We will also use seven key terms for describing, remembering, and applying the various alchemical operations. There are: *calcination, dissolution, separation, conjunction, fermentation, distillation,* and *coagulation.** These words can very effectively liberate us from our conceptual neurotic bias the moment we experience them

*Turn to pages 25–26 for a definition of these terms if they are unfamiliar.

happening in our psyche and also simultaneously in nature with the blessing of Imagination. Hillman writes:

> Every alchemical phenomenon is both material and psychological at the same time, else alchemy could not claim to be salvific of both the human soul and material nature. (2014, 15)

This is quite a claim. If the world is indeed one seamless psyche, what happens alchemically within us must somehow also happen in the wider world of ecology and nature. Otherwise, we fall into the split of Cartesian dualism, believing that psyche exists only in us but not in the world itself. If we manage to experience a Gaian alchemical conjunction will the world spring to life so much that a spontaneous feeling arises in us to love and protect our wider body, our animate Earth? If so, then the alchemical process is after all very down to Earth: very practical, very pragmatic, and very much needed.

☙ YOUR GAIA PLACE

> *I only went out for a walk and finally concluded to stay out*
> *till sundown, for going out, I found, was really going in.*
> JOHN MUIR

For Gaia alchemy to do its work it is absolutely essential for you to have a Gaia place of your own, with which you'll become increasingly familiar as you work with this book.

What is a Gaia place and how can you find yours? It's a place where you can relax and connect deeply to nature, where your heart feels glad, where you'll make important discoveries, both inner and outer. Most people's Gaia places are out of doors. Even a small back garden can offer many micro-Gaia place possibilities, but a window box or a favorite indoor plant can work very well too.

As you scout around for your Gaia place, notice if a particular locale sparks even the slightest glimmer of gladness in you. If this feels like a good Gaia place for you make sure that it is physically as close as possible to where you spend most of your time so that you can easily get yourself there. You can have more distant Gaia places, which you might visit months or even years later, some less wild perhaps, closer to home, and others farther out in wilder country for extended visits and overnight communion under the sparkling light of the stars. However, your principal Gaia place needs to be very close to you. Mine, from where I write, is a small English jungle garden, untouched now for thirty years, right next to our little cottage here on the grounds of Schumacher College on the Dartington Hall estate.

You'll know if you've found your Gaia place because you'll miss it when you haven't been there for a while. When you think of things you have seen and remember insights that came to you there you'll feel a warmth in your heart, a comfort in your body, and a sense of delight to have found such nourishment in your Gaia place, your home in the bosom of nature. My friend the philosopher David Abram writes beautifully about this ancient ecological consciousness we can rediscover in our Gaia place:

> Humans are tuned for relationship. The eyes, the skin, the tongue, ears, and nostrils—all are gates where our body receives the nourishment of otherness. This landscape of shadowed voices, these feathered bodies and antlers and tumbling streams—these breathing shapes are our family, the beings with whom we are engaged, with whom we struggle and suffer and celebrate.
>
> For the largest part of our species' existence, humans have negotiated relationships with every aspect of the sensuous surroundings, exchanging possibilities with every flapping form, with each textured surface and shivering entity that we happened to focus upon.
>
> All could speak, articulating in gesture and whistle and sigh a shifting web of meanings that we felt on our skin or inhaled through our nostrils or focused with our listening ears, and to which we replied—whether with sounds, or through movements, or minute shifts of mood.
>
> The color of sky, the rush of waves—every aspect of the earthly sensuous could draw us into a relationship fed with curiosity and spiced with danger. Every sound was a voice, every scrape or blunder was a meeting—with Thunder, with Oak, with Dragonfly. And from

all of these relationships our collective sensibilities were nourished. (Abram, 1997, ix)

You could say that David has described the deep ecology of your Gaia place, so now it's time to go and find yours. It's good to establish a threshold to your Gaia place, somewhere just outside it or on its edge, and ponder David's words there. The threshold is where you pause, slow down, and prepare yourself to enter the sacred precincts of your Gaia place. The threshold can be marked by a rotting log, or perhaps by an arching branch, or by a space between two trees. Whatever and wherever it is, find it and let it help you embrace the humble attitude that will lead you into deep experiences in your Gaia place.

You might make an offering of some kind to the other-than-human beings that dwell in your Gaia place: perhaps a flower, a stone, or some other natural object; or perhaps you'll offer art, movement, dance, writing, or music. I like to offer small pebbles I find by the sea.

Visit your Gaia place on a regular basis, every day if you can, in all weather. Regard it as your mentor and teacher. Develop a rapport with your Gaia place. Allow it to communicate its subtle messages of color, scent, taste, touch, and sound. Allow its birds and other beings to word-

Figure 1.1. By M. Merian from Michael Maier's *Atalanta Fugiens,* 1618.

lessly saturate you with their qualities and their presences. Let yourself be known by your Gaia place. Converse with it, gleaning its subtle meanings much as you would enjoy a conversation with a close friend. You may find yourself communicating with trees wordlessly or with great volubility, or perhaps with birds and other animals that come close to you. Love your Gaia place and let it love you.

After a while you'll feel so deeply at home and relaxed in your Gaia place that you'll begin to free yourself from our cultural conditioning against seeing the whole of nature as alive and sentient. Eventually you may feel the entire planet nurturing you with life energy, as in figure 1.1, an alchemical image from Michael Maier's book *Atalanta Fugiens* published in 1618, in which Gaia suckles the young child of our Gaian consciousness.

∾

At various moments in the book I'll suggest that you visit your Gaia place to try out certain exercises and contemplations. Hopefully you'll find that Gaia feels more and more soulful and alive in the light of the union of alchemy and science that you'll encounter with this book in your Gaia place. Then perhaps deeper meanings of Gaia alchemy will dawn on you in ways that enliven you and fill you with the joy of discovering that the anima mundi—the soul of the world—is objectively real. In such moments of awakened *cognitive imagination*, a phrase coined by Henri Corbin, whom we shall meet later, we touch the Philosopher's Stone, the *Lapis Philosophorum*—the psyche of the world—and we are healed.

2

Psyche and Alchemy

THE STRUCTURE OF THE PSYCHE

So what is psyche? In this book we'll use Jung's understanding of the structure of the psyche to integrate scientific aspects of Gaia with the deeper realms of psyche revealed by alchemy. Let's begin with his model of the structure of consciousness (shown at the top of fig. 2.1).

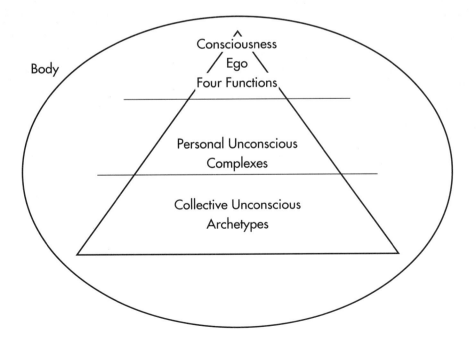

Figure 2.1. A basic model of the structure of the psyche.

Consciousness, according to Jung's model, is structured as a four-fold, as a *quaternity*, of four "functions" arranged as pairs of opposites: thinking and feeling; sensing and intuition. Thinking is our dominant cultural function, which evaluates situations with reason and logic. Feeling is not about emotion but rather about evaluating the value or importance of a thing. How good is it? What is its intrinsic worth? A lived sense of ethics (one's own unique sense of right and wrong) and of beauty and its opposite are required for our feeling function to be well developed. Sensing is about our connection with physical reality via our sensory experience, and intuition helps us "to look 'round corners" as Jung would say. Intuition allows us to know (without knowing how) about where a thing is going, where it came from, or what it really is now and what it could be in future.

By working with his many patients over many years Jung found that we are each born with a dominant function and that we need to make a special effort to develop the opposite "inferior" function in order to be whole. The remaining two functions tend to act as auxiliaries or assistants to the dominant function. If I am good at thinking, my feeling will not be too well developed, for example, but I will use my sensing and intuition to further my aims, as is the case in science. Jung's model (which I elsewhere call the Jungian Mandala) should be taken as no more than that. It is only a general guide to our conscious psychological orientation. Jung himself insisted that this scheme be taken as no more than a compass to help orient ourselves within the mysteries of nature and the human psyche.

◇◇◇◇◇ A Conversation with Jeffrey Kiehl ◇◇◇◇◇

JEFFREY: People strongly oriented toward thinking-sensation will really have a hard time working with alchemy. They often look at alchemy as a collection of historical remnants. They're not able to grasp the numinous depths of alchemy because alchemy arises out of the imagination and intuition, their weakest function.

STEPHAN: Sensing is opposite to intuition, so these folks can't get there through their intuition. You have to get them there through their feeling.

JEFFREY: Exactly. It's not guaranteed that if somebody is so invested in their thinking and sensation functions that they're going be able to go into alchemy imagistically. They're heavily weighted toward the neocortex and they can't get back into the limbic system, which is the imaginal part of the brain.

STEPHAN: Does that mean that when reptiles are walking around they're feeling images?

JEFFREY: Probably living more in a dream state. Animals may be dreaming us.

◇◇◇◇◇◇◇◇◇◇◇◇◇◇◇◇◇◇◇◇◇◇◇◇◇◇◇◇◇◇◇◇◇

Below the level of consciousness (see fig. 2.1) we find the unconscious, which, as we shall see, is essential for working alchemically. Here is one of Jung's many definitions of this mysterious realm:

> Everything which I know, but of which I am not at the moment thinking; everything of which I was once conscious but have now forgotten, everything perceived by my senses, but not noted by my conscious mind; everything which, involuntarily and without paying attention to it, I feel; think, remember, want and do; all the future things that are taking shape in me and will sometime come to consciousness: all this is the content of the unconscious. (Jung [1951] 1972, para 382)

These words define our personal unconscious, which knows, among other things, what we don't know consciously about our trauma rooted complexes that can make us suffer so much.

Elsewhere in Jung's extensive writings we learn that the unconscious is an even vaster transpersonal collective domain that he called the collective unconscious, which contains the archetypes, those powerful autonomous centers of psychic energy that seem to arise from the unknown frontier between matter and psyche, from the "psychoid" realm. He wrote:

> For years I have been observing and investigating the products of the unconscious in the widest sense of the word, namely dreams,

fantasies, visions and delusions of the insane. I have not been able to avoid recognizing certain regularities that is "types." There are types of "situations" and types of "figures" that repeat themselves frequently and have corresponding meaning. I therefore employ the term "motif" to designate these repetitions. . . . [These] can be arranged under a series of archetypes, the chief of them being . . . the "shadow," the "wise old man" the "child" (including the child hero), the "mother" ("Primordial Mother" and "Earth Mother") as a supraordinate personality . . . and her counterpart the "maiden" and lastly the "anima" in man and the "animus" in women. (Jung [1959] 1981, para. 309)

Jung also writes:

The collective unconscious—so far as we can say anything about it at all—appears to consist of mythological motifs or primordial images, for which reason the myths of all nations are its real exponent. (Jung [1951] 1972, para 325)

Furthermore:

The archetypes have, when they appear, a distinctly numinous character which can only be described as "spiritual" if "magical" is too strong a word. (Jung [1951] 1972, para 405)

In summary, Jung suggests that the collective unconscious contains the sum total of all human experience down the ages clustering around thematic centers, which Jung called archetypes, such as the shadow (one's own negative or neglected qualities), the persona (the "mask" we show the world), the anima (the soul of a man), the animus (the soul of a woman), and the Self (the deep experience of integration of our own wholeness with that of the cosmos). We sense that we are in the presence of a sacred, or numinous, presence when we experience an archetype, a situation that sometimes overwhelms us with realization and meaning.

Jungian analyst Anthony Stevens provides us with a helpful diagram of Jung's understanding of the human psyche as a whole in figure 2.2. Here is Stevens's own description of his diagram:

> The model should be visualized as a globe or a sphere, like a three layered onion. At the center, and permeating the entire system with its influence, is the Self. Within the inner of the three concentric circles is the collective unconscious composed of archetypes. The outer circle represents consciousness, with its local ego orbiting the system rather like a planet orbiting the sun, or the moon orbiting the earth. Intermediate between the conscious and the collective unconscious is the personal unconscious, made up of complexes, each of which is linked to an archetype: for complexes are personifications of archetypes: they are means through which archetypes manifest themselves in the personal psyche. (Stevens 1994, 48)

This is all very well, but can Jung's hypothesis of a collective unconscious be verified scientifically? Jung was trained as a medical doctor and thus gathered extensive empirical evidence for the existence of the collective unconscious, which he sometimes referred to as the objective psyche. One strand of evidence concerns a young schizophrenic man who told Jung in 1906 that when he moved his head while looking out of a window in the corridors of his sanatorium he could see the sun's phallus moving from side to side and that this movement produced all the winds of the Earth. To his surprise, Jung later discovered that the young man's vision corresponded very closely to the liturgy of an ancient Mithraic cult, which likewise speaks of a tube hanging down from the disc of the sun as the source of the "ministering wind." Jung convincingly shows that it was impossible for the young man to have had any prior knowledge of this Mithraic text or indeed of any such primordial ideas. Furthermore, Jung quotes a similar medieval concept in a Latin text, which speaks of how the spirit (the Holy Ghost) descends through the disc of the sun as a "mighty rushing wind." He also cites another medieval notion that it was this wind as the Holy Ghost in the form of a dove that impregnated the

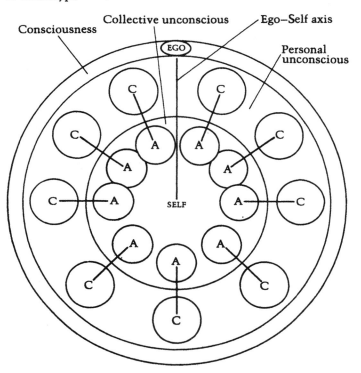

Figure 2.2. Jung's structure of the psyche
© A. Stevens, *Jung, A Very Short Introduction,* 1994.
Reproduced with permission through PLSclear.

Virgin Mary via a tube descending from heaven (Jung [1951] 1972).

Jung also noticed that ancient myths from diverse cultures all over the world fall into readily recognized patterns and categories according to the kinds of images they produce. For Jung this was strong evidence that these images are living exponents of the collective unconscious.

Jung analyzed many images produced by his patients when they were engaged in his process of active imagination, in which he encouraged them to flow freely with their fantasies while he kept his influence to the absolute minimum. Jung encouraged his patients to express their fantasy images in writing, dance, music, and various kinds of artwork as part of their therapeutic process. Several years later, to his astonishment, he found that these products had many key themes in common. The quaternity (square and cross) and rotation (circle, sphere) were prevalent, as were the opposition of light and dark, upper and lower among other such discernible themes. In particular, he noted a strong tendency toward a centering process, which he observed as "the never-to-be surpassed climax of the whole development, characterized as such by the fact that it brings with it the greatest possible therapeutic effect." These centered images of wholeness are known as mandalas and are major representations of the archetype of the Self in cultures past and present from all over the world.

From these and other lines of evidence, Jung concluded that:

> The collective unconscious contains the whole spiritual heritage of mankind's evolution, born anew in the brain structure of every individual. His conscious mind is an ephemeral phenomenon that accomplishes all provisional adaptations and orientations, for which reason one can best compare its function to orientation in space. The unconscious, on the other hand, is the source of the instinctual forces of the psyche and of the forms or categories that regulate them, namely the archetypes. All the most powerful ideas in history go back to archetypes. This is particularly true of religious ideas, but the central concepts of science, philosophy and ethics are no exception to this rule. In their present form they are variants of archetypal ideas, created by consciously applying these ideas to reality. For it is the function of consciousness not only to recognize and assimilate the external world through the gateway of the senses, but to translate into visible reality the world within us. (Jung [1951] 1972, para 342)

Here we learn that instinct isn't as low and as bestial as we usually think it is. Some of our instincts are indeed like that, but others are of a much nobler quality. The central one of these is our urge for wholeness and healing, which for Jung is regulated by the archetype of the Self, the central organizing archetype in the collective unconscious whose purpose is to foster wholeness and completion in ourselves and throughout the entirety of nature. The Self is an active agency with specific goals of its own that have to do with developing a great diversity of life forms and styles of awareness. We humans find fulfillment when our everyday consciousness (our ego) becomes aware of the Self and its purposes, with which we establish a relationship. Archetypes such as the Self are common to all humanity. They are condensed forms of all the experiences of our species throughout our entire tenure on our planet and almost certainly even further back into the earliest days of the first living cells. The archetypes have their roots in nature and are thus the voices of nature herself.

If all of this sounds fanciful and improbable to you, then bear in mind that neuroscience has shown that we humans have two quite distinct ways of understanding our world. Each hemisphere of the brain offers us differing views of the world, which we combine in many ways in our various life situations as needed. This model can be useful for contrasting these differing approaches, but it is far too simplistic to fully account for the working of the human mind. As Iain Mcgilchrist points out, we need both hemispheres to imagine and to reason.

The approach associated largely with our brain's left hemisphere is rational and reductionist, operating under the sway of linear logic, cause and effect thinking and direct sensorial attention to detail. It is narrowly focused on seemingly isolated lifeless objects.

This approach has given us science with all its benefits and pitfalls. It tends to immerse us in the experience of being detached observers. The detached state, in which we are fundamentally disconnected from the world, is utterly devoid of meaning and purpose. On the other hand, the way of seeing associated with our right cerebral hemisphere contemplates nature as a series of flowing images full of life and meaning. It sees the world with an embodied openness by means of empathy, intuition, and feeling. It is empathically connected with the unique individuality of every living being.

The right hemisphere is that of the imaginal. This beautiful word was coined by French writer and philospher Henri Corbin, based on his studies of Arabic and Persian texts written by Islamic theosophers of the past. Corbin coined the word *imaginal* to make it quite clear that he was referring to a dimension of reality not discernible by our everyday awareness, which creates the "imaginary" world of our deepest fantasies that have a quality of objectivity about them. The concept corresponds well with Jung's collective unconscious. According to Corbin, the sages from whom he drew his ideas cultivated what he called their cognitive imagination to such a high degree that they accessed the archetype of the Self dwelling deep in the *mundus imaginalis,* in the "imaginal" realm. This is also the realm of the alchemists.

One way in which alchemists access the imaginal realm is by contemplating the variety of symbols it produces. Here we must note an important difference between sign and symbol. Signs point to things already completely known. Think of road signs pointing to a destination, whereas symbols point to numinous entities in the collective unconscious that can never be fully known or understood but bring insight, life, energy, and experience.

Perhaps the symbol that carries the greatest charge of numinosity in all cultures around the world is the mandala, which integrates every aspect of the psyche into a great coherently functioning whole. The alchemists often declared that the aim of their work was to find the "Philosopher's Stone." This is an enlightened, supremely nature-connected state of mind often depicted as a mandala or as a series of interlocking mandalas. As we shall see, the alchemists drew on energies and insights from the collective unconscious or the imaginal realm to achieve this state of mind. This brought them powerful conscious experiences of the sacredness of nature. Later, we will encounter a particularly interesting example drawn by none other than alchemist and scientist Sir Isaac Newton.

⬦⬦⬦⬦⬦ A Conversation with Jeffrey Kiehl ⬦⬦⬦⬦⬦

JEFFREY: By looking at alchemical images our imaginal process is activated and we find ourselves in a part of psyche that has been neglected in modern times. We can do this through dreams as well as with alchemical images. The images motivate, *move* us by awakening an emotion to treat Gaia well.

STEPHAN: Alchemical images lead us into a state of mind in which everything falls into place—into the insight that the world is truly magical. Organisms, ecosystems are images too.

JEFFREY: Yes, there's lots of nature in alchemical images. The sea, green land, trees, sky, lions, dragons. They all wake us up to nature.

◇◇◇◇◇◇◇◇◇◇◇◇◇◇◇◇◇◇◇◇◇◇◇◇◇◇◇◇◇◇◇◇◇◇

WHAT IS ALCHEMY?

Alchemy is thousands of years old and appeared in some form or another in all advanced cultures including European, Arabic, and Asiatic when minimal or no physical contact between these peoples was taking place. It is well known that the alchemists wanted to transform physical lead into physical gold in their laboratories. The more profane among them did this to enrich themselves financially, but the best of them had a much deeper motivation, namely to extract the Philosopher's Stone (the Self) or the elixir of life from the raw matter, the *prima materia,* of nature herself.

The most enlightened alchemists came to believe that there was a divine spirit in matter that could be extracted by means of physical operations in their retorts and alembics. This same sacred spirit could be brought into a state of greater realization through interaction with human consciousness, which would also be transformed in the process.

Many alchemists recognized and employed seven key transformational steps in their work, which we will refer to again and again in this text. These are:

1. Calcination—burning away the dross in matter and in ourselves leaving behind only what is essential in both
2. Dissolution—dissolving this essence in the depths of the unconscious
3. Separation—allowing the products of the dissolution to separate into their distinctive natures
4. Conjunction—allowing these distinctive natures to come together into a coherent wholeness

5. Fermentation—allowing this new coherence to rot down so that an ever deeper essence can be manifested

6. Distillation—cultivating this deeper essence into a wider style of awareness

7. Coagulation—the products of distillation spontaneously arrange themselves into the deepest meaning and belonging we are capable of perceiving

The alchemists lived in prescientific times when nature was still seen as animate and alive, so they did not yet suffer from the materialist prejudice of our modern mechanistic worldview in which matter is considered utterly lifeless, dead, and inert. Edward Edinger gives us a glimpse into the meaning and importance of alchemy:

One might ask, why alchemy? What is its relevance for the modern mind? And the answer is that alchemy gives us a unique glimpse into the depths of the unconscious psyche, a glimpse no other body of symbolism provides in quite the same way. . . . The alchemists were fired with the beginnings of the modern spirit of enquiry, but yet, as investigators of the nature of matter, they were still half asleep. So in their zeal to investigate those newly opened vistas, they projected their fantasies and dream images into matter. . . . The alchemists were rooted in the Western psyche which we've inherited, so their imagery, their fantasy, their dream, is our fantasy and our dream. (Edinger 1994b, 7–8)

This freedom from prejudice meant that the objective psyche was able to project its living images through the alchemists into their symbols and their operations of heating, distilling, and precipitating various chemical (and psychological) substances.

Jung adds his own enlightening perspective:

So it was with the old adepts who, not knowing anything about the nature of chemical substances, reeled from one perplexity to the next: willy nilly they had to submit to the overwhelming power of the numinous ideas that crowded into the empty darkness of their minds. From these depths a light gradually dawned upon them as to the nature of the (alchemical) process and its goals. Because they were ignorant of the laws of matter, its behavior did not do anything to contradict their archetypal conception of it. Occasionally they made chemical discoveries in passing, as was only to be expected, but what they really discovered, and what was an endless source of fascination for them, was the symbolism of the individuation process . . . In their efforts to fathom the secrets of matter they had unexpectedly blundered into the unconscious, and thus, without at first being aware of it, they became the discoverers of a process that underlies Christian symbolism among others. . . . It did not take more than a couple of centuries for the more reflective among them to realize what the quest for the stone was actually about. Hesitatingly at first, hint by hint, and then with unmistakable clarity, the stone revealed its identity with man himself . . . with the Self. (Jung [1951] 1981, para. 393–394)

Jung spent much of the second part of his long life engrossed in deep contemplation of his large collection of original pigskin-bound alchemical manuscripts written in Latin. He extensively cross-referenced the weird images and terminology he discovered in these tomes, deciphering them for us as messages from the collective unconscious that, if we let them, can foster the most wondrous development and widening of our conscious experience.

Jung discovered that alchemy is a conduit through which the individuation processes inherent in the collective unconscious can become a conscious experience for each of us to discover in our own way. He realized the immense importance of alchemy's richly layered interweaving of meaning and symbol for our psychological growth and well-being, for our *individuation,* our journey to our own unique perception of and location in the wholeness of nature and Gaia. Jung's psychology draws heavily on his insight that alchemy is a spiritual heritage that activates a connection with the Self when one works consciously with alchemical ideas, images, and symbols. These are gifted to us by the miraculous living agency of the collective unconscious.

The alchemist is the child in us who pays attention to the living stream of nature as revealed by dreams, myths, and stories experienced as the promptings of a second psychological center within us that runs deeper than our limited yet essential everyday ego. Historically, such people were mostly unaware that they were using their conscious minds to "translate into visible reality the world within us." Eminent modern psychologists such as Jung, James Hillman, and others have discovered what most alchemists of the past didn't know for themselves: that alchemy is in fact a depth psychology of immense importance for healing our relationship with nature and with each other in these troubled times.

According to the C. G. Jung Center of Evanston, Illinois, depth psychology involves "approaches . . . open to the exploration of the subtle, unconscious, and transpersonal aspects of human experience. A depth approach . . . explores the unconscious and involves the study and exploration of dreams, complexes, and archetypes. Depth psychology is non-pathologizing and strength affirming."

Alchemists were attempting to understand the deepest nature of matter. In the process, they became channels for archetypal (and therefore numinous) ideas. These ideas expressed themselves in forms particular to the cultural settings in which they arose and the styles of consciousness to which this gave rise. Hence, we see in the images handed down to us in European alchemy alembics, shields, swords, and other paraphernalia characteristic of the fifteenth and sixteenth centuries, as well as artifacts from earlier times. The images that came through the alchemists are still available for us to work with to foster our own individuation, which happens when we cultivate a deep connection with Gaia and all of nature by establishing a healthy and ongoing relationship with the collective unconscious. Alchemical images are guides from the collective unconscious about how to reach the full potential of our individual consciousness (our "individuation"), which in these times of deep crisis concerns developing as rich a consciousness of Gaia as we are able to discover and enact. This is a process open to anyone, irrespective of class, intelligence, or race. Jung again:

Alchemical symbols . . . seek to translate natural secrets into the language of consciousness and to declare the truth that is the common property of mankind. (Jung [1951] 1981, para 395)

It is important to realize that the alchemists did not create their images, but rather that they *received* them directly from nature herself (from the collective unconscious) because of the sincerity of their quest to understand and experience the deep soul of nature in their laboratory work with matter. It is good to remind oneself of this when one works with alchemical images, for to be effective we need to experience them as coming from an objective realm of psyche which wants to foster our individuation—our growth into wholeness within Gaia's body and the cosmos.

The alchemists thus cultivated vitally important ancient aspects of the psyche left behind and forgotten by modern science and by the modern world as a whole. Connecting with this hidden part of ourselves gives us the widest possible mental perspective and helps us find the deepest meaning in our lives as members of the Gaian community of life. As we've seen, Jung called this lost aspect the Self, which he sometimes referred to as the "two-million-year-old self." This is our long-forgotten ancient, aboriginal, archaic personality, which links us to the distant past, to our early human ancestors, to the evolution of the first living cells on our planet, to the formation of our solar system, and to the supernova explosion that created it. Ultimately, this leads us back to the energy behind all things.

This ancient one in us responds with deep feelings and intimations of meaning to ancient myths and stories; to tales of gods and goddesses, hidden temples, and wise sages living in primeval forests; to symbols and alchemical images. This deeper personality, our two-million-year-old self, offers us wisdom and knowledge in the form of images, such as this part of a larger alchemical tableau published in 1588 by Reusner in his book *Pandora* (fig. 2.3, p. 30).

Here we see the winged Mercurius, the living spirit hidden in the depths of matter, being extracted from a lump of seemingly inert material by a figure wearing a crown whose head is encircled by a glowing

Figure 2.3. From Reusner's *Pandora* 1588.
Redrawn for this book by Julia Ponsonby.

halo. The image symbolizes the extraction of meaning and life force (the winged Mercurius) by individuated consciousness (the crowned figure) from what appears to our ordinary awareness as inert matter—just dead stuff.

In a more contemporary reading of the symbol, the lump of matter is the inanimate Earth as revealed by science before the advent of Gaia theory. The crowned figure is a Gaia alchemist, and the winged figure, Mercurius, is the immense meaning that dawns on us when the amalgam of alchemy and Gaian science brings us profound lived experiences of our animate Earth.

The two wings of Mercurius symbolize the opposites—the paradoxical nature of reality—which for us, as we shall see in this inquiry, are what I call archetypal Gaia and scientific Gaia. These become reconciled in the body of Mercurius. He is the very essence of the deepest meaning appearing to us as the transcendent synthesis of these opposites as alchemical Gaia. You might note that his particular manifestation of Mercurius carries a nasty stinging tail, a warning that he turns dangerous if we don't treat him with the deepest respect.

Jung valued these legends, myths, and stories very highly, for he found them to have immensely healing effects on many of the psychologically wounded people he helped during his long life.

Even though the beginnings of modern science are embedded in the alchemists' experiments with chemical substances in their efforts to find the Stone, today's scientists regard the discipline as primitive, backward, misguided, and utterly irrelevant for gaining reliable knowledge about the world. Our mainstream culture considers alchemy to be a meaningless jumble of incoherent ideas about the nature of matter, which is why some people today see this science of the spirit as nothing more than misguided primitive chemistry with little or no scientific worth or validity.

Yet the master alchemists of the past, including Paracelsus, Michael Maier, Gerhard Dorn, and Basil Valentine achieved deep knowledge of themselves and of the inner life of nature by unifying the powerful and deeply inspiring psychological experiences gleaned in their alchemical work with their direct sensory contact and connection with nature. One of the pioneers of modern science, Roger Bacon (1219–1292), a founder of what is now known as the scientific method, combined alchemical exploration with an emphasis on experiment and mathematics as a means of exploring nature. There is Isaac Newton, who spent much of his time and energy on deep alchemical explorations. Could it be that he received his world-changing scientific ideas about gravity (and also the calculus) from the deeply creative energies of the archetypal world with which he connected as an alchemist? If so, then to foster their creativity, every scientist should follow in his wake and become an alchemist.

If alchemical ideas truly are archetypal, then this brings into question the viewpoint that would see alchemy as no more than a superficial and rather dubious ego product of a particularly imaginative yet somewhat deranged subset of people within the general population. People endorsing this worldview would perhaps explain the impressively close similarity of alchemical ideas, images, and themes across cultures and individuals by diminishing the wondrously healing depths of psyche from which these productions emanate to the mere quasi-mechanical functioning of shallow egos helplessly trapped in the vast spaces of a meaningless cosmos. I for one abandoned the strict scientific materialism instilled into me by my education once I became aware of its alienating effects and after encountering the numinosity of alchemical-psychological insights for myself. Jung also disliked this approach:

> There are people, of course, who think it unscientific to take anything seriously; they do not want their intellectual playground disturbed by graver considerations. But the doctor who fails to take account of man's feeling for values commits a very serious blunder, and if he tries to correct the mysterious and well-nigh inscrutable workings of nature with his so-called scientific attitude, he is merely putting his shallow sophistry in place of nature's healing process. (Jung [1944] 1981, para 33)

By *doctor* Jung means a doctor of the soul who heals our psyche, which is the greatest healing that can be bestowed upon us. He warns that we cannot bring our souls back to health, back into connection with Gaia, without feeling, without a powerfully lived sense of the value and importance of nature and of harmonious human relations with her and with each other. By "mysterious working of nature" he is referring to the strange and autonomous life of the unconscious and not to the more mechanistic aspects of nature, which science allows us to understand and control. Jung ably showed how to bring a scientific attitude to understanding the unconscious, as if one were observing how a hugely gifted cosmic artist expresses their underlying meanings, purposes, and intentions in pattern, sequence, form, and theme in a multitude of diverse productions.

The Four Elements

One of the most important of these themes that keeps coming up in alchemy is the quaternity—that is, the number four. This relates to the four Classical elements: air, fire, earth, and water. These correspond in ways open to personal interpretation with the four alchemical colors: nigredo, albedo, citrinitas, and rubedo, which are the so-called stages of the alchemical process, but which I have learned from Hillman and others are more like states of mind. Since we are engaged alchemically with the issue of developing a Gaian consciousness, we need to realize how these quaternities are as much about physical nature as they are about psyche, since in the end these two aspects of life are indelibly and mysteriously connected.

Nigredo (black), for an alchemist, means **Earth** and the physical solidity of our planet, which connects seamlessly with an inner feeling of being on solid ground. Earth is often dark, even black, which brings to mind the alchemical nigredo—that state of confusion, of not knowing who or what you are or what nature might be. There's plenty of cognitive functioning, but no feeling as yet. Since the nigredo is connected with the unconscious it is also full of rich, dark healing energy that we can learn to harness in the boilers and retorts of our Gaian alchemical transformation.

Albedo (white), which comes after nigredo (black), is about a lightening of the darkness as realizations begin to dawn in us about what the alchemical process is all about and as more and more experiences of the powerfully purposeful livingness of nature descend on us in the woods and mountains and in our Gaia place. **Air** seems to be the element best suited to this state, since as beings of air we can soar high above our inner and outer landscapes and see them more clearly for what they are.

Citrinitas is a lovely warm yellow such as you find on the breast of a yellow canary or on a British yellow wagtail. This state brings a strong feeling of certainty that one is on the right track and is perhaps associated with the flowing circulatory qualities of our blood and of Gaia's as her **water** cycle, both ultimately powered by the yellow sun.

Rubedo is considered alchemically as a state of being filled with a zest for life. Eventually, after much dedicated work, one might glimpse it for a few moments before it collapses back into the unconscious. It is a feeling of being intensely and fearlessly alive in a world full of meaning to which one feels the deepest commitment even as one knows for sure that this meaning is beyond our comprehension. The alchemists used **fire** in their retorts to transform their view of nature and found that fire is the element that best describes the energy and calm, directed passion of the rubedo.

There is so much more to be learned from this kind of contemplation of the four elements in alchemy. Jung, for example, discovered in his own research that the four elements and colors emerge out of a much deeper unity of intense wholeness out of which all opposites appear. The alchemical task, he suggests, is to harness the marvelously healing energy of that unity by bringing together the four elements into wholeness in our lived experience. Gaia alchemy follows this direction, but brings Gaia center stage by realizing that this unification cannot happen unless we unify with the bustling, self-regulating, fourfold ecology of our animate Earth's biosphere, atmosphere, hydrosphere, and lithosphere.

Holistic Science

Such a union of alchemy and quantitative science might have developed to a high degree during the succeeding centuries into a truly holistic science that would have harmed the planet to a much lesser extent than the kind of one-eyed science we have ended up with today, which mostly ignores psyche at such great cost to ourselves and our animate Earth.

Such a development might have flourished long ago under the patronage of King Frederick V of Bohemia who in 1619 established Prague as his capital where he reigned for a year with his wife, Elizabeth, daughter of England's King James I. Frederick and Elizabeth brought together many of the most distinguished alchemists of the day in Prague with the intention of making their domain an alchemical kingdom where nature could be studied in a cohesive way with all our human functions in full collaboration. Here was an opportunity to explore the possibilities of a style of knowledge that combined mathematics, spirit, matter, and psyche into one integrated vision of reality. As it turned out, all this had little chance of bearing fruit—and all because of religious conflict.

Frederick was a Protestant who felt secure in the knowledge that his father-in-law, the king of England, would send troops to defend Prague from any threat from the Catholics. Sadly for us all, this was not to be. Instead, Catholic forces successfully laid siege to Prague in the battle of the White Mountain during the third year (1620) of the Thirty Years War (1618–1648), a hugely destructive conflict between Protestants and Catholics that raged over central Europe, killing around eight million people from warfare, famine, and disease. Frederick and Elizabeth fled to the Netherlands, and the alchemists they had so carefully assembled in Prague were either murdered by Catholic soldiers or were forced to flee and were scattered. Tagging along with the Catholic forces, perhaps not as a soldier but rather as an observer or even as a spy, was none other than the brilliant French philosopher and mathematician Rene Descartes (1596–1650). Decartes hated the organic, magical worldview of the alchemists with a vehement passion born perhaps of the early death of his mother and his strict Jesuit upbringing.

Descartes was part of a movement in Western thought that gradually began to conceive of the sensory qualities we perceive in nature such as taste, color, touch, and sound as deeply unreliable inventions of our consciousness that we project onto nature, mistaking these projections for the actual state of how things are in themselves independently of us. Galileo (1564–1642) stated this most clearly in his book *Il Saggiatore* in which he writes that:

> I think that tastes, odours, colors and so on are no more than mere names so far as the object in which we place them is concerned, and that they reside only in the consciousness.

Descartes took this view to an extreme by stating that the only qualities that are real in nature are those that can be measured (such as length, breadth, weight, and duration) while everything else—namely those qualities that can't be measured, such as our sensory experiences, feelings, intuitions, and emotions—tell us nothing about the true nature of reality. These "secondary qualities" were considered merely subjective and therefore utterly worthless for gaining reliable knowledge about the world. They were named as such later on by John Locke (1632–1704), who also referred to those aspects of nature that can be measured as its "primary qualities."

It was Descartes who struck the final blow that demolished the alchemical worldview by severing the sacred wholeness of nature into two irreconcilable and completely disconnected halves, two utterly separate incommensurable substances: human thinking—the *res cogitans*—on one side and the inert, dead, soulless world of matter—the *res extensa*—on the other. The assault on alchemy was so successful that alchemical science gradually faded away as alchemists lost faith in their enterprise and abandoned their retorts and alembics, degenerating instead into baseless philosophizing once they had lost touch with the rich physical reality of nature (Jung [1944] 1981, 227).

Cartesian dualism has done much damage to the world, to psyche, and to alchemy itself. But how did this materialist philosophy come to be? Did Descartes invent it from scratch, or does this perspective have a much more ancient provenance? To answer this question first we need to go into a little more history. Then, to shed some valuable light on the workings and intentions of the unconscious, we'll learn something about Descartes's dream life and discover how he might have worked fruitfully with his unconscious to heal the rift in himself, thereby sparing us all the dominance of his mechanistic perspective. And after all this we'll be ready for our deep immersion into Gaia alchemy.

3

Descartes's
Sky God

The report shows a planet in which the human footprint is so large it leaves little space for anything else. Three-quarters of all land has been turned into farm fields, covered by concrete, swallowed up by dam reservoirs or otherwise significantly altered. Two-thirds of the marine environment has also been changed by fish farms, shipping routes, subsea mines and other projects. Three-quarters of rivers and lakes are used for crop or livestock cultivation. As a result, more than 500,000 species have insufficient habitats for long-term survival. Many are on course to disappear within decades.

JONATHAN WATTS, 2019

We live in a time of a huge ecological and social crisis of our own making. Climate change is real and is already causing massive suffering and disruption. We are wiping out huge numbers of our fellow species at worryingly accelerating rates, further destabilizing the Earth's ability to mitigate the damage we are doing to her climate. We have also been rapidly destroying the rich cultural diversity of our own species, obliterating the many languages and multifarious indigenous ways of seeing the world that contribute to our wisdom and to our humanity.

◇◇◇◇ A Conversation with Jeffrey Kiehl ◇◇◇◇

JEFFREY: Indigenous people pay close attention to animals. When we are in touch with soul and we follow her she's shows us where we're supposed to go. We learn from animals. We listen to the hoot of the Owl. We look for the Raven. That's soul showing up saying "pay attention, pay attention."

STEPHAN: Whenever Raven flies over us and croaks at a significant moment that's soul showing up.

JEFFREY: Yes. Indigenous peoples know that. We've forgotten, but they know it because they're so grounded. Once, while talking to Frank, a Navajo elder, I realized how grounded he is. A group of us were at Jerome's [Jerome Bernstein] house sitting on his back porch in Santa Fe, and a rainbow appeared. Jerome said to me, "Well, as you're a scientist. Tell us what that rainbow is over there." Well I happen to have studied the rainbow a lot in my life. So I launched into a lecture on light scattering off the raindrops and the number of times the light goes around the interior of the droplet and why you get the different colors and why double rainbows appear (it was a double rainbow we saw). I talked about the mathematics one uses and so on. Jerome looked at Frank and said, "Frank, tell us how Navajo experience the rainbow." Frank spoke of the mountain where the rainbow was coming from and about the meaning of the mountain. He spoke of the rainbow bridge where the spirits come across and where the end of the rainbow is. What spirits do in the land—the connections with spirits in the land. He described an entire cosmology. We all sat transported to a different world. But he was very nonchalant when he spoke, very relaxed. No showmanship. He was explaining what his people experience whenever they see a rainbow. Frank finished, and Jerome said, "So, two different ways of looking at the same phenomenon." And we all agreed that the much richer way of looking at that rainbow was Frank's. There was a lot of soul there, you know, in Frank, in his explanation of how Navajo see the world. When they see a rainbow, they're seeing spirit, they're seeing cosmos. They're seeing the land and the spirits in the land. It's so rich. Yet when we

Westerners see a rainbow, we say "oh, what a pretty rainbow" but we don't experience the cosmology. We don't feel anything soulful and deep at all.

STEPHAN: That's what we need to do. We need to see and feel the soul of the world—the anima mundi.

JEFFREY: The alchemists did feel it. When they looked at matter and the phenomenal world they were seeing and experiencing the anima mundi. We don't do that anymore, no, but our Gaian consciousness does. We could say Frank has Gaian consciousness.

STEPHAN: We can use the anima mundi view to transform science. We've got to bring soul into science. We need to retell your scientific account of the rainbow as story, step by step. Everything you know about the rainbow from science must be there including the maths, all as soul, all as story. Then we merge the two as an alchemical *coniunctio*. This is a modern *coniunctio*, which it is our challenge to create, to give birth to right here in our own times.

◇◇◇◇◇◇◇◇◇◇◇◇◇◇◇◇◇◇◇◇◇◇◇◇◇◇◇◇◇◇◇◇◇

More and more people are realizing that we are harming ourselves and our world because of a fundamental split in our psyche, which has been hugely exacerbated and exaggerated during the major cultural developments of the last four hundred years—in particular by the scientific revolution. This is the split between what we see as the "inner" living world of our mental and emotional experience and the seemingly separate, inert "outer" world of dead nature and matter. This split looks more and more certain to be fatal for civilization because our disdain for nature is wrecking the global ecology upon which we are utterly dependent for food, clean air, shelter, and indeed for all our basic needs. We must heal the split fast, for time is running out.

From our very beginnings as a species around 300,000 years ago we instinctively unified psyche and matter. We kept these opposites together in many ways, including with ritual, meditation, and art, but ultimately to no avail, for now the split is of such titanic proportions that it is making us destroy the very basis of our existence, namely the recent pre-industrial configuration of Gaia with her richly teeming biodiversity and her remarkably stable Holocene climate of the last 11,600 years or so since the end of the last ice age. The split has by now widened into a vast chasm that so fatally threatens us on a collective level.

But how did the split—our modern immensely dangerous disconnection between psyche and matter—come about? It's a long and complicated story that has been traced back to what happened to the Goddess cultures of Old Europe and beyond at the end of the Neolithic (the New Stone Age), which began around 10,000 BCE and ended about 5,500 BCE. Settled agriculture is the defining characteristic of the Neolithic in Old Europe and beyond as far as the Middle East and into the Indus valley.

It was a time when the ancient, mostly nomadic hunter-gatherer lifestyles of the previous tens of millennia were replaced by well populated communities centered around permanent structurally robust dwellings and public buildings. The relatively high numbers of people in these settlements were supported by skilful tilling of the soil for growing crops such as grain and the domestication of animals for food and work. As Anne Baring and Jules Cashford explain in their book *The Myth of the Goddess—Evolution of an Image,* the primordial hunter-gatherers' sense of deep unity with nature was not in any way lost during the Neolithic agricultural transition—instead it blossomed and developed into a deep reverence for the Mother Goddess, who was:

> An image that, more obviously than before, inspires a perception of the universe as an organic, alive and sacred whole, in which humanity, the earth and all life on earth participate as "her children." As the Great Mother, she presides over the whole of creation as goddess of life, death and regeneration, containing within herself the life of plants as well as the life of animals and human beings. There is the same recognition of an essential relationship between an invisible order, embodied earlier in the cycles of human and animal life, and now in the cycle of the seasons and the agricultural year. (Baring and Cashford 1993, 48)

Many figurines from that period show the Goddess embracing or otherwise in deep relationship with a God, revealing that the Goddess was a hermaphroditic entity for these Neolithic peoples. This powerfully holistic perception presages an identical insight that surfaced within medieval alchemy many millennia later in which the hermaphrodite symbolized the profound union of matter and psyche—the indwelling of psyche within the very heart of nature herself.

The great authority on the Neolithic of Old Europe, Marija Gimbutas, provides archaeological evidence that these were egalitarian, nonpatriarchal, matrilineal cultures in which inheritance was passed down through the women whose social importance was emphasized by the fact that they played major roles in religious ceremonies. Nowhere in the artifacts of these people do we find images or other references to weapons or chieftains or war. Instead, their many and various artistic creations attest to a deep love of the Goddess and of the animals and plants she engendered and cared for.

Gimbutas shows how these essentially peaceful, nature-revering cultures were overwhelmed and destroyed by sky-god worshiping, war-loving nomadic peoples. These warrior horsemen swept over them with terrible destructive force from their steppe homelands between the Dneiper and Volga rivers to the east. Recent evidence reveals that these invaders and the Neolithic peoples they subjugated were actually two genetically distinct human subgroups, suggesting a genetic basis for the very different degrees of aggressiveness in the two cultures. We know for sure that that the male warriors of the sky-god people were fond of extreme violence, for the same genetic evidence shows that they killed the men of the Neolithic cultures, subjugated their women, and fathered children by them. Thus were the egalitarian Goddess cultures destroyed and replaced by a deeply patriarchal society based on the absolute superiority of men over women and of humans over nature (Barras 2019).

This violent, profoundly divisive patriarchal attitude of the mounted invaders from the eastern steppes spilled over into the Old Testament, in which, as Julian David shows in his book, *A Brief History of God,* the old hermaphroditic male-female deity of wholeness, Elohim, was replaced by the male sky god Yahweh, whose nature-dominating, anti-feminine impulse carried through into early mainstream Christianity (though not into the teachings of Jesus, who was very much an egalitarian ecologist).

The sky-god image insinuated itself into the central dogmas of both Catholic and Protestant Churches via Augustine, who integrated Platonism with Christianity, after which the "real" did not reside in this world but rather in an ideal metaphysical or spiritual world. From there the sky god morphed again in the seventeenth century, becoming the metaphysical foundation of the scientific revolution mostly thanks to the writings of René Descartes.

The sky god in Descartes's psyche was no longer a furious thrower of thunderbolts as Yahweh had been. Instead, he had become a cool-headed, highly intellectual mathematician and engineer who had set up the universe as a gigantic clockwork long ago, then sat back in his throne to amuse himself by watching his creation tick its way predictably down the ages. To make sure that humans didn't forget him, he proved his existence now and then by enacting a miracle in the lowly fallen realm of sinful matter.

In Descartes the sky god had at last found and wielded his sharpest and deadliest ax to cut loose our ties to the Goddess, to the living soul of nature, and to our own souls, thereby consigning us to merely surviving in a meaningless universe over which the sky god could at last reign supreme over humanity by imposing tyrannical government and a purely mechanistic science upon the world.

Since Descartes was a devout Catholic he was very careful to make sure that this arrangement did not upset the Church's dogma of an immortal soul (psyche) and mortal body (matter). This was not too difficult since the Church had already gone a long way toward creating the final split between these opposites by denigrating matter, and so to begin with the churchmen didn't notice that Descartes's system would end up dispensing with Jesus, Mary, and even God himself a few hundred years later.

This telling of the story is probably too critical of the Cartesian approach, for there is no doubt that mathematical-mechanistic thinking is immensely valid. It has proved itself to be of great value as a tool for improving our lives and, in our time, for developing planet-healing technologies and ways of living. At last, we are realizing that this kind of thinking is very useful, but only as a tool to help us deal with certain very limited aspects of the world that bear some resemblance to how machines work, such as the way in which my tendons and muscles move my skeleton. However, the mechanistic approach is deeply dangerous if we imagine it tells us anything at all fundamental about the actual nature of the world. Stretching mechanistic thinking this far has snapped the world in two. We need look no further than the current global crisis for evidence of the damaging effects of our outdated mechanistic ontology.

◇◇◇◇◇ A Conversation with Jeffrey Kiehl ◇◇◇◇◇

JEFFREY: In the process of going down this one-sided rational linear logos oriented pathway with Descartes we have lost the feminine. Gaia is the feminine. We have to reconnect with the feminine.

STEPHAN: And the masculine?

JEFFREY: That too needs to be worked on because it is too one-sided.

STEPHAN: The masculine in our culture, in science, gives me a sort of faraway view of things. A dryness that leads me to be as inwardly bleak as the moon, a bleakness that also infects the Earth. It cuts all the flesh off the earth until we are only left with bare rocks.

JEFFREY: A barren wasteland.

STEPHAN: So let's find way back to something wholesome. We can't abandon our thinking—that would be crazy—but we're thinking in a different way now, in a much more feminine way. We have to see our equations exuding a feminine beauty.

JEFFREY: We need *levitas*, the opposite of *gravitas*.

STEPHAN: Gravity is really Gaia's love holding everything down. She's a huge, massive living being holding everything down with her gravitas and we're part of that. Once we feel it we have the right to go into our imagination and get into levitas, but always remembering her and in her service.

JEFFREY: When you do that you are doing what the alchemists have done throughout time: marrying heaven and Earth.

Although the Cartesian division of reality into two irreconcilable opposites would eventually, in our day, lead to the banishment of psyche from our worldview, Descartes himself believed in the existence of angels and God. He also recognized the importance of dreams. Two of these dreams of his changed our world, so we need to look at them.

They came to Descartes along with what was probably a neurological vision during the day of November 10, 1619. Descartes was twenty-three years old and held up in a room at Ulm in southern Germany on his way to Bohemia to join the Catholic forces of Ferdinand II. This monarch was preparing to oust the Protestant King Frederick V from his capital in Prague—an ancient city, which, as we saw earlier, Frederick had filled with some of the most eminent alchemists in Europe. It is possible that Ferdinand had sent Descartes to Prague as a spy, to help root out those detestable alchemists who worshiped a living nature.

Knowing that no one would disturb him, Descartes was enjoying the warmth of his stove-heated room that night, completely untroubled by any concerns. He went into a deeply contemplative state, during which it dawned on him to question whether everything he had learned about the world might in fact be no more than a set of collective errors amounting to an edifice of outlandish falsehood and mistaken ideas.

Descartes was psychologically astute enough to realize that he had been influenced by the collective bias of the social milieu of his times. He had the important realization that what our culture considers to be real could in fact be a highly contagious style of collective delusion. He saw another possibility and dedicated himself completely to cultivating it.

He knew very strongly that this new way had to do with the careful observation of nature by means of a quantitative-mathematical approach, for he felt that God reveals himself to us through number, quantity, and measurement. He was right, but in a limited way, since measuring is only *one* way we can discover truths about the world, not the *only* way. Sadly, by not perceiving this, he went badly wrong with great cost to himself and to the world.

The day and night in question had a profound effect on him that he never forgot. Here he is writing twenty-three years later in his *Meditations on First Philosophy* about that fateful day, November 10, 1619:

> Some years ago I was stuck by the large number of falsehoods that I had accepted as true in my childhood, and by the highly doubtful nature of the whole edifice that I had subsequently based upon them. I realized that it was necessary, once in the course of my life, to demolish everything completely and start again from the foundations if I wanted to establish anything at all in the science that was stable and likely to last.

Descartes had given so much energy and attention to dissolving his preconceptions that he had achieved a great degree of freedom by that evening. He went to bed in great excitement and fell asleep, whereupon the unconscious took over the work, for believing, because of his meditation that day, as A. C. Grayling says, "that deep truths were within his grasp." Descartes had two dreams that night interspersed with a strange semi-hypnogogic event, all of which stirred him to his depths, urging him to press much further with his inquiry.

Descartes's biographer, Baillet, reports these events in volume 2 of his book *La Vie de Monsieur Descartes* published in 1691. I summarize here what he says, but you can find a full account in A. C. Grayling's book *Descartes*.

Here are Baillet's words about the first dream, in which Descartes:

> Felt his imagination struck by the representation of some phantoms, which frightened him so much that, thinking that he was walking in the streets, he had to lean to his left in order to reach his destination, because he had a great weakness in his right side and could not hold himself upright. He tried to straighten himself, feeling ashamed to walk in the fashion, but he was hit by turbulent blasts as if of a whirlwind, which spun him round three or four times on his left foot. Even this was not what alarmed him; the difficulty he had in struggling along made him feel that he was going to fall at every

step. Noticing a school open along his route he went in, seeking refuge and a remedy for his problem. He tried to reach the school chapel, where his thought was to pray. But realizing that he had passed an acquaintance without greeting him, he sought to retrace his steps to pay his respects, but was violently repulsed by the wind blowing into the chapel. At the same time he saw another person in the school courtyard who addressed him by name and politely told him that if he wished to find Monsieur N he had something to give him. Descartes took it that the thing in question was a melon from a foreign country. What was more surprising was that the people clustering around that person in order to talk with him were straight and steady on their feet, although he himself was still bent over and unsteady on the same ground. Having almost knocked him over a number of times, the wind had greatly lessened.

Descartes awakes right after this dream in the middle of the night with a pain in his left side, feeling that the dream had been sent him by an evil spirit. Wide awake, he prays for a full two hours for God to forgive his sins (which were probably not as serious as he thought) and begs for him not to send thunderbolts from heaven, which would be his just punishment for such bad behavior.

Then he thinks he falls asleep into a second dream, but in fact neurophysiological evidence suggests that this was "exploding head syndrome" in which one hears a very loud bang while asleep that wakes one up. He awakes in fear and sees red and gold sparks of fire flying hither and thither in the darkness before him. These comfort him greatly, for he has seen these before many times, and so he falls peacefully asleep on his right side with no anxiety at all.

Now he dreams that he is in his chamber and notices a curious old book upon his table. He has no idea how it got there. He opens it and discovers to his delight that it is a dictionary and feels very happy to have found such a useful reference book. Then he notices another book, which has mysteriously appeared nearby. This turns out to be called the *Corpus Poetarum,* a collection of poems by many authors. He opens the book and comes across the following phrase:

Quod vitae sectabor iter?
What way of life should I follow?

Then a stranger appears and gives him a piece of paper with a poem whose first words are:

Yes and No

The stranger tells him that this is an excellent poem and Descartes recognizes it. He knows that it is in the *Corpus Poetarum* and that it comes from one of the *Idylls* of Ausonius, a Roman poet of the fourth century BCE. As Descartes searches for this poem in the *Corpus Poetarum* the dictionary reappears, but it is not as complete as before. He can't find the "yes and no" poem, but he looks for the first poem which the stranger would very much like to see. As he does so, he comes across some copperplate portraits, which he greatly admires out loud, but before he finds the poem, both the stranger and the book vanish.

Baillet implies that Descartes regarded this dream to be prophetic, for the next day an Italian painter visits him, which suggests to Descartes that the copper plates in the dream poetry book foretold this event.

Descartes begins interpreting this last dream while still asleep. He decides that the dictionary means "all the sciences gathered together" (Baillet's words) and that the book of poems represents the union of Philosophy and Wisdom. When he awakes Descartes continues to interpret this third dream. He thinks that the book of poems represents Revelation and Enthusiasm, and the "yes and no" he interprets as Truth and Falsehood in "human enquiry and science" (Baillet again). So pleased is Descartes with these interpretations that he believes that the Spirit of Truth has sent him this dream "to open to him the treasures of all the sciences" (Baillet once more).

But would the modern world have been different if Descartes had interpreted this dream another way?

4

Descartes
Meets Alchemy

Paying attention to the imagery of the objective psyche (such as alchemy) generates auspicious reciprocal effects.

EDWARD EDINGER

There is so much more I want to tell you, but you can't bear it now.

JOHN 16:12

In one of his videos about alchemy filmed in Prague, Terence McKenna narrates an intriguing fantasy devised by a Czech friend of his in which Descartes is seriously wounded in a duel with an alchemist in the streets of that beautiful ancient city just after the Battle of the White Mountain. The alchemist takes pity on Descartes, takes him home, and nurses him back to health.

The Gaian alchemical view helps me to see how the two become firm friends and how during Descartes's long period of convalescence they each discover the merits of their opposing worldviews. Restored to health, Descartes eventually becomes the champion of a truly holistic science in which the mathematical and alchemical worlds combine to produce a view of nature as a living presence amenable to mathematical representation and scientific investigation, yet which is far more alive and mysterious than reason alone can ever know. What follows is how a crucial conversation between the two friends might have gone at the alchemist's house near Prague, 1622.

DESCARTES: *How do you work with these fantastical alchemical images you've been showing me these past few months?*

ALCHEMIST: *We need a poetic attitude to investigate the meaning of alchemical images, which are paradoxical, both a "yes" and a "no." By doing that we break through to a new attitude which makes us feel more alive, more connected to something dynamic that produces these images. We are not dealing with logic here.*

DESCARTES: *With the "yes and no" are you speaking of the dream I have told you of many times—the one of the dictionary and the book of poems on my table in my chamber?*

ALCHEMIST: *Exactly. Now you are getting the idea. You will never understand what your dream poetry book is telling you about using the dictionary, will you? The dictionary can tell you nothing about poetry.*

DESCARTES: *And no doubt you will assert the same of the "yes and no" on the piece of paper given to me by that mysterious dream stranger?*

ALCHEMIST: *Indeed. I would commend his message to you as a paradoxical statement from the imaginal realm urging you to break through your domineering logical constructs into a more fluid way of seeing nature as intelligent and alive.*

DESCARTES: *So you would reject my interpretation of the dream?*

ALCHEMIST: *Not completely, but you have let logic take control of the poetry book, that is, of your poetic soul, which connects you with nature as a living psyche. The poetry book is not about Truth and Error in the practice of science—no—instead it urges you to complement your powerful logical mind with the paradoxical poetic symbolism of the imaginal realm so that you can be whole. Then you will see how damaging is your idea that all of nature is just the res extensa as you call it, just dead matter.*

DESCARTES: *You are somehow convincing me and I am feeling very disoriented in myself. I must apply my four principles to this matter.*

ALCHEMIST: *A great idea. Remind me, what is the first principle?*

DESCARTES: *To only accept notions that are so clear and distinct that they cannot be doubted.*

ALCHEMIST: *Well, you do not doubt that your dreams have meaning, do you? You have always paid attention to your dreams. You even sleep late in the morning to make sure you dream well and then write down your dreams in your little notebook. The clear and distinct notion here is that dreams have meaning. So have we cleared the first hurdle?*

DESCARTES: *Well, I suppose so, in a manner of speaking. But dreams and logic are quite distinct.*

ALCHEMIST: *But you grant that dreams have their own style of logic?*

DESCARTES: *Yes, from my own experience I am bound to agree.*

ALCHEMIST: *And the second principle?*

DESCARTES: *Is that to understand anything well I need to examine its parts in detail.*

ALCHEMIST: *And do we not do the same as we analyze your dream? Do we not look into the meaning of each part with great care: the two books, the "yes and no"?*

DESCARTES: *Indeed we do—I cannot refute it.*

ALCHEMIST: *Then that takes care of your second hurdle. What of the next?*

DESCARTES: *To proceed in an orderly manner from the most easily known objects to the most complex.*

ALCHEMIST: *Have we not done this with your dream? Which is the most easily known object in it for you?*

DESCARTES: *The dictionary.*

ALCHEMIST: *And the most complex?*

DESCARTES: *The "yes and no."*

ALCHEMIST: *And can we not go step by step from the dictionary to the poetry book to the "yes and no," gathering more meaning as we go from the simplicity of the dictionary's logic to the paradoxical statements of the poetic, the imaginal, which are more complex and more difficult to understand? Ponder well on it.*

DESCARTES *(after a long silence): Hmm, I begin to feel a faint* *glimmering of what you are getting at. There seems to be another capacity for perception in me which senses something beyond the "yes and no."*

ALCHEMIST: *The poetic wakes up in you?*

DESCARTES: *Perhaps, perhaps indeed. My fourth principle is to review my thinking very carefully so as to make sure nothing is left out.*

ALCHEMIST: *That is a fine principle. Have we not diligently applied it to your dream by looking deeply into each aspect of it over and over again until we reached some kind of satisfaction?*

DESCARTES: *Well, this conversation is proof enough of that. So are the many previous ones we have had on this topic.*

ALCHEMIST: *So where are you now with all this?*

DESCARTES: *Well, you have looked after me with great kindness and we have become great friends. I respect your intelligence and you have shown great aptitude for issues of logic and science. Therefore I cannot believe that what you say about alchemy is nonsense since you are no fool. Because* **you** *are an alchemist I must now take it seriously, even though it baffles me*

ALCHEMIST: *Well, dear René, perhaps now after these years of our friendship together I am ready to reveal to you that there is an alchemical laboratory hidden in this very house.*

DESCARTES: *Truly? Why didn't you tell me sooner?*

ALCHEMIST: *I didn't feel you were ready.*

DESCARTES: *I am curious to see it, although I am not still completely convinced by alchemy. There's no mathematics in it, and how can the world be a living soul?*

ALCHEMIST: *Let's not argue about all that again. Just come and see.*

They walk down a narrow passage in the Alchemist's house until they come to a beautiful Persian carpet. The Alchemist pulls this to one side revealing a large trap door. He opens it and begins to descend some broad wooden steps. Descartes follows him down into the room below.

DESCARTES: *What a beautiful room. I wasn't expecting to see such a large rose-framed window overlooking such fine woods and mountains.*

ALCHEMIST: *There are other windows behind these curtains. I will draw them to let the sunlight in.*

As the daylight filters in, Descartes spies an impressive gray-haired woman sitting in an old wooden chair near the open window. He notices her clothes—they are not of his times. They are far simpler, more economic in line and material. She wears glasses with thick, wide lenses that look nothing like seventeenth-century spectacles.

MARIE-LOUISE VON FRANZ: *Welcome, Monsieur Descartes. I have come here specially to see you.*

DESCARTES: *Pray, madame, who are you?*

MARIE-LOUISE VON FRANZ: *I am Dr. Marie-Louise von Franz, a close student of Carl Gustav Jung. I come from the future.*

DESCARTES: *How is this possible?*

MARIE-LOUISE VON FRANZ: *With alchemy all sorts of things are possible.*

DESCARTES (taking a chair opposite her): *But who are you?*

MARIE-LOUISE VON FRANZ: *Let's say that I am a doctor of the soul who has come from the future to help you understand that first dream of yours.*

DESCARTES (shuddering): *I don't need help with that dream.*

MARIE-LOUISE VON FRANZ: *But you have altogether ignored it.*

DESCARTES: *It was too disturbing . . . it . . . it . . . frightened me greatly.*

MARIE-LOUISE VON FRANZ: *Then would you like to analyze it with me? Perhaps what we discover will do you good.*

DESCARTES: *Can you rid me of the blood-chilling fear I feel when I think of it?*

MARIE-LOUISE VON FRANZ: *That will depend on you.*

DESCARTES: *I don't want to go into the dream again. I don't want to poke an old wound.*

MARIE-LOUISE VON FRANZ: *The opposite of fear is truth.*

DESCARTES: *You seem very erudite, very wise.*

MARIE-LOUISE VON FRANZ: *Then let's start with the fact that you were walking in the streets toward an unknown goal.*

DESCARTES: *Yes, I wonder why I was walking in those dark streets. Why was I so disoriented?*

MARIE-LOUISE VON FRANZ: *The dream tells you that you must leave your introverted life and enter the life of ordinary people. You need to do something for them. You must use your considerable gifts to help them. You must serve them. But for the moment you don't know how.*

DESCARTES: *Why was I bending so tortuously on my left side?*

MARIE-LOUISE VON FRANZ: *Because you have neglected your feminine side, which the dream represents as "sinister," on the left—as the feminine, which you have undervalued, neglected, and persecuted—which is none other than your unconscious.*

DESCARTES: *Neglected and persecuted? My unconscious?*

MARIE-LOUISE VON FRANZ: *The dream tries to balance you out by taking you over to the left, to your feminine poetic relatedness with the physical world and to your buried ability to feel its immense living value. Right now, you are unconscious of both.*

DESCARTES: *Balance? Then why was I spun around on my left foot by that powerful whirlwind?*

MARIE-LOUISE VON FRANZ: *You refused to listen to the ghosts. So they turned into a storm. They spun you round three or four times to tell you of the paradox of the three and four of which you are completely unaware.*

Through the miracle of alchemy, in just a few minutes Descartes's consciousness develops through the equivalent of five years' intensive analysis with Marie-Louise von Franz, one of Jung's finest pupils.

MARIE-LOUISE VON FRANZ: *The storm is the tension in your time between the Protestants and the Catholics, which is tearing your world apart. The tension opens up a yawning gap and you are gripped by a mad enthusiasm to fill it with your universal mathematics and with your mechanistic theory of a soulless universe based on your new scientific thinking. That hubris will be dearly paid for by future generations—human and nonhuman.*

DESCARTES: *The storm whirled me around three or four times.*

MARIE-LOUISE VON FRANZ: *So that you could have a comprehensive view. You have been far too focused on mathematics and reasoning.*

DESCARTES: *Stuck in a style of thinking that has made the world no more than a machine. I see it now.*

MARIE-LOUISE VON FRANZ: *Your mechanistic thinking will rip the physical and the psychic worlds apart to the detriment of all life on the planet. All this will happen in large part because you have been unable to integrate the feminine into your life.*

DESCARTES: *And that man whom I turned back to greet? Who was he?*

MARIE-LOUISE VON FRANZ: *He is an important part of your personality that you have consistently overlooked. He is the shadow part of yourself who will lead you into the deepest happiness if only you would listen to him. That man represents your undiscovered self. Your alchemical Self. Your introverted thinking has impelled you to escape life so much that you are even terrified of falling in love. This is a sorry state of affairs for you and for the world you will influence with that great mind of yours.*

DESCARTES: *What strange and marvelous feelings wake up in me right now in this time with you, Dr. von Franz. I feel more myself, more alive. Earth seems somehow alive too.*

MARIE-LOUISE VON FRANZ: *You need to be rooted and in contact with our beautiful Earth, with the ancient Gaia you learned about in those old myths when you were a boy. The melon you are asked to give Mr. N. is of course very significant in this regard.*

DESCARTES: *How so?*

MARIE-LOUISE VON FRANZ: *Melons grow close to the Earth, so the image guides you toward what you long for inwardly without even knowing it: to become deliciously caught in earthly reality, in the feminine, which for you is the way into the deepest understanding. Can you perceive the depth of that view?*

DESCARTES: *I can now. I experience a beautiful feeling of the wholeness of the world, which is simply indescribable. I see now how everything deeply hangs together—the inner world of dreams and the outer world of matter.*

MARIE-LOUISE VON FRANZ: *The dream images are doing their work very nicely at long last. The rational mind does not know how to relate to the profound inner realities of the psyche where the deepest treasures are.*

DESCARTES: *I begin to see my error. I'm starting to love this Earth and her creatures, her waters, her winds and storms and her rocks.*

MARIE-LOUISE VON FRANZ: *But there is an even deeper message.*

DESCARTES: *Which is?*

MARIE-LOUISE VON FRANZ: *The dream warns you about the evil contained in the lack of balance between feeling, intuition, sensing, and thinking in the new intellectual attitude you are preparing to unleash upon the world.*

DESCARTES: *So . . . that is why I awoke feeling endangered by an evil spirit—the evil spirit of excessive rationality, which kills off the soul of the world.*

But wait. One of those ghosts approaches from my right—it talks to me.

MARIE-LOUISE VON FRANZ: *Your right side is now a window into the very soul of nature. What does the ghost tell you? Let it speak.*

GHOST: *Let me show you who I am.*

DESCARTES (hesitatingly): *Well then, come forth ghost. Speak. I can bear to see you now.*

The ghost comes out of the shadows and slowly turns into an Indigenous person from the Amazon rain forest.

GHOST: *You have denigrated us, spat on us, insulted us, and yet we are your deepest nature so we love you still.*

DESCARTES (experiencing a great surge of insight and a great open feeling in his heart): *What healing you bring me. An even deeper knowledge grows in me that the Earth and all of nature are alive. In your presence, ghost, this knowledge thickens and gets stronger.*

I see now the crimes that my culture will inflict on you if I carry on with my one-sided intellectual attitude. Forgive me, ancient one.

GHOST: *Dear Heart, I restore you now to this oldest way of seeing. May this view never leave you and may you give the world great gifts from her treasure store. I am here always to guide you.*

He walks toward Descartes and dissolves into his body.

DESCARTES: *Dr. von Franz, I cannot thank you enough. Without you I would never have experienced such expansive freedom and such a widening and deepening of my awareness. Like a snake my heart has shed its skin and I am free. The Earth is alive.*

MARIE-LOUISE VON FRANZ: *There is more, dear Descartes, much more. But you have already come a long way. Now at long last you've entered the living stream of life. Look there, another ghost appears.*

DESCARTES: *Another ghost in the shadows. Come forth, phantom!*

GHOST: *I come from the future, from the twenty-first century. I am the disasters that your mechanistic worldview has imposed upon the world. You refused to listen to the wisdom of the alchemists and instead pushed ahead with your devastating idea of a soulless universe regardless of the painful cries of the trees and the birds. Our living planet, our only home in the vastness of the cosmos, is close to collapse in my century because of your mechanistic worldview and your division between humans and nature. Gaia is in great danger of overheating, of becoming mostly desert, of becoming a wasteland in which billions of people will suffer and die without hope. Millions of God's species will tumble into extinction.*

DESCARTES: *How my heart wrenches and bleeds to hear it. Ow!*

GHOST: *But I am delighted to find that you have now rejected your mechanistic bias. So all this mess will be avoided. I can't wait. I must rush back to what must be a paradise in my own century.*

The ghost vanishes.

MARIE-LOUISE VON FRANZ: *You see how you rejected these vitally important aspects of life—your feeling, your poetic perception? You failed to grasp them and so they haunted and terrified you in the form of those ghosts.*

DESCARTES: *How interesting and most strange. These ghosts are now my greatest helpers.*

MARIE-LOUISE VON FRANZ: *Now my work is done and I must return to my own times.*

Marie-Louise von Franz begins dissolving and disappearing.

MARIE-LOUISE VON FRANZ: *You have experienced the deep transformative life and power of the psyche.*

This is alchemy.

Solve et Coagula!

Farewell. Write your book with the greatest love and care for Gaia, our gorgeous Earth, dear René.

DESCARTES: *Farewell, Marie-Louise, wise woman of the stars. May we meet again in some as yet unknown land. You are my guide and mentor, now and always.*

She is gone.

The alchemist gently guides Descartes toward the window.

ALCHEMIST: *Come now, dear René. Come and rest on this ample sofa by the open window and sleep awhile.*

Let the soft breezes of the distant mountains soothe away your cares.

Let the rosy scents wafting in from these lovely flowers by the window bless you too.

When you awake the world will be bright and new,

Everything sparkling like the freshest dew.

Fifteen years have passed. Descartes is now forty years old. He is sitting under the apple trees in his alchemical garden in southern France on a beautiful spring day. Full of love for the living Earth, he looks behind him to a first-floor window of his house. His wife greets him lovingly with that smile he so much adores as she holds their baby daughter in her arms. In the background his alchemical retorts and alembics evoke the alchemical Mercurius ever more powerfully and effectively.

He takes up his pen and begins to write his book, the one that would have taught us how to love, learn, and be in this beautiful Gaian planetary paradise with virtually no impact on her sacred wild living roundness.

And this is the title of his book: *Natura Sapientia: L'union Expérientielle de L'alchimie et des Mathématiques pour Comprendre et Aimer Notre Terre Vivante.*

"Wise Nature: The Experiential Union of Alchemy and Mathematics for Understanding and Loving Our Living Earth" René Descartes, Figeac, South West France, 1636.

And now four hundred years later, thanks to this alternative trajectory that Descartes might have pioneered with his great book, our own perceptions would be more Gaian, our science more holistic, and our planet healthier, wilder, and more biodiverse than we experience her now in the tragic reality of our times.

5

The Unus Mundus

Gaia Archetype and Gaia Science

The idea of the unus mundus is founded on the assumption that the multiplicity of the empirical world rests on an underlying unity, and that not two or more fundamentally different worlds exist side by side or are mingled with one another. Rather, everything divided and different belongs to one and the same world. . . . even the psychic world, which is so extraordinarily different from the physical world, does not have its roots outside the one cosmos [which] is evident from the undeniable fact that causal connections exist between the psyche and the body, which point to their underlying unitary nature.

C. G. JUNG [1956] 1974

Gaia alchemy heals the Cartesian split by making matter and psyche intensely aware of each other as an unbroken wholeness in the *unus mundus*. As fact and image meld within us, an integrated style of consciousness is born—an epiphany happens that combines our deeply buried Indigenous soulful outlook with a modern mentality informed and shaped by the stunning discoveries of the contemporary sciences of the Earth.

In this book we explore how the opposites, science and alchemy, can be brought together to complete the sacred marriage between matter and psyche, which was interrupted so long ago by the scientific revolution and the Church. This child of this inner marriage is the Gaian consciousness we must all quickly find before the split wipes out civilization through climate change and the decimation of biodiversity.

We are running out of time to celebrate the wedding, for a mutual recognition between opposites often happens slowly, sometimes only in a momentary flash when a marvelously freeing sense of the intensely purposeful aliveness of reality itself descends upon us like a valedictory blessing. In these blessed moments we experience the inner light of nature shining within us and in all things.

To do this, we'll follow the path of integrating two versions of Gaia: archetypal or mythological Gaia and scientific Gaia, which are Gaian opposites (fig. 5.1). When this happens we can experience a third, transcendent, Gaia that I call alchemical Gaia. Archetypal Gaia relates of course to the objective psyche (the collective unconscious), while scien-

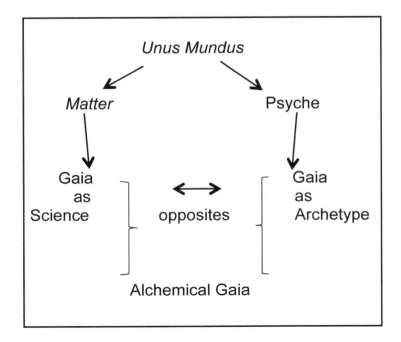

Figure 5.1. Alchemical Gaia as a union between scientific and archetypal Gaias.

tific Gaia is based on James Lovelock's Gaia theory. Alchemical Gaia requires the union of the two into a transcendent function in which the resulting state of affairs in consciousness is a blend of alchemy and science, transforming both into a deeply ecological style of consciousness lost to our culture so long ago but which is so deeply needed in this time of crisis.

ARCHETYPAL GAIA

Hemmed round by rationalistic walls, we are cut off from the eternity of nature.

C. G. JUNG

Archetypal or mythological Gaia, unlike its apparent opposite—scientific Gaia—is not a product of the rational mind, for in essence archetypal Gaia is not a system of rationally elucidated feedbacks. To experience archetypal Gaia we need to connect with an intuitive perception that comes from deeper, more ancient regions of the psyche where primordial thoughts, events, and emotions common to all humanity accumulate as persistent images and memory traces. In other words, to experience archetypal Gaia we need to connect Corbin's concept of cognitive imagination with our mythological intelligence, with Imagination, the collective unconscious, the objective psyche.

Our thinking function only serves to hinder us in this domain. Yet, this focus on an ancient style of perception brings us into a world alive with birdsong, of swaying branches laden with the green shoots of spring, and the clear blue sky of an English April morning, for me right here, right now as I write—revealing a living world that science can help us to appreciate ever more fully.

The best person to introduce us to archetypal Gaia is my friend the mythologist, scholar, and Jungian analyst, Jules Cashford. In only seventy-three pages of her masterpiece, *Gaia: Story of Origin to Universe Story,* she gives us a superb immersion into the depths of Imagination and this primordial manifestation of Gaia. Jules taught, with James Lovelock, the very first course of all at Schumacher College, which was on Gaia, where a motley group of exceptional people from all over the world explored Gaia as both science and myth, a happening that has blossomed for me some thirty years later into Gaia alchemy, a new kind of science awake to the phenomenal power and presence of psyche in the world of nature.

Jules reminds us of William Blake's famous saying: "To the Man of Imagination, Nature is Imagination itself." But what is Imagination with a capital *I*? Poets evoke Imagination best of all. I am no poet, but here is an example of Imagination from my own experience. I close my eyes and remember the blue Mediterranean I saw in Greece long ago. An immense love comes over me, light in texture, full of an open, expansive longing, which is somehow fulfilled by my memory of the sea itself with its turquoise waters and the clear blue sky above. The feeling expands into a lived realization of the palpable existence of the entire planet as one miraculous, living, breathing being. Such Imagination events have a particular quality—they reveal something absolutely real about the world as a substance that is both inward and outward simultaneously.

⬦⬦⬦⬦⬦ A Conversation with Jeffrey Kiehl ⬦⬦⬦⬦⬦

JEFFREY: According to Jung, archetypes are the images of instincts, which are biological. They're probably the closest to Gaia. This is one of Jung's great contributions: he felt that there's something in us that pulls us to the numinous, which is the religious function. In the Judeo-Christian mythology you would say there is a natural instinct for us to want to connect to God. If you want to stay out of a particular religion you could say that there is a natural pull, a natural process that wants us to experience the transpersonal. The archetypes provide the images that facilitate that experience. The instincts are very organic—they are the product of evolution—they're the biological roots of psyche. The Self, as the archetype of wholeness, is the image of the instinctual religious function. Its purpose is to give us an experience of the transpersonal—a numinous experience.

STEPHAN: So all this is rooted in matter?

JEFFREY: Yes. That's why Jung said that the archetypes are rooted in the earth itself.

STEPHAN: So the religious instinct must be there in matter itself?

JEFFREY: That's deep panpsychism, which is the insight that psyche is everywhere. Archetypes and instincts dwell in the psychoid realm, which is even more primordial than psyche. Psyche and matter arise out of the psychoid. The psychoid marries psyche and matter. My proposal is that the whole thing rests in the unus mundus.

◇◇◇◇◇◇◇◇◇◇◇◇◇◇◇◇◇◇◇◇◇◇◇◇◇◇◇◇◇◇◇

Thinking, however, takes another route. Eschewing Imagination, it would analyze the Mediterranean into its parts, flensing it into shards and fragments labeled as atoms, molecules, and parts per thousand of sodium chloride. This is all very well, as long as Imagination imbues these abstract concepts with a strongly animistic sense of connection. Consider what a mess reason and thinking have created in the world by banishing Imagination as the central guiding perception in our consciousness. Clearly, we might have been more compassionate, more in tune with nature, and more at peace with ourselves if we'd kept Imagination in the picture. Jung says that: "hemmed round by rationalistic walls, we are cut off from the eternity of nature." Without that sense of eternity, we live without meaning and become mere exploiters and destroyers of nature. Imagination, if turned inward, connects us with the deepest healing potentials in our psyche.

Jules writes that W. B. Yeats refers to images:

> as "living souls" which come upon us with a life of their own, trailing their own histories and destinies. He continues that "whatever the passions of man have gathered about becomes a symbol in the Great Memory"—which is "the Memory of Nature herself"—and that these symbols are available to the Imagination in human beings. (Cashford 2014, 17)

We learn from Jules that "Imagination is the ultimate in human thinking and has laws of its own no less rigorous than those of logic"

(Cashford 2016, 8). Reason dominates us too much. We must realize that Imagination (Corbin's imaginal, his cognitive imagination) is just as essential as reason for our well-being and wholeness.

The rigorous laws of Imagination tell us that Gaia is the physical, animate Earth herself, and at the same time the animating soul and living energy coursing through the entire cosmos. Jules reminds us that Gaia is the "structuring principle of the universe," which is not limited only to the Earth. She says:

> Gaia was an image or idea far beyond what we generally mean by "Earth": she was the Mother who brought forth the universe from herself, so all children were children of the universe, formed from her substance. Earth, then, was inherently lawful (Themis) carrying the memory of the whole (Mnemosyne)—the Great Memory—and embodied the changing rhythms of time (Cronos, the last of the Titans who name means "Time"). It followed that lawfulness and memory and temporal rhythms also belonged to all her creation. In contemporary terms, Gaia was a vision of the universe as one dynamic living whole. (Cashford 2010, 23)

This is archetypal Gaia. One might think that such an immaterial idea of Gaia is primitive and backward and that we were right to let it go when science took hold, banishing this archaic Gaia to the outer darkness of our awareness. But how can we be so sure that our "primitive" forebears were not feeling and perceiving something real when they spoke, each in their own way according to their cultural complex, of the universe as born from a great cosmic Earth Mother? Perhaps they knew something absolutely real that we moderns must rediscover, allowing their wisdom to permeate our science and technology so that we and our planet can reach our full potential together.

If this is true, then the Mother Earth myth or story gives us a clue about the nature and qualities of archetypal Gaia. So let's explore the central Mother Earth myth of our own culture—that of Gaia herself—which comes to us from the ancient Greeks.

Here is a highly simplified retelling of the Gaia myth based on

Hesiod's *Theogony* from around 700 BCE. As we go through the story, be aware of how a new level of consciousness bubbles up from the depths of the unconscious with the appearance of each new god. The movement from Ouranos to Cronos to Zeus becomes a journey through new ways of seeing, each of which engenders a new definition of normality in the culture.

Jules points to this developmental process:

As we follow the story of Gaia unfolding into creation it is remarkable how, in the Imagination of the ancient Greeks, Gaia was a dynamic force at each stage of creation . . . Gaia giving birth to children who give birth to their children and so on are also stages of differentiation of human consciousness: how we separate things from each other, draw distinctions between them, give them a name and a role—drawing out the actual from the potential so we can understand them and let them live. (Cashford 2010, —25)

It seems that Gaia wants consciousness to develop; she seems to want to broaden and deepen consciousness through the evolutionary trajectory of the universe, and so it may well be that the growth of consciousness in all nature is deeply implicated in her mysterious purposes.

It would be best to read the following story in your Gaia place. Go there now if you can.

Make yourself calm and comfortable in your place of magic and healing.

Allow your perceptions to open and to widen. Listen to the wind, to bird song. Feel the temperature of the air—breathe in and savour the aromas it carries. Touch the ground, the bark of trees, the soft patina of an outspread leaf. Delight in the richness of colors. Feel the weight of your body on the ground.

Gently guide your thinking mind to the sidelines where it won't harry you with its doubts and worries and allow yourself to delve into a living sense of archetypal Gaia.

First, before the world existed, there was Chaos—vast and dark. Chaos was alone in the great void of its own loneliness.

To make company for itself, to abolish its loneliness, Chaos gave birth to Gaia who is both the vastness of the cosmos and our sacred, deep-breasted Earth, both imbued with soul.

Gaia gave birth to three children: Love (Eros), the underworld (Tartarus), and the heavens with all its stars (Ouranos). She also gave birth to the hills and mountains and to Pontus, the great swirling ocean.

Ouranos and Gaia made love. Gaia gave birth to the six gods and six goddesses known as the Titans: including Themis (law), Rhea (flow), Mnemosyne (memory), and Chronos (time). The Titan Epimetheus, also her son, created all Earth's living beings except for man, who was created by his brother, Prometheus.

Gaia also gave birth to three ugly, violent giants, each one with fifty heads and a hundred flailing arms. Ouranos, their father, couldn't stand these brutes. He heaved hard and pushed these ugly giants back into Gaia's belly to stop them from seeing the light.

Gaia groaned and stretched in pain. She couldn't seem to give birth again to those giant children of hers who were back in her belly and who needed to be in the light.

She pondered how to ease her misery.

So out of herself she made a fearsome iron sickle, gray and dull, toothed, sharp as a razor, shaped exactly like the sickle moon.

She handed the sickle to Cronos, who dreamed of nothing more than deposing his own father, Ouranos.

Cronos hid, holding his sickle at the ready.

Ouranos appeared and sprawled himself out next to Gaia asking for love.

Seeing his chance, Cronos leaped out and hacked off his father's genitals with that cruel sickle while Ouranos and Gaia were locked in a love embrace. Ouranos leaped back in shock and he and Gaia were separated.

Ouranos rushed off toward the sea carrying his father's genitals, which dripped drops of blood into Gaia's soil. The drops became the three Furies who ruthlessly punish moral crimes, faithlessness, and murder.

Cronos reached the glistening seashore and threw the severed genitals into the ocean with all his might. They turned into Aphrodite, goddess of love and relationship, who emerged from the foam of the sea.

Cronos was now in charge, as he had always wanted. He mated with his sister Rhea (flow). She gave birth to six children (whom we know as the Olympian gods and goddesses): Hestia, Demeter, Hera, Poseidon, Hades, and Zeus.

Gaia, who knows all since all comes from her, prophesized to Cronos that he would be supplanted in turn by one of his own children.

To prevent losing his power Cronos swallowed his offspring, but not Zeus, whom Gaia hid in a remote cave deep in the sun-soaked Cretan countryside redolent with the scents of wild lavender and sage.

Rhea gave Cronos a baby-sized stone wrapped in swaddling clothes, telling him that this was Zeus. Cronos swallowed the stone thinking that he was devouring the last of his children.

Sometime later, in faraway Crete, Zeus had grown into his manhood. After much persuasion Gaia convinced him to induce Cronos to release his children from his dark innards.

Cronos refused, so for ten long years a war raged between Zeus and his father. Gaia gave Zeus thunderbolt and lightning to fight the battle.

Zeus won. Drunk with victory, he threw Cronos and rest of the Titans into the underworld to be held eternally captive there.

Gaia wanted Zeus to release the Titans, for like the giants before them, they needed to be out in the world. Zeus refused. So another war raged, but this time between Gaia and her grandson.

Zeus won and took control. He heeded the advice of his grandmother and placated her by mating with the Titan Themis (law) who gave birth to the Fates and the seasons, and also with the Titan Mnemosyne (memory), whose children are the Muses.

And so, despite many setbacks, the cosmos develops as it should with Gaia, nature, the gods and goddesses integrated into one evolving living whole.

We see how, in this ancient myth, each new god from Ouranos to Cronos to Zeus transforms consciousness, bringing new perspectives that perhaps not even Gaia could have entirely foreseen. Could she have known that the three giants she spawned would be thrust back into her belly by her son and lover Ouranos? This event stops the flow of creation, and so she needs a solution to this hiatus in the growth of consciousness.

Her answer is to throw Ouranos's generative power into the ocean, the cradle of biological life, to restart the processes of development. But who is to do the deed? Cronos seems fitting, since time must be invoked to set the evolutionary journey of consciousness and the cosmos into movement again. Gaia forges a sickle for Cronos made from the moon, who was the physical embodiment of time for ancient people because of how, in her waxing, she slowly appears out of the darkness of space, year on year and month on month, eternally.

Cronos uses the sickle to cut off Ouranos's genitals while Ouranos and Gaia make love. The shock of the event separates the pair, suggesting that the development of consciousness can continue because the masculine energy of discernment is now sharply discriminated from the feminine energy of nurturing and relationship. Thus are born the cosmic parents found in so many myths of origin around the world.

As Cronos runs off, drops of blood fall into Gaia's soil, bringing forth the three Furies who make us aware of our most grievous transgressions so that consciousness can develop within powerful moral guidelines. When Ouranos's genitals sink into the ocean they fertilize the sea, who gives birth to Aphrodite, the Goddess of love and relationships who initiates the intimacy between living beings needed to sustain Gaia's ecological communities, empowering the biological world to weave itself together with our planet's rocks, atmosphere, and waters into a coherent self-regulating living whole.

Cronos now rules with a new form of consciousness more grounded in the pulse and thrum of nature's rhythms than before when timeless Ouranos was in charge. Cronos mates with his sister Rhea (flow), setting many diverse strands and tempos of time flowing through the cosmos and throughout Gaia's evolving biosphere.

The children of Cronos and Rhea are the Olympian goddesses and gods, the last of whom is Zeus, whose name, as Jules tells us, "means

'Light' and 'Day,' or rather, in its original verbal form, the moment of 'Lighting up' ('Theos,' god, was said in the moment of revelation). So the (Olympian) gods form the structural principles of Sea, Underworld and Sky (as Light, Day and Storm), while the goddesses explore the relation of humans to the given conditions of life, the habitation of earth in the human realm" (Cashford 2010, 27).

Here we see a further differentiation of consciousness via the humanizing feminine principles of the goddesses. However, if the new consciousness brought by Zeus is to blossom, he must depose his father, Cronos. In this way, a more discriminating style of consciousness can be born. Gaia tells Cronos that one of his children will depose him, but Cronos can't countenance the changes that the new consciousness will bring. He eats his children, banishing them into the depths of the unconscious in a move counter to all that Gaia wants to achieve. All except Zeus, whom Gaia saves and nourishes in the peace and tranquillity of the ancient Cretan countryside, deep in one of her sacred caves where she prepares him to be the next ruling principle of consciousness. When it's clear that Cronos won't go without a struggle, Gaia arms Zeus with lightning (sudden insight) and the thunderbolt (reverberating understanding) for the battle with his father.

Zeus wins and banishes all the Titans, including Cronos himself, to the underworld just as Ouranos had done when he pushed the three ugly giants back into Gaia's belly and just as Cronos himself had done when he swallowed his own children. Gaia is furious. This is the third time that a newly emerged kind of consciousness has pushed valuable older ways of knowing into the unconscious because it can't seem to understand that old and new energies need to be integrated. So Gaia fights it out with Zeus who is again victorious. Of this, Jules writes that:

The new image of the divine, embodied in Zeus . . . separates out from its source and initiates a new set of values. Light is set *against* the lower world, and the new rule of oppositions is born, characteristic of patriarchies everywhere. However, in Greece, the old order is brought into relation with the new, so the original inheritance is never entirely lost. (Cashford 2010, 28)

Zeus, realizing this need to connect with the older wisdom, unites with the feminine Titans, Themis and Mnemosyne (law and memory), two of the original cosmic principles without whom further development cannot happen. Zeus also mates with the ancient goddesses of Earth and Moon, with his own sister Demeter (Goddess of the harvest and the fertility of the Earth) and with the nymphs (the nature spirits of woods, mountains, rivers, and streams), thereby bringing these ancient ways of being and knowing into his new regime of consciousness. Thus, even though Zeus brings forth a consciousness that is more reflective, detached, and able to look back on itself and understand its context, Gaia, Mother of All, archetypal Gaia, continued to be revered and respected in ancient Greece. Jules summarizes the situation thus:

> Gaia continued to be honoured as a living presence whose laws were written into the lives of all creation. It followed that Gaia's law was related to the moral law of human beings, or, as we might say, Nature and human nature, were not separately configured, as they have become today . . . the order of Nature was for the Greeks a dynamic moral order implicating human life. (Cashford 2010,—31)

Over the long ages of our human presence on this planet most ancient cultures experienced Earth as a sacred Mother whose immense significance they felt by aligning themselves with the mysterious meanings in her cycles and seasons and in the many complex connections and relationships between all her beings, experiencing her as an earthly living personhood made of soul and spirit, who gives birth to and sustains the entire cosmos in every moment.

We find such an understanding in the Bushmen of southern Africa, who are the direct descendants of our earliest human ancestors. Bushman myths and stories involving goddesses and the feminine spirit reveal something of the earliest manifestations of archetypal Gaia in our species. Laurens van der Post—the great South African anthropologist and explorer—recounts a pertinent Bushman story told to him as a young child in Africa by his beloved native nurse in his marvelous book *The Heart of the Hunter* (1965).

What follows is my simplified retelling of that story.

There was once a Bushman of ancient times who had a wonderful herd of black and white cattle, the color pattern with the most potent mystical associations for his people. The man looked after his cattle with deep devotion, making sure that no lions, hyenas, or other wild animals disturbed them in the least as they grazed in the wild bush country of southern Africa. He enjoyed the most delicious milk from his cattle, a milk so pure and subtle that whenever he drank it he felt a deep connection with the First Spirit and realized how sacred and divine was the wild, pure bush country where he lived.

One morning he went to milk his cows as usual but found that all their udders were completely dry. He thought that perhaps the previous day's grazing had not been nutritious enough for his animals, so the next day he took them to a place rich in succulent young grasses and pungent healing herbs. But by morning the udders were dry again.

Deeply disturbed, the man spent that night hiding near his cattle, waiting to see what would transpire. Soon enough, a silver thread descended from the stars and a group of lovely sky maidens descended down it to earth. Laughing and singing, they milked all his cows, filling their calabashes with the sumptuous frothy milk.

The man leaped out to catch them, but they easily escaped him and clambered up the silver rope back to the stars carrying their calabashes. All except one, that is, whom the man managed to catch. She was the most beautiful of them all.

Soon they were married and all went very well for the man and his celestial wife, who worked in the fields while he tended his cattle. He loved her dearly, but one thing troubled him. When he caught her, she had with her a beautifully woven basket with a tight-fitting lid. Before she married him, she made him promise never to look inside the basket until she allowed him to do so. She made it quite clear that if he disobeyed things would go awry for them.

Many months passed, and one day when his wife was out working in the fields he saw the basket standing alone in a corner of their hut. He could stand it no longer. Gripped by a rush of heedless curiosity, he ripped off the lid, looked inside, and rolled about in fits of laughter.

That evening his wife came home and knew immediately what had happened. "You've looked in the basket," she said, a look of horror on her face.

"You silly thing," said he, laughing again. "There's nothing there. It's completely empty."

"Are you sure—nothing at all?" she said with a quavering voice, almost fainting. "Absolutely nothing!" boomed his voice.

With that, she turned around and walked out of the hut into the night, never to be seen or heard of again.

Laurens's African nurse finished the story with these words: "And do you know why she went away, my little master? Not because he had broken his promise, but because, looking into the basket, he had found it empty. She went because the basket was not empty. It was full of beautiful things of the sky she stored there for them both, and because he could not see them and just laughed, there was no use for her on earth anymore and she just vanished."

The sky goddesses in the story are manifestations of archetypal Gaia—the ordering principles of the cosmos. They come from the sky because these principles are intangible to our ordinary perception. The goddesses want to become Gaia made flesh by drinking the nutritious nectar from the udders of the herdsman's sacred black-and-white cows.

You can't capture a goddess unless she wants you to, so perhaps the most beautiful of the sky Goddesses deliberately allowed herself to be caught by the herdsman whom she knew could one day become a great healer.

Marinating in her love each day brought him a little closer to being capable of consciously feeling the immense reality and value of the sky secrets hidden in her basket, which contained images of the First Spirit who is the animating principle of nature and the cosmos, also known as the anima mundi, the soul of the world—archetypal Gaia. Only by seeing this could he and all humanity be returned to our original wholeness here on Earth.

But his insight wasn't fully ripened that fateful day when he lifted the lid. It was too early in his development. His consciousness wasn't fully cooked, and so he saw only an empty basket. Just like him, most moderns wouldn't see anything in the basket either, even if it had been brought to us by a Goddess from the sky.

Archetypal Gaia is invisible to our culturally conditioned modern perception in which we see the world as dead matter. We've lost the sacred image of the world as a living whole, and so we despoil and destroy it to feed our greed for material things.

We can imagine how it might have been had the herdsman only waited until his wife was ready to show him the contents of her sacred basket. Years would have passed, decades perhaps, or maybe only days—we cannot know. But it's certain that the herdsman would have become wiser and more conscious day by day thanks to the subtle influence of his wife helping him grow into his wholeness.

One day when his insight had at last fully ripened, she would have invited him out of their hut into the sparkling morning sunshine of the southern African dry season, with emerald spotted wood doves calling nearby and bateleur eagles soaring far above in that great vault of peerless blue sky. As soon as he sees the basket before him on the dusty ground, he feels an electric thrill running through his mind and body. Now at last, the moment has come. Slowly, she lifts the lid, and bowing, she signals for to him to peer inside.

He sees a black round of darkness surrounded by a circle of finely woven basket work. The blackness makes his heart beat with holy recognition of the wholeness of nature. A slowly circling mandala appears out of the blackness and turns into a vision of Gaia, of our living planet swirling in heavenly beauty through the vastness of space. Profound knowledge and deep connection with Gaia's mysterious intelligence, purposes, and moral order awakens in him, making him ready to be the healer he was long ago destined to be.

We moderns are like the herdsman. We are not yet psychologically developed enough to perceive the true nature of things. We have lost the skill of perceiving the soul of the world, the First Spirit of the Bushmen. We must find it again quickly before our time runs out. It's a hard lesson with a precious result; one we must learn for the sake of the future. Awful as it was, the coronavirus reminded us how to live within Gaia's limits, to slow down, consume less, and connect more with each other and with our animate Earth.

Van der Post, like Jung and many others, felt that this loss of soul is the root of all our problems. They worked hard to bring the perception of soul back into the awareness of globalized, Westernized people, which is why we are working with Jung's psychological and alchemical insights in this book, attempting to bring science and alchemy together again, those infant twins who should never have been separated so long ago by that fateful, purely intellectual movement spearhead by Descartes and others.

Another helpful description of archetypal Gaia is given to us by Joseph Campbell in his book *Primitive Mythology* in which he speaks about the basal Neolithic perception of the feminine energies of nature based on the many female clay figurines found in many parts of Europe from that period. He says of them that:

> They give magical psychological aid to women in childbirth and conception, stand in house shrines to receive daily prayers and to protect the occupants from physical as well as spiritual danger, serve to support the mind in meditation on the mystery of being, and, since they are frequently charming to behold, serve as ornaments in the pious home. They go forth with the farmer into his fields, protect the crops, protect the cattle in the barn. They are the guardians of children. They watch over the sailor at sea and the merchant on the road. (Campbell [1959] 2011, 139)

Clearly, we've lost touch with archetypal Gaia and her healing, protective, and inspiring energies, and so we lay the world to waste as a result. Jung pointed out that in a severe situation such as our current global crisis, compensatory images will be given us by nature—by the collective unconscious—in an attempt to correct the imbalance, as we discovered in Descartes's dreams. This inward compensation is a fine example of Jung's discovery of the psyche's innate ability for self-regulation in its constant search for wholeness through the reconciliation of opposing tendencies. As we shall see, self-regulation is a key trait shared by all living beings including this physical Gaia, our animate Earth.

We would therefore expect that a hugely powerful healing image should have emerged into view as the global ecological-social crisis deepened in recent times. With a kind of cosmic irony, the great compensatory image did indeed appear: Gaia. Most unexpectedly, this was not revealed to a poet, religious leader, or philosopher, but to a scientist in 1965: James Lovelock, perhaps the only scientist alive at the time capable of integrating such a profound image from the depths of nature—from archetypal Gaia—into his own psyche without losing one jot of scientific rigor. It is ironic, because for centuries science has taken great pains to repress archetypal Gaia. John Maynard-Smith, the genial genius of evolutionary biology, once accused Lovelock of promoting his scientific Gaia as "that evil religion," before he himself became more sympathetic to certain scientific aspects of Gaia.

The alchemical insight which we are exploring here (much to the disdain of some of my fellow scientists, no doubt) is that Lovelock did not *invent* the idea of Gaia as a self-regulating living planet. Rather, he *received* it from the depths of the psyche—from archetypal Gaia, so desperate was she to wake us out of our mechanistic slumber just when the ecological and climate crises were gearing up into a serious intensity.

James Lovelock knows about regions of psyche that are deeper and more primordial than reason. He knows how to intuit the presence of archetypal Gaia. The importance he attaches to intuition for developing a deep understanding of Gaia came home to me during a conversation I had with him a few years ago.

In the early winter of 2017, we were walking together along Chesil beach in Dorset, near his new home. He was then ninety-eight years old, as lively in mind and sprightly in body as ever. We talked about the importance of intuition for connecting with Gaia. Even though he didn't say it in so many words, it seems to me now that he was telling me how he intuitively nourishes his relationship with archetypal Gaia.

"The only way to really understand Gaia, Stephan, isn't through science and reasoning. It's through intuition."

"What is intuition, Jim?"

"Imagine we're deep in the jungle and at this very moment we

see a tiger in front of us. We react without even thinking about it. Another part of our mind takes over, a nonrational functioning that guides us to safety. We'd be dead if we had to think: 'that's a tiger— hmm, probably dangerous. Let's calculate its probable trajectory, and so on.' Some other part of our mind takes over and we know what to do without thinking. That's what intuition is like."

"You mean that the mind that reacts to a danger is somehow connected to the intuitive mind that can sense what or who Gaia is?"

"Yes, they are connected. Intuition comes in flash—in a moment of insight."

"Can we cultivate intuition?"

"Oh yes. It's best learned when we are children."

"Did you learn it as a child?"

"From my father. He was deeply connected to nature. He knew how to live off the land, how to catch rabbits. He knew the names of wild plants, and which berries one could eat. He could see the trails of mammals, he knew where birds nested. He knew their names.

"I get it—your father was a tracker! A sort of modern Bushman!"

"And he taught me how to tickle for trout."

"Tickle for trout?"

"By wiggling my fingers under water in a quiet river's eddy where trout like to wait for food. If you did it right, the trout would be fooled into mistaking your fingers for worms. But you can only learn it as a child. Only a child is able to evoke an intuitive connection deep enough to attract the fish."

"You mean that searching for the intuitive experience of Gaia is like tickling for trout?"

"It's just like that. To sense Gaia we need to be like a child tickling for trout."

We walk in silence for a while, gazing out over the gentle, sunlit sea. The conversation turns to other Gaian things. We go in, have lunch, then tea. It's late. The Lovelocks must be tired. Time to go.

The image has stayed with me all this while, a gift from the sage by the sea. The river water is the great flowing psyche of nature. Our fingers, they're our intuitive feelers in this flow. The trout, that's the world-saving insight that can be granted if we feel our way into the stream of our planet's vast life with the openness of a child. Science can take us partway to Gaia, that's clear. But to feel her fully, as fully as we are humanely able, we must be like children, for only then can we dwell in the living sense of archetypal Gaia.

We must learn to tickle for trout.

SCIENTIFIC GAIA

Doing science with awe and humility is a powerful act of reciprocity with the more-than-human world.

ROBIN WALL KIMMERER

A Gaian alchemical rendering of the oft-repeated story of how the idea of a living Earth first occurred to James Lovelock focuses as much on the synchronicities (meaningful coincidences) that occurred along the way as it does on the science. I will briefly retell the story in this more animistic way while introducing you to the basic scientific ideas behind Gaia that we'll need to work effectively with this book.

In the early 1960s NASA wanted to send a lander to Mars to confirm the commonly held notion that there was life writ large on the surface of the red planet. Lovelock was famous as an inventor of superbly sensitive scientific instruments, so it was quite natural that NASA should invite him to join them in Pasadena, California, to help them develop life-detecting instruments for their missions to Mars.

The unquestioned mainstream scientific understanding at that time—the early 1960s—was that our Earth is no more than a dead lump of rock floating through space carrying a thin patina of living beings on its surface, which have to adapt to the environmental conditions (such as temperature, acidity, and rainfall) imposed upon them by the surrounding rocks, atmosphere, and water. It was unthinkable then that these living beings could have any significant impact on their environment, let alone regulate global aspects of it such as its surface temperature.

Full of excitement, Lovelock rushed off to NASA, only to find that the life detection experiments proposed by the biologists there were painfully inadequate, partly because they were too reductionist. What if the lander happened to touch down on a lifeless patch of the Martian surface and totally missed a richly thriving haven of Martian life perhaps as close as twenty meters away and yet totally out of reach? Lovelock realized that these experiments relied exclusively on testing the landing site for the presence of life and that this oversight could so easily produce a resounding and extremely expensive false negative. Lovelock sensed that a totally different approach was needed. He knew that he had to think of an experiment that would somehow detect Martian life at the level of the entire planet. But what was that experiment?

Lovelock invented a beautifully holistic life detection experiment out of this question, which is applicable not just to Mars but to any planet. His answer was to look for the presence of chemical disequilibrium in the planet's atmospheric gasses. A disequilibrium would be a signal for widespread surface life, since living beings would soon discover how to use the atmosphere as a source of raw materials and as a dumping ground for the waste products of their metabolism. In contrast, a planetary atmosphere at chemical equilibrium would signal very little or absolutely no life on the planet's surface.

Philosopher Dian Hitchcock, hired by NASA to assess the logical consistency of the experiments to be placed on the Mars landers, now enters the story. With her fierce rationality and feminine sensitivity she helped Lovelock to stress test his life detection idea and thus made a vital contribution to the birth of scientific Gaia. It seems significant from an alchemical point of view that scientific Gaia was born from a collaboration between masculine and feminine archetypes in the form of these two ground-breaking researchers.

To test out his idea, Lovelock needed data on the atmospheric composition of Mars, which he knew could be obtained relatively easily here on Earth by pointing a telescope with an infrared spectrometer attached at the red planet. No need for a mission to Mars. NASA was not pleased to hear this, so wedded were they to their life-detecting landers.

And yet how strangely synchronistic it was that unbeknown to Lovelock and Hitchcock, two French scientists—Pierre and Janine Connes—had just recently collected exactly the data Lovelock needed from the atmospheres of Mars and Venus using the Pic de Midi telescope in the Alps. Soon after, in September 1965, the astronomer Lou Kaplan brought in printouts of these Pic de Midi data for Lovelock and Hitchcock to look over. From these data they immediately saw that the atmospheres of Mars and Venus are mostly carbon dioxide—a sure sign of chemical equilibrium and hence of the absence of life writ large on the surfaces of both planets.

The Pic de Midi data set spurred Lovelock to musing. Earth's atmosphere contains gasses produced by life, such as oxygen and methane as well as oxygen and nitrogen, that react violently together in the presence of sunlight. Both reactions strip oxygen from the atmosphere, and yet we know from geological evidence that the gas has remained at a roughly constant level of around 20 percent in our atmosphere for hundreds of millions of years. How could this be?

Lovelock was "tickling for trout" as he felt his way toward the deeper meaning lying hidden in the Pic de Midi data. Then, as he was talking to Diane Hitchcock about these data, an immense insight came to him in a flash:

> It was at that moment that I glimpsed Gaia. An awesome thought came to me. The Earth's atmosphere was an extraordinary and unstable mixture of gasses, yet I knew that it was constant in composition over quite long periods of time. Could it be that life on Earth not only made the atmosphere, but also *regulated* it—keeping it at a constant composition and at a level favorable for organisms? (my emphasis, Lovelock 1991, 22)

In his autobiography, *Homage to Gaia* (2000), Lovelock writes that his mind was well prepared "emotionally and scientifically" to receive the intuition that life regulates key aspects of our planet's surface such as temperature. This idea involved such a powerful shift of perspective—from a dead to a living, self-regulating Earth—that even his most brilliant colleagues could not grasp the new concept at first. Lovelock writes that "I blurted out my intuition to my colleague Dian Hitchcock and to the cosmologist Carl Sagan. There was little comment at the time."

However, back in England lived a person capable of understanding Lovelock's intuition and its importance for science, humanity, and the entirety of our living planet. That person was William Golding, Lovelock's friend and neighbor in the little Wiltshire village of Bowerchalke. Golding just happened to be none other than a Nobel Prize–winning novelist, a polymath who had studied physics, and a person deeply familiar with the myths of ancient Greece.

The fact that these two geniuses happened to live in the same tiny English village certainly seems synchronistic, as was the fact that they decided to go for a long walk together after they had met by chance on the way to the village post office soon after Lovelock had returned from NASA with his unnamed idea of a self-regulating Earth.

It was during this fateful walk that Golding suggested to Lovelock that he call his hypothesis after Gaia, the ancient Greek divinity of the Earth. After an initial misunderstanding (he heard "gyre," not "Gaia"), Lovelock felt that Golding's suggestion was just what he had been looking for. He adopted the name Gaia wholeheartedly in a moment of deep recognition. Thus was born the Gaia hypothesis, which states that life has been in charge of regulating the surface conditions of the planet Earth over vast spans of geological time.

Lovelock's Gaia hypothesis evolved into his Gaia theory once sufficient evidence in favor of the hypothesis had come in from his pioneering mathematical model known as Daisyworld and from hard scientific data from the real world. Gaia theory proposes that our planet is a complex, lifelike system able to regulate key surface conditions such as its temperature, acidity, and the distribution of key elements within the narrow limits that organisms can tolerate. This is thanks to intricate feedbacks that have operated over billions of years between all biological life (the biota), rocks, atmosphere, and water (the abiotic realms). Here is one of Lovelock's many definitions of Gaia theory:

Gaia theory is about the evolution of a tightly coupled system whose constituents are the biota and their material environment, which comprises the atmosphere, the oceans and the surface rocks. Self-regulation of important properties, such as climate and chemical composition, is seen as consequence of this evolutionary process. (Lovelock 1989)

Elsewhere Lovelock writes that:

Through Gaia theory I now see the system of the material Earth and the living organisms on it, evolving so that self-regulation is an emergent property. In such a system, active feedback processes operate automatically and solar energy sustains comfortable conditions for life. The conditions are only constant in the short term and evolve in synchrony with the changing needs of the biota as it evolves. Life and its environment are so closely coupled that evolution concerns Gaia, not the organisms or the environment taken separately. (Lovelock 1995, 19)

Gaian self-regulation is an emergent property that arises unexpectedly at the level of the planet as a whole. This occurs as the result of all the interactions among the parts of the Gaian system, namely the biota on the one hand and the atmosphere, waters, and rocks on the other. In this view, there is no providential Gaia steering the system from above or beyond. Instead, scientific Gaia emerges from multifarious, unconscious, "automatic," down-to-earth, cause and effect, scientifically verifiable interactions among these major components of our planetary system.

It's fair to say that the scientific community reacted unfavorably to his Gaia hypothesis. Lovelock knew that he needed to invent a mathematical model of a self-regulating planet, but how to do this was no easy matter. He pondered and mulled over this problem for about a year with no result.

Then another particularly interesting synchronistic event took place, which gave Lovelock the inspiration he needed. On Christmas Day,

1981, he walked into his laboratory at home. To his surprise, he found a copy of the science journal *Nature* lying open at random on his desk revealing some succinct mathematical equations by Carter and Prince for the growth of small plants (plantains) on an English lawn. His unconscious had already brought him memories of his work for NASA on the use of black and white panels for regulating the temperature of satellites. Then, with a typically brilliant Lovelockian flash of insight, he realized that he could use the plantain equations to model the spread of black and white daisies on a simplified planet, where, just as with the satellite panels, black daisies would warm themselves and the planet by absorbing solar energy and white daisies would cool themselves and their world by reflecting the sun's energy back to space. This is Daisyworld, the first ever mathematical model of a Gaian planet, which Lovelock used to model feedbacks between life (the daisies) and their nonliving environment (the surface temperature of their planet) with just six coupled differential equations taken from biology and physics.

Daisyworld's sun behaves just like our real sun by increasing its luminosity gradually over geological time. Both daisy types have the same biologically realistic bell-shaped growth response to surface temperature: below 5 degrees Centigrade it is too cold for growth and above 40 degrees Centigrade it is too hot, with maximum growth at 22.5 degrees Centigrade. However, the daisies don't just respond to the planetary surface temperature. They also affect it due to the reflectivity of their petals: as we have said, white daisies reflect solar energy to space and hence cool themselves and their planet, whereas black daisies warm themselves and their world. The biological equations are neatly neo-Darwinian, for they make light and dark daisies compete for space on the planet's surface.

Once he had the Carter and Prince equations it only took him an hour to program Daisyworld using a refined form of Basic on his computer. The results amazed him (fig. 5.2).

Time runs along the horizontal axis in both graphs while the vertical axis in the lower graph shows the abundance and diversity of both daisy types while in the upper graph the vertical axis plots planetary temperature.

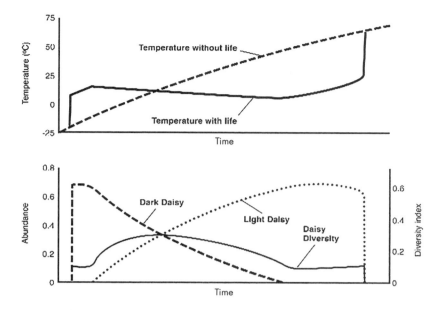

Figure 5.2. Daisyworld reveals its remarkably stable emergent temperature regulation.

The lower graph shows how dark daisies dominate when the sun is very cool, at which point they warm themselves and the planet. As the sun brightens, light daisies gradually become more abundant and help to cool the planet. For a vast span of time, a mixture of both daisy types coexist, though the light daisies gradually become more abundant as the sun brightens while dark daisy abundance decreases. Eventually the sun is so bright that all the dark daises have gone extinct (because it is too hot for them) and only white daisies persist. Eventually the sun becomes so bright that even the light daisies go extinct and the surface temperature shoots up to the lifeless temperature. This is the death of Daisyworld.

The upper graph shows how the surface temperature is regulated well within the limits tolerable by life over a huge span of time despite the increasing solar luminosity because of changes in the relative abundances of the two daisy types. Notice the marked difference between the surface temperature with and without life. The stability of Daisyworld is all the more remarkable given that systems of coupled differential equations are notoriously prone to produce chaos and instability.

◇◇◇◇ *A Conversation with Jeffrey Kiehl* ◇◇◇◇

JEFFREY: Jupiter's metal is tin, which shines a bit, so we are talking about reflective processes. We're in the albedo—it's all about reflective properties. In Gaia albedo is about white clouds reflecting sunlight, which is a very important part of how Gaia regulates her temperature. In Daisyworld models, changes to the albedo of the planet helps regulate Gaia's flow of energy. Gaia alchemy allows us to reflect on Gaia.

STEPHAN: Are we the only species that can reflect on Gaia?

JEFFREY: I think dolphins can self-reflect. I believe elephants can too. Both have a sense of self.

STEPHAN: Magpies as well.

JEFFREY: Yes, magpies. There are other animals that have self-reflecting abilities but we are probably somewhat unique in our degree and depth of self-reflection. The magpie could also be an extremely intelligent and reflective being. The only thing I really know is that we are.

STEPHAN: Exactly. So we give the magpie and all the other species maximum scope for self-awareness. But we're going into dissolution with our ability to reflect deeply on Gaia with flowing energy.

JEFFREY: We've got to be fluid.

STEPHAN: So in scientific terms we start thinking in terms of feedback loops.

JEFFREY: Yes. The flow of mass, the flow of energy.

STEPHAN: The flow of information.

JEFFREY: And entropy.

STEPHAN: Cybernetics and feedback.

◇◇◇◇◇◇◇◇◇◇◇◇◇◇◇◇◇◇◇◇◇◇◇◇◇

I worked on ecological extensions of Daisyworld with Lovelock for about five years. The model's emergent temperature regulation amazed me, but also of great interest is a powerful alchemical principle at work here that points to the archetype of fruitful interaction between opposites.

Detailed analysis of the Daisyworld model by mathematician Peter Saunders revealed the presence of what he calls integral rein control, a principle that was then discovered to operate in many physiological systems including the regulation of glucose in our bodies.

In essence, the idea is that Daisyworld's highly effective temperature regulation emerges because dark daisies prefer to be cool yet they warm themselves and their environment while light daisies prefer to be warm but cool themselves and their surroundings. Thus each daisy type gives the other what it needs but cannot provide for itself on its own.

The alchemists of old knew of this principle and illustrated it with the alchemical image the double pelican (fig. 5.3) in which each alembic distills a product in its upper globe that it feeds into the lower globe of its opposite number. The result is emergent wholeness and health for both of them, shown by the fourfold stars behind the upper globes.

This type of synergy between opposites can be found in any situation where effective regulation is at work, including the psyche, where the collective unconscious—the objective psyche—gives consciousness its view on our progress toward individuation while the unconscious learns and grows through contact with consciousness.

Daisyworld, together with hard scientific evidence from the real world, shows that life does indeed have major impacts on climate. These have convinced scientists to accept Gaia theory in principle, but only after rebranding the theory as "Earth System Science," since they object to the notion that our planet is in any sense a Goddess let alone animate, alive, or even lifelike, in contrast to Lovelock's own view that "Gaia is the largest manifestation of life."

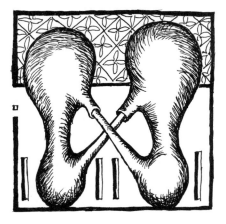

Figure 5.3. The Double Pelican.
Drawn for this book by Julia Ponsonby.

6

Carbon and Gaia's Temperature Regulation

The chemical element carbon offers us a direct route into experiencing Gaia alchemy through science, for carbon is centrally involved in weaving together our planet's biology with her climate. Carbon dioxide (CO_2) and methane (CH_4) are two key greenhouse gasses cycled in and out of the atmosphere by life, thereby helping to determine the temperature of our planet's surface. Living beings bond carbon atoms into vast chains that form the backbones of all life's organic molecules including giant molecules of DNA, polysaccharides, and fats, among many others.

Gaia's surface temperature is a vital signature of her health: too hot and her oceans would boil off to space leaving behind a scarred, dead planet somewhat like Venus, which lost its water billions of years ago when it seems likely that a runaway greenhouse feedback evaporated all the oceans; too cold and we end up with a frozen Snowball Earth. As a greenhouse gas, carbon dioxide is a key player in the ancient self-regulating dance between life, rocks, atmosphere, and water that has kept the surface temperature of our planet within habitable bounds for huge stretches of time. How does this self-regulating dynamic work?

Carbon dioxide molecules have been continuously arriving in the atmosphere through volcanoes and other fractures and punctures in Earth's surface ever since Earth cooled enough to form a crust. This happened about a hundred million years after the sun and the planets in our solar system coalesced out of the orbiting dust of a huge star, which exploded into a supernova about 4600 million years ago. The early sun was about 30 percent less bright than today, but there is good evidence that there was liquid water on our planet's surface some 4000 million years ago, or even earlier. This suggests that an atmosphere thick with greenhouse gasses such as carbon dioxide must have kept Earth warm enough to maintain liquid water on her surface all those many, many, many thousands of millions of years ago* despite a much dimmer sun.

From those early days right up to our own times, the amount of carbon dioxide in the atmosphere has slowly decreased while the luminosity of the sun has gradually increased. Despite evidence for some hot periods and also times of extreme cold, there must have been a balancing act between these opposing forces of cooling and warming that has worked reasonably well over geological time to regulate our planet's temperature within the narrow limits tolerable by most life forms. Is this relatively stable temperature no more than an amazing bit of good luck? Or could there be a giant planetary thermostat at work that has regulated global temperature throughout geological time?

The current view among scientists disposed favorably toward Gaia is that we live in a "probable Gaia" in which life-sustaining, self-regulating feedbacks had a good chance of emerging and persisting over billions of years once life became a planetwide phenomenon. Recent breakthroughs by Arwen Nicholson and colleagues in the mathematical simulation of nascent planets supports the view that emergent self-regulatory dynamics are likely to kick in and persist just as soon as candidate Gaian planets spawn widespread life.

Scientists have discovered that this ancient temperature regulating dynamic involves countless interactions among rocks, atmosphere, sediments, water, and the teeming biodiversity in our continents and oceans. A key finding is that calcium silicate rocks such as granite are essential components of this central temperature regulating feedback. One pathway for granite formation opens up when water-saturated slabs

---

*Since we are exploring vast periods of time, it is this author's opinion that these are more understandable when using the British system for displaying large numbers. For example, 3500 million years ago means three thousand five hundred million years ago. Please note that in science and in this book one thousand million is equivalent to one billion.

of sea floor basalt carrying their overlaying carapaces of sediments are pushed deep into Earth's interior where two tectonic plates meet. Here, under intense temperatures and pressures, the water-rich rock liquifies, producing a melt less dense than the surrounding material. This lighter granitic melt rises toward the planetary surface, cooling as it goes. Various crystals precipitate out of the melt at specific temperatures: feldspar, mica, amphibole, quartz, and others, all as a result of chemical transformations in the melt. Finally, when the melt has shed enough heat, it solidifies into granite rock, becoming the foundation of the continents.

In the following description of Earth's process of temperature regulation, see if you can discern which alchemical processes are at play. Recall that these are: calcination, dissolution, separation, conjunction, fermentation, distillation, and coagulation. You may also wish to return to this chapter again after reading later passages of the book.

Earth's regulating feedback involves a powerful chemical attraction between calcium ions in granite and carbon atoms in carbon dioxide gas in the air. Seen through the poetic eyes of a Gaian alchemical imagination, calcium ions become calcium princesses who are held tight in granite castles and wait for their carbon princes to rescue them from the monotony of their crystalline existence that has held them in unchanging fixity for many millions, sometimes billions, of years. In this Gaian alchemical perspective, we transform the science into a love story in which calcium princesses yearn to unite with their carbon princes with whom they dream of journeying into the swirling worlds of biosphere rivers and oceans after being liberated from the granite castles that held them in such monotonous constancy.

To begin with, each carbon prince rides free in the atmosphere with two oxygen atoms as his assistants in a molecule of carbon dioxide gas. How does a flighty, insubstantial gas manage to liberate calcium princesses from the impenetrable solidity of granite rock? Rain—the very opposite of solid rock—is the answer.

Carbon dioxide molecules in the air are captured and dissolved by raindrops as these tumble downward through the sky. Within each raindrop molecules of carbon dioxide and water combine to form two new chemical beings: negatively charged bicarbonate ions (HCO_3-) and positively charged hydrogen ions ($H+$). Billions of these interactions happen in every single raindrop as they fall earthward from the sky. Some of this natural acid rain falls on calcium silicate rocks such as granite and basalt. The hydrogen ions in the raindrops begin to eat away the rock because their tiny positive electrical charges attract them toward negatively charged ions on the rock surface. Although to us the granite is impenetrably solid, for atomic beings the rock is almost entirely empty space peppered here and there with large centers of electrical energy, which we call ions. This electrical energy is either positive or negative. Positive and negative charges attract; like charges repel. Here, in the very heart of the rock, we find a deep alchemical principle at work where opposites interact to create our physical reality and almost certainly the physical aspects of psyche as well.

Like bees around a honeypot, hordes of hydrogen ions cluster around massive negatively charged ions in the rock such as those of oxygen and silicon, neutralizing and disrupting the electrical attractions that hold the rock together. As a result, the rock dissolves, releasing legions of calcium princesses into the rainwater on the rock surface along with other ions such as those of silicon. Free at last, each calcium princess now loosely associates in the water with two bicarbonate ions, each of which holds a carbon prince at its center. The result is a watery solution of calcium bicarbonate. By removing the greenhouse gas carbon dioxide from the atmosphere, this alchemical dissolution, known as silicate rock weathering, cools Gaia's surface.

So far, the story has involved interactions between chemical beings such as hydrogen, calcium, and carbon. Now it is time to explore the Gaian dimensions of the story by focusing on plants, bacteria, fungi, lichens, and other biological beings living on the granite who mine the rock for nutrients such as phosphorus. This life-induced rock mining (or biologically assisted rock weathering as it is known in science) happens in various ways. Plants send their roots into the rock, splitting it into small fragments that dissolve in the carbonic acid brewed when carbon dioxide dissolves in rainwater. Lichens secrete rock-dissolving acids that speed up the weathering. Some bacteria secrete complex sugary molecules into tiny cracks in the rock, which swell up like balloons, splitting the rock. Countless beings: plant roots, earthworms, millipedes, fungi, bacteria, and many others exhale carbon dioxide onto the rock as the end product of their respiration, increasing the amount of the gas available for making rock-dissolving carbonic acid when rainwater percolates down to the roots from the air above. A whole host of soil animals breathe carbon dioxide onto the rock as the end product of their decomposition of dead organic beings. These include nematodes, woodlice, millipedes, fungi, and bacteria. Stable soils made by these organisms above the granite help all these interactions to happen more quickly than on rocks barren of life. In these ways, calcium princesses are released from the granite into the surrounding rainwater much faster than without life. As a result, they more quickly encounter their longed-for carbon princes.

◇◇◇◇◇ A Conversation with Jeffrey Kiehl ◇◇◇◇◇

STEPHAN: Alchemical images are about nature because alchemy is all about our relationship to Gaia. So for me, Gaia alchemy is the ultimate approach to Gaia. We can get a certain way with science, and science is fantastic but I don't think it takes us far enough. We need to throw science into the alchemical vessel of story and image so that it's tinctured with the ancient feelings for the animate Earth, which our ancestors would have had so long ago.

JEFFREY: What stands behind science is a deeper numinous experience of Gaia—of our ecosystems—of our planet. That's always behind the science because science comes from that experience. Science has its own particular way of knowing. It's important to remember that it's only trying to understand the world quantitatively, which is very important. We've learned a lot about Gaia through science, but it doesn't hold spirit, soul, or anima. It doesn't hold the numinous. That's what alchemy brings. It's a complement to the rational, scientific way of looking at things.

STEPHAN: Before we had science we had alchemy. The alchemists were the first people in our culture to explore the nature of matter.

Of course, they projected their unconscious into matter. The most advanced of them were beginning to realize that mathematics could be part of their quest. And they could have developed a holistic science in which the quantitative approach would have been as fully developed as now along with anima the psyche, the numinous dimension. These two aspects of ourselves could have been more fully integrated by now. What we are trying to do with Gaia alchemy is to make that development happen now. This could have happened four hundred years ago, but we had a hiatus of four hundred years for various historical reasons. Our task as Gaia alchemists is to carry on the development that stopped four hundred years ago.

◇◇◇◇◇◇◇◇◇◇◇◇◇◇◇◇◇◇◇◇◇◇◇◇◇◇◇◇◇◇◇◇◇◇

The closest union between our two alchemical atomic lovers (carbon and calcium) is yet to be. For the time being each calcium princess makes a loose association with two carbon princes, who cluster around each princess. Each carbon prince is bonded to three atoms of oxygen, and two of these oxygens are bonded to a respective hydrogen atom. The double positive charge on each calcium princess attracts two carbon-bonded oxygen atoms into her ambit, the entire ensemble making one molecule of calcium bicarbonate (fig. 6.1).

This chemical being only exists dissolved in water, which makes the attractions between calcium and carbon-bonded oxygen so loose, fleeting, and forever moving that the two royals are constantly changing partners.

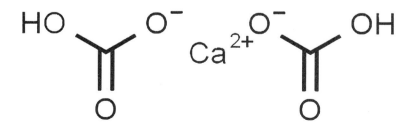

Figure 6.1. A calcium bicarbonate molecule.
There is a carbon atom where each set of four lines join.

The life-enhanced amplification of granite dissolution (or biologically assisted granite weathering) cools Gaia by removing planet-warming molecules of carbon dioxide from her atmosphere perhaps up to one hundred times faster than is the case on bare lifeless rock. It would take biologically assisted granite weathering merely one million years to completely remove every single carbon dioxide molecule from the atmosphere if all inputs from volcanoes and other natural sources were completely shut off, plunging the planet into the frozen death of a permanent Snowball Earth. A million years is no time at all for Gaia. From the perspective of our almost 4600-million-year-old planet, one million years is equivalent to the time it takes me to blink a few times in relation to my potential lifetime of eighty years or so. Rain flushes legions of bicarbonate molecules through the soil and groundwater into rivers and then finally to the sea. As they travel through these domains of fresh water, the two royals (calcium princesses and carbon princes) encounter each other in ever-flowing partner-swapping dances under the careful gaze of their oxygen and hydrogen assistants. They move together like human dance partners in Scottish reels or ceilidhs until they finally reach the ocean.

Here, floating in the ocean surface, tiny single-celled algae, such as the coccolithophores (which means "carriers of little stone berries"), usher the calcium bicarbonate molecules into bridal chambers deep within their photosynthesizing bodies. Coccolithophore bridal chambers are alive. They intelligently control the precipitation of the aqueous calcium bicarbonate into beautifully sculpted mandalalike coccoliths of solid calcium carbonate—chalk—which they extrude in overlapping plates onto their cellular surfaces (fig. 6.2).

Multitudes of dead coccolithophores, along with hosts of loose coccoliths, sink into ocean basins forming vast deposits of chalk. When compacted, these turn into the even denser rock known as limestone. Movements of tectonic plates oftentimes subduct these calcium carbonate deposits deep beneath a continent where the chalk melts under the intense temperatures and pressures in the subterranean regions of our planet's body.

If it was indeed an alchemical marriage that took place in the

Figure 6.2. An electron microscope image of coccolithophores. Each one is a single
photosynthetic cell covered in mandalalike plates of calcium carbonate known as coccoliths.
Reproduced with permission through Science Photo Library.

sunlit coccolithophores' bridal chambers, could it be that the royal union now ends in separation here in the deep hot bowels of the Earth? The melting chalk releases carbon dioxide gas, which volcanoes spew out into the atmosphere. Meanwhile, the calcium princesses are left behind in the molten chalk. They become part of a newly forming rocky melt destined to become fresh granite as it rises and cools. Perhaps this is no divorce after all, but merely a temporary separation. Eventually, in perhaps two hundred million years or so, the two royals will meet again when the newly formed granite is exposed to the atmosphere and hence to biologically assisted weathering. This great journey is then repeated.

Science shows us that this entire dynamic has regulated Gaia's temperature over geological time. The crux of it is that living beings are very sensitive to temperature. When they sense a temperature increase caused by an upturn in greenhouse gas emissions from volcanic activity, their response is to grow more and to reproduce more profusely. Plants grow better in higher temperatures since warmer temperatures produce more evaporation from the ocean and hence more rain. There is also more of the vital plant food, carbon dioxide, in the air.

The warmer conditions promote vibrant growth among all the granite weathering biota, which work to reduce temperature by increasing attractions between carbon princes in the atmosphere and calcium princesses in the granite as described above. When temperature declines, granite weathering is significantly reduced because life grows less well in cooler conditions. Lower temperatures mean less water evaporating from the oceans and hence less rainfall on land. Together with reduced amounts of the plant food carbon dioxide in the air, this results in less granite weathering. Volcanoes gradually return carbon dioxide to the atmosphere, eventually warming the planet once again, increasing biologically assisted granite weathering again, which tips the feedback toward cooling in a classic self-regulating (negative) feedback loop (fig. 6.3).

The picture on the bottom of the facing page shows you how the self-regulating feedback works. Notice that there are two kinds of arrow: solid and broken. A solid arrow denotes a direct coupling between two components of the system. For example, if carbon dioxide in the atmosphere increases then so will Gaia's temperature. Conversely, if carbon dioxide in the atmosphere decreases, Gaia's temperature diminishes. A broken arrow denotes an inverse coupling between two components. There is only one of these in this simplified feedback: an increase in biologically assisted rock weathering leads to a *decrease* in carbon dioxide in the atmosphere, and vice versa. Try going round the feedback a few times to convince yourself that it regulates Gaia's temperature within narrow limits. Without this great feedback operating in the background, life might have vanished on our planet many millions of years ago.

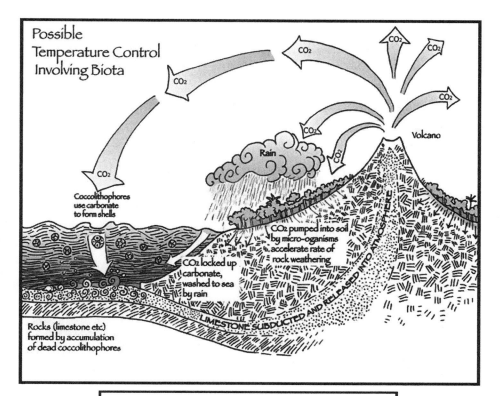

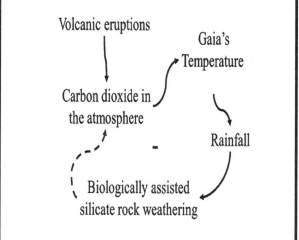

Figure 6.3. The long-term carbon cycle (*top*) is
Gaia's background temperature regulating feedback (*bottom*).
The dash in the bottom figure denotes a negative (i.e., self-regulating) feedback.

7

A Gaia Alchemy Meditation
Creating and Using the Gaiascope

Let's now begin our approach to Gaia alchemy by integrating the four functions of consciousness from depth psychology, the four elements from alchemy, and the four components of the living Earth from the science of Gaia theory. The four alchemical elements map quite nicely onto the four functions of consciousness: thinking with air; intuition with fire; feeling with water; and earth with sensing. These then map onto our scientific understanding of Gaia, in which self-regulation of key aspects of our planetary surface emerges from feedbacks between atmosphere (air), life (biosphere), rocks (lithosphere), and water (hydrosphere). The mapping is best shown diagrammatically in figure 7.1.

The three levels go inward—from depth psychology into alchemy into matter—and out again in mutual reinforcement among the levels, with alchemy interfacing between matter (physical Gaia) and depth psychology (psyche).

The *Lapis Philosophorum* (Philosopher's Stone) at the center is the Self. It is the mercurial consciousness that arises in us when we integrate our four functions and three levels as much as we can in service of creating a personal lifestyle and a wider culture that knows how to live wisely with Gaia. Thus, by placing alchemy between psyche (depth psychology) and matter (scientific Gaia) our aim is to restore the value of alchemical images as a means of reactivating Imagination to help us reconnect with the living qualities of our planet in these desperate times.

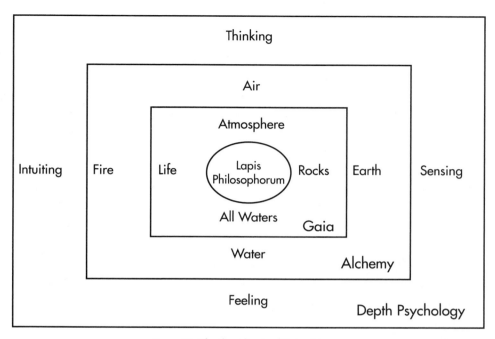

Figure 7.1. The three levels of Gaia alchemy.

You can use this diagram to make a physical artifact with your own hands to help you connect more deeply with Gaia through an interweaving of craft, art, Gaian science, alchemy, and depth psychology. I call it the Gaiascope.

✿ CREATING YOUR OWN GAIASCOPE

It's a simple device, but hidden within it are huge possibilities for discovering many deeply healing and enlightening qualities of our living Earth. The Gaiascope works best when used in conjunction with regular periods of profound immersion in your Gaia place in the company of its biodiverse air, rocks, soils, and waters.

It's easy to make a Gaiascope. It consists of nothing more than three broad, flat rings, one inside the other concentrically arranged so that each ring moves independently of the others. Each ring has four key words at each of its cardinal points. These are the words we encountered in figure 7.1.

The four words in the innermost ring (which is actually a disc) are: atmosphere, rocks, all waters, and life. This is the disc of scientific Gaia. The middle ring is the ring of alchemical understanding and carries the names of the alchemical four elements: air, earth, water, and fire embodying a blend of literal and symbolic meanings. The outer ring is the ring of psyche representing the four functions of consciousness: thinking, sensing, feeling, and intuiting.

To make a Gaiascope, use a good quality compass to draw two outer rings and an inner ring or disc on white card of about a millimeter's thickness. Here are the dimensions I used, but please feel encouraged to choose your own:

Radius (center to outer ring): 14.6 cm

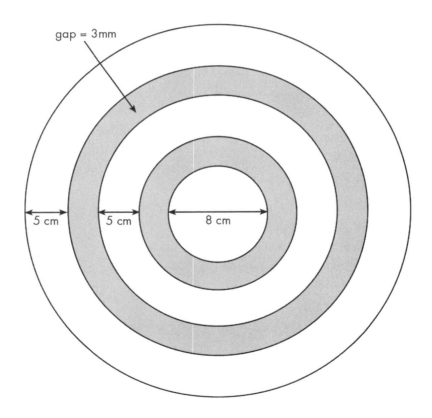

Figure 7.2. Dimensions of the Gaiascope.

Width of middle ring: 5 cm
Width of inner disc: 8 cm

Draw two additional circles appropriately placed to create three millimeter gaps (which you will later cut away) between the rings to give them space to move past each other easily. Cut the rings out using a sharp craft knife and decorate your Gaiascope with drawings and patterns. I found myself spontaneously pouring lashings of soul and feeling into my Gaiascope as I made it. It was an act primarily of soul, not of reason. Making my Gaiascope was a time of great discovery, that which I shall never forget.

Here is my Gaiascope (fig. 7.3) set up in the configuration we saw in figure 7.1 to show you how it works.

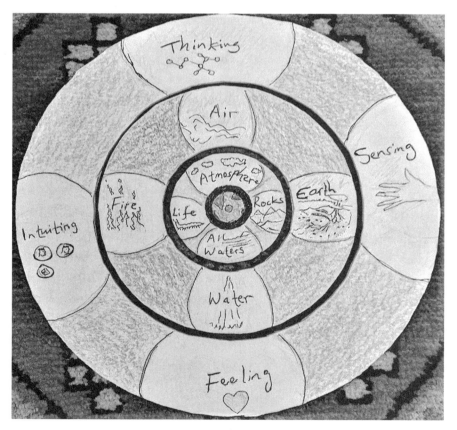

Figure 7.3. My first Gaiascope.

USING YOUR GAIASCOPE

The Gaiascope is a moving mandala that combines words from the three different realms in many different ways to reveal Gaia's deepest qualities. Here we'll work with sets of three words ("triplets") one word from the inner disc of scientific Gaia, another from the middle ring of alchemy, and finally one word from the outer ring of the four psychological functions. Since each of these can move independently there are sixty-four configurations of triplets in the Gaiascope. Interestingly, as my friend and colleague Andy Letcher pointed out to me, this is the same as the number of hexagrams in the I Ching. Andy also reminded me that Ramon Lull, the famous thirteenth-century alchemist from Mallorca, had created a similar but much more complex system of movable concentric circles for exploring the many attributes of God.

We need to evoke our poetic-imaginal awareness for our Gaiascope to work well. I've noticed that approaching my Gaiascope with my thinking-sceptical attitude reduces it to just some silly painted cardboard hoops, killing its ability to bring me a living sense of Gaia.

There are many ways to awaken the meditative attitude needed to truly benefit from the Gaiascope. I like to prepare by stepping into my Gaia place and connecting again with sky, rain, air, rocks, soil, and with the teeming life of its ecology. Going for a nice slow saunter in nature with no particular destination and an open mind is also very good preparation.

When returning indoors after my preparation, I like to clear a suitable space on my desk for my Gaiascope. I put away the keyboard, phone, diary, and things like that. Then, I place a fossil ammonite, a Tibetan silver coin, a pine cone, and a round, flat, dark brown serpentine pebble around it. I suggest you do something similar with an air of playful reverence and mindfulness before using your Gaiascope.

One way I work with my Gaiascope is to begin by reading a science word from the inner disc and then quickly moving my attention to the adjacent alchemical word in the middle ring and thence rapidly to the adjoining psychological word in the outer ring.

There are no rules, so sometimes I do it differently and just pause for a while to savor the depths and breadths in each word before moving to the next. I've been amazed to find how easily and how often these triplet brews of science, alchemy, and psychology bring about deeply healing and illuminating Gaian perceptions in me.

At other times the words in the triplets insist on being read in different orders, each with its own meaning. Notice when this happens and follow the process.

I've also noticed that sometimes the triplets speak of the current extinction-climate crisis. When this happens, I feel the tragedy of our times but soon remember that Gaiascope does its best when connecting us with Gaia's pristine qualities as they were around ten thousand years ago just after the last ice glacial period ended. Gaia's unspoiled mountains, forests, oceans, deserts, and ice caps sweep into me, bringing fresh vision and a willingness to work peacefully and democratically to solve the crisis for the sake of all beings.

Some triplets will speak to you more eloquently than others. Some will be difficult to connect with initially but will yield their secrets if you persist. Some will become favorites that will quickly take you into deep connection with Gaia.

Now we are ready to explore. You might perhaps like to configure your Gaiascope as mine is on page 99. If so . . . let's begin.

Contemplate the right horizontal triplet of your Gaiascope.
Read each word slowly . . .
as if reading haiku.

Rocks . . .

Earth . . .

Sensing . . .

When you are ready, contemplate the lower vertical triplet.

All Waters . . .

Water . . .

Feeling . . .

Now focus on the left horizontal triplet.

Life . . .

Fire . . .

Intuiting . . .

Lastly, gaze on the upper vertical triplet.

Atmosphere . . .

Air . . .

Thinking . . .

Now move the inner disc one place to the right so that the Gaiascope as a whole presents you with eight new word triplets.
    Take time to savor and explore the Gaian perceptions that come to you now from each of these new triplets. They will show you new aspects of Gaia not revealed before.

∞

You could try leaving leave the Gaiascope in this configuration for an entire twenty-four-hour cycle. Come back to it from time to time during the day to ponder it further.

∞

Then, when you've marinated yourself in this particular Gaian alchemical configuration, move the inner disc one place to the right and start again.

Basic Guidance for Using the Gaiascope

The exercise above is just one way to interact with the Gaiascope. You will find many more ways of your own to explore Gaia's depths in its company. You could mentally scramble the order of the words in the triplets, for example, or perhaps contemplate the six words of two triplets at a time.

Although there are no rules, I would suggest always choosing words from the inner disc and the two rings beyond. An equal number of words from each of these is essential for bringing balance between the three realms of science, alchemy, and psychology so that they synthesize well into deep Gaian perceptions.

In my experience, the triplet is the minimum word structure capable of producing these deep Gaian alchemical understandings. I've tried two words (one from each of two rings) and it doesn't work quite so well. Only triplets and longer strings work best in integrating the three realms that have been so tragically separated in our culture.

I've noticed too that the triplets are very good at stopping my internal dialogue, especially when I am in the woods. I bring my Gaiascope to mind as I walk and mentally arrange the rings into different triplet combinations. As I amble through the woods near our little cottage, I contemplate the words inwardly, and the triplets bring direct perceptions of Gaia into the present moment. Suddenly, a sense of rocks as a style of Earth's feeling appears all around me as I walk through the trees.

FURTHER GAIASCOPE VARIATIONS

You could explore all sixty-four word triplets in the Gaiascope systematically if you are so inclined. To do this, choose a word from the inner disc of Gaian science and another from the outer ring of the psychological functions and keep these locked in place as you move the middle ring of alchemy, feeling the qualities of each word triplet as it appears.

Now move the outer ring one step to the left and hold it in that position and once again move the inner ring of alchemy four times. Do the same with the remaining two psychological functions on the outer ring and you will have explored the sixteen triplets associated with each Gaian science word in the inner ring.

Now change to another Gaian science word and repeat the process just described, exploring the qualities of each triplet as you go. Then do the same for the other two Gaian science words on the inner disc. By the time you have done all this you will have encountered all sixty-four triplets and, if things have gone well, you might have experienced many of Gaia's deepest qualities.

Another way to do this is to cut out two new inner discs from your surplus card material, giving you four blank circular surfaces. Now write one of the four Gaian science words clearly on each surface and decorate with some artwork. Replace the central Gaian science disc with the disc showing a single Gaian science word and begin your exploration.

Take your time. This is not something to do in a rush. It might take you weeks to visit all the triplets. You could perhaps write out all sixty-four triplets systematically in a notebook and tick each triplet once you've spent a goodly while contemplating it.

Another approach is to introduce an element of randomness (or perhaps synchronicity?) to your interactions with the Gaiascope by using a four-sided (tetrahedral) die to determine how to move the rings. Our son Oscar has made me a wooden four-sided die for just this purpose.

The number you'll need to use when the die settles is out of sight at the base of the die. Just tip the die to see it or deduce it from the numbers on the die's visible faces. There's something rather splendid about the fact that the number you need is hidden from view. For me, it's a key to discovering secret treasures in the Gaiascope.

The first throw of the die tells you which ring needs to move. A throw of 1 indicates the inner disc, a throw of 2 the middle ring, and a 3 indicates the outer ring. Since there is no fourth ring, ignore a throw that gives a 4. Just throw again until you get a number between 1 and 3.

The next throw tells you whether to move the ring in question to the right or to the left. Throwing 1 or 2 means move left, throwing 3 or 4 means move right.

The final throw determines how many places to move the chosen ring. Only use a number between 1 and 3. Ignore a 4, since that would make the ring return to where it started.

I find that four throws gives me plenty to work with. Throw the die and configure the Gaiascope. Contemplate each of the four new triplets until the quality of the whole configuration of the Gaiascope makes a distinct impression on you. It's not easy to reach this point, so don't worry if the quality slips and slides in and out of your awareness. Just experience it as much as you can and throw the die again. Remember, this is a meditative practice.

Whatever configuration comes up next is a new permutation of Gaia's wholeness. Each configuration of the Gaiascope is Gaia expressing herself differently.

New Gaian perceptions will slowly open up as you contemplate the qualities of each new throw in relation to the previous throws. Give it time. Sometimes insight comes, sometimes not.

When your session with the Gaiascope—whether systematic, random, or something else—is coming to end, you could try settling and melding all the qualities of the session's triplets, word strings, and configurations into the little Gaia image at the center of your Gaiascope. Let them brew there awhile, then let them seep out into the world to heal it while also empowering you to find your path for acting beautifully in our world on behalf of all her beings.

May the many healing images and perceptions facilitated by the Gaiascope increase your sense of our Earth's majesty, mystery, and beauty, and may the images give you the resolve to do what you can, large or small, with love, to help heal our ailing planet in these times of woe.

8

Gaia and the
Tabula Smaragdina

I feel the need to offer an intellectual justification for engaging in this Gaian alchemical inquiry in which we begin to explore Gaia alchemy by unifying scientific Gaia and archetypal Gaia as we have just done with the Gaiascope. I sense that a rational argument is required to convince our thinking minds of the validity of the enterprise, now that they are so agile after four hundred years of one-sided cultivation in the subtle art of impeding Imagination. We must not exclude thinking as it is as vitally needed in the journey just as much as our sensing, valuing (feeling), and intuition, and so we need to satisfy our thinking that there really is something worthwhile in our efforts to bring alchemy and science (or, more broadly, mind and matter) together to heal both Gaia and ourselves.

My own conclusion after thirty years of contemplation and study is that we can indeed bring thinking with us as we step into the living world of psyche. This is the world where we rediscover a level of being we knew as children, but which we have now mostly lost sight of under the accumulating material and psychological bric-a-brac of modern living.

The arguments we require have been recently supplied by my friend, Jungian analyst and scientist Andrew Fellows, who provides, in his recent much recommended book, *Gaia, Psyche and Deep Ecology* (2019), a very useful conceptual map of the relationships between mind and matter, which for our inquiry translate into archetypal Gaia and scientific Gaia.

Andrew shows us how the Cartesian split is still a major issue for science and modernity (perhaps *the* major issue), even though the great discoveries of quantum physics in the early days of the last century offered clues for finding a new way of understanding the paradoxes deep in the relationship between mind and matter.

Wolfgang Pauli, a Nobel laureate in physics, struggled with various manifestations of this problem (including his inability to feel due to his overdeveloped intellect) to such an extent that he sought out psychological help from Jung to help resolve his confusion. The result was a profound and long collaboration between them, from which came the Pauli-Jung conjecture proposing that there is a layer of reality deeper than both mind and matter, both of which appear from this deeper layer as twin manifestations of an ancient, underlying, intelligent, teleological whole. This whole is itself beyond time and space, but has divided itself into two halves that must rediscover each other in manifold ways throughout time and space for reasons concerning its own self-realization. This deepest reality is the unus mundus, of which Jung says:

> Since psyche and matter are contained in one and the same world, and moreover are in continuous contact with one another and ultimately rest on irrepresentable, transcendental factors, it is not only possible, but fairly probable, even, that psyche and matter are two different aspects of one and the same thing. (Jung [1951] 1972, para 148)

The Pauli-Jung conjecture brings meaning into the world of matter. This is why synchronicity is foundational for the conjecture, since it involves the meaningful coincidence of events not at all connected through the standard channel of cause and effect. The fact that meaning is a foundational aspect of our everyday reality suggests that meaning itself is very much a quality of Jung's "irrepresentable, transcendental factors" of the deep underlying unity from which all opposites arise. This is the unus mundus.

The unus mundus might seem to be a purely speculative metaphysical concept with no basis in fact, but there is solid evidence for its existence from physics. The empirical existence of the quantum vacuum has been confirmed by physics, and it is out of this vacuum that elementary particles such as electrons emerge into existence before falling back, dissolving, and losing their identity. The entire material universe constantly fluctuates between appearing from and disappearing into the vacuum—a scientific finding that totally demolishes our mundane supposition about the solidity, permanence, and mundanity of the everyday world around us. Andrew offers a simple diagram (fig. 8.1) that helps us to approach these insights.

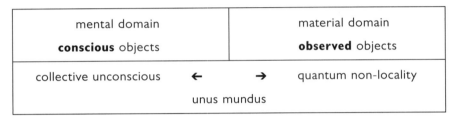

mental domain	material domain
conscious objects	**observed** objects
collective unconscious ← → quantum non-locality	
unus mundus	

Figure 8.1. The unus mundus divides into two domains which remain connected.
© 2019 from *Gaia, Psyche and Deep Ecology* by Andrew Fellows.
Reproduced by permission of Taylor and Francis Group, LLC, a division of Informa plc.

Interestingly, since time and space merge in the unus mundus, they must also merge in the collective unconscious, which must therefore hold memories of past events wherever in the cosmos they might have happened. We can become aware of these memories and events as conscious objects in the mental domain, just as the perceived objects of solid matter bubble up into our awareness from quantum nonlocality in the material domain.

Alchemical images are memories from the collective unconscious—Gaia's inward dimension of meaning—while empirical facts about Gaia revealed by science as observed objects constitute our experience of Gaia's material domain. To use the terminology of the great Russian pre-Gaian scientist Vladimir Vernadsky (much beloved by Lynn Margulis, the eminent American evolutionary biologist whom we briefly met earlier in this journey) her material domain is constituted by her biosphere, atmosphere, hydrosphere, and lithosphere. Archetypal and scientific Gaia must therefore be intimately connected in what we are calling Gaia alchemy. Since both arise from the unus mundus, they have to be.

How do we genuinely explore these links holistically, with all four functions—sensing, intuiting, thinking, and valuing or feeling—at once? The litmus test for the reality of the alchemical venture is the extent to which it helps us to improve life around us, both human and other-than-human. If all we do is to sow yet more bitterness and strife as a result of our supposed alchemical work, then we are not engaged in real alchemy. In fact, we are doing no alchemy at all.

Andrew proposes his Psyche-Gaia conjecture (fig. 8.2) as an extension of the Pauli-Jung conjecture in the deep ecological direction that is so relevant and so much needed for healing the split in our modern world. By *Gaia* he means what we here are calling scientific Gaia— that is, scientifically validated empirical data about the functioning of our planet.

Psyche	Gaia
conscious objects	observed objects
emergence (complexes etc.)	emergence (climate etc.)
symbolism	*chemistry*
archetypes	
Self	
unus mundus	

Figure 8.2. Andrew Fellow's Psyche-Gaia conjecture.
© 2019 from *Gaia, Psyche and Deep Ecology* by Andrew Fellows.
Reproduced by permission of Taylor and Francis Group, LLC, a division of Informa plc.

Andrew's Psyche-Gaia conjecture follows Jung's insight that the unus mundus differentiates into a central and centralizing autonomous focus of meaning and energy within the collective unconscious, which Jung called the archetype of the Self along with a host of other archetypes that mold and structure the seeming opposites of mind and matter (psyche and Gaia in Andrew's terms) within the realm of our conscious experience.

The Pauli-Jung and Psyche-Gaia conjectures resonate well with insights that dawned on some alchemists some four hundred years ago. We can see this by contemplating a hugely important alchemical image known as the *Tabula Smaragdina* (fig. 8.3) made by Matthieu Merian and printed by Daniel Mylius in his *Opus Medico-Chymicum* of 1618. This contains all the major psychological insights of alchemy depicted with great beauty and potency in a single image.

We have only to place an inverted, transposed, and slightly modified version of Andrew's Psyche-Gaia conjecture next to the *Tabula* image to see the correspondences (fig. 8.4).

Although the parallels are by no means exact, you can see that an original unity is represented at the top of both images. This is the unus mundus in the Pauli-Jung and Psyche-Gaia conjectures. It corresponds

Figure 8.3. The *Tabula Smaragdina*, 1618.

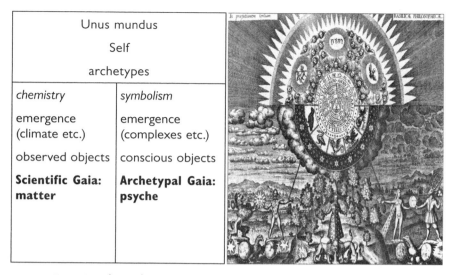

	Unus mundus		
	Self		
	archetypes		
chemistry	*symbolism*
emergence (climate etc.)	emergence (complexes etc.)
observed objects	conscious objects
Scientific Gaia: matter	**Archetypal Gaia: psyche**

Figure 8.4. The Psyche-Gaia conjecture and the *Tabula Smaragdina* side by side.

with what the alchemists called the One Mind. In the *Tabula* it is represented by the outermost ring of sun rays at the top of the image. In both images this primordial domain exists beyond our perceptions of time and space. This is why a horizontal line distinguishes it from realms lower down. These, by contrast, do exist in time and space. However, the reader should understand that the unus mundus or One Mind is in no way fundamentally separate from time and space, but of course it is beyond us to grasp this intellectually. The One Mind is sacred, eternal, and essentially unknowable by us in its vast essence. Yet, psychological development through alchemy and many other means helps us to uncover our innate capability for intuitively experiencing its profoundly liberating qualities. In other words, the One Mind is beyond human reality but not separate from it.

In the *Tabula* twenty-nine cherubs and three larger oval entities appear out of the One Mind as it begins its process of differentiation in the direction of time, space, and materiality. These entities correspond to the archetypes in the Pauli-Jung and the Psyche-Gaia conjectures. Gazing down both images, we see how the One Mind differentiates into two fundamental polarities that yearn to be reunited so that wholeness can manifest in the world of matter and in the world of psyche or the collective unconscious in diverse modes of sentience including those of bacteria, plants, fungi, Protoctista,* ourselves as humans, and our fellow animals.

One's first impression is that the left side of both the *Tabula* and of the Psyche-Gaia conjecture correspond to the rational mind and hence to scientific Gaia respectively, whereas the right side in both images seems to correspond to the mysterious living dynamics of the psyche or collective unconscious and hence to archetypal Gaia. When we look in more detail, we find that the lower left side of the *Tabula* features a solar man in daylight, while on the right we see a lunar woman at nighttime.

The two spheres under the man hold Fire and Air, both of which represent psychological and spiritual development. In these, thinking and reasoning are fully integrated into an expanded outlook that goes beyond them both. However, this wider outlook needs their contributions to be whole. These two spheres are guarded by a phoenix, representing the ability of the psyche to rise up out of its own ashes into wider, intelligently compassionate ways of loving nature.

The two spheres under the lunar woman contain Earth and Water, representing the deeply synchronistic workings of nature and the collective unconscious or objective psyche. This is the part of us that knows the value of dreams and is able to tune in to their poetic guidance for living our lives. The Earth and Water spheres are guarded by an eagle, a bird who symbolizes our indissoluble connection with the physical Earth, while Earth and Water themselves point deeply into the mysterious physicality of things. To be whole, our reason must collaborate with the unconscious just as this lunar world must collaborate with deepest respect with our reason. This is the way that these and all other opposites can work together to heal both ourselves and our relationship to Gaia.

Notice that there is a seven-rayed star under the foot of both the man and the Red Lion on the left side of the image, and also on the

---

*Single-celled beings with cell nuclei such as amoebae and paramecia, as well as both uni- and multicellular algae

right breast of the lunar woman (whose name is Luna), out of which the Milky Way pours its blessings into the Earth. We will see later that this seven-rayed star is of immense importance for our work since it accords to the seven stages of transformation discovered by the alchemists, which they supposed every dynamic process in nature (both material and psychological) must undergo in order to find completion.

Both the man and the woman have a star and a moon on their breasts, showing how both need each other's qualities to be complete, which is the union of Air and Fire under the man and Earth and Water under the woman.

Now, if you will, here is an invitation to spend a little time contemplating the *Tabula*.

Just gaze upon the Tabula image for a while, wherever you are, whether your Gaia place or in nature or perhaps in a quiet room with this book.

Breathe easily and relax as you enter a semi-dream state in which you are fully aware of the outer world as well as of more subtle levels of your inner world.

The Tabula image is a doorway into a wider sense of being and understanding which it will help you explore and discover.

See how the Red Lion gives the solar man a bright sun, which comes from the seven-rayed star underneath the Lion's foot?

See how both Lion and solar man stand on the wings of the Phoenix, beneath which the energies of fire and air are raging?

A gently rising sensation enters into you, which begins to loosen the tension in the chain of unknowing manacled to solar man's left hand, which, as we now realize, is an aspect of ourselves.

As this feeling increases the clouds of unknowing that have obscured the upper part of the image begin to disperse.

See how the lunar woman is receiving the gift of the moon from an antlered man? He is the Fugitive Stag. He was once a man, but Artemis, Goddess of wild nature, changed him into what he now is after he watched her bathing naked in a cool forest pool.

See how the wide stream of the Milky Way pours from the

seven-rayed star on her breast, bringing Earth to life? The downward flowing energies of Earth and Water beneath her feet begin to dissolve the chain that binds the lunar woman to her clouds of unknowing as you realize that she is part of you.

Now almost freed of their chains, the solar man and lunar woman can at last see each other.

They feel a deep attraction, a fully integrated sense of love on both material and spiritual levels.

Feel their union within you, no matter how small, no matter how great. Allow yourself this moment of profound relief and wholeness as solar man and lunar woman meet at last after an almost eternal separation.

Notice how an alchemist has appeared between them from the union of solar man and lunar woman. Their coming together has manifested him.

He is in the center of the image, standing on two Lions.

His garment is black studded with white stars on our right side, white studded with black stars on our left.

He holds a hatchet in each hand. With these hatchets you see him cutting the chains that have bound both solar man and lunar woman to their respective clouds of unknowing.

Behind him there is a forest.

You notice how each tree in the forest carries a symbol. Those in the first two rows carry signs of the zodiac, those in the last row the signs of the metals. The central tree bears the alchemical sign for gold. As the central tree grows it parts the clouds.

As the clouds part you see seven large stars arrayed in great beauty in a circular arrangement above the central tree. These are the seven stages of psychological-alchemical transformation inherent in solar man and lunar woman and in the whole of nature.

You feel a strong urge to explore the celestial beauty of these stars as you absorb the qualities of their lovely colors set against the darkness of the night sky studded with smaller stars.

Dwell now with whatever realization, great or small, the seven stars bring you.

After relishing these realizations for a time, take a deep breath and slowly bring back what you have learned as a gift for the world to which you return with a heart full of insight, love, and compassion for humanity and all of nature.

Dennis Hauck in his book *The Emerald Tablet* (1999) gives us an excellent description of the *Tabula,* and so I will follow his account carefully in what I'll write here about the rest of the image. Above the seven stars we see a semicircle containing five birds. Each bird is connected with a planet, that itself represents a particular quality in the realm of spirit that we are now about to enter. In this spiritual realm we encounter a mandala which, as Hauck points out, resides in and influences both halves of the image, the Above and the Below. He shows us how this mandala consists of seven concentric spheres, again representing the seven stages of alchemical transformation. We must deeply experience these stages within ourselves before we can reach the center of the mandala where we encounter the symbol of Mercurius within an upturned triangle. This final figure represents the Philosopher's Stone, or as Hauck says "the Monad or the One Thing which is the Stone."

How are we to make sense of these arcane images and symbols in relation to Gaia our living planet? The unus mundus is the nondual state that we can experience via psycho-spiritual practices such as meditation, depth psychological work including alchemy, and many other pathways. The Philosopher's Stone is this nondual state that appears when the opposites are in right relation. Spirit and matter, psyche and matter—these are dual states, whereas unus mundus is pure being. Words can't describe unus mundus, for words are far too dualistic and therefore cannot help but split into pieces whatever they describe. Poetry gets close, and music and the visual arts are also good at guiding us into these realms if we know how to let them take us there.

We have plenty of theories about Gaia, which come out of our thinking and our sensory experience, but as yet we don't have an equally strong value-rich intuitive Gaia. Alchemy gives us a pathway into these intuitive perceptions of Gaia we so badly need to resolve the crisis.

Gaia herself is nondual. In nondual Gaia there is no "you and

Gaia." There is no duality, there is only being, only presence. In this nondual Gaia state there are no concepts, no thinking, just presence. In Buddhism this is *Shunyata*. This experience is transitory for most of us, if we ever experience it at all. If we do, we feel compelled to bring back the memory and qualities of nondual Gaia into everything we do in the world with all its joys, suffering, beauty, and disappointments.

Perhaps nondual Gaia is associated with the symbol of the Stone because stones seem to us to be so utterly permanent. Mercurius is the Stone at the center of the *Tabula* representing nondual Gaia because the Stone can transmute into anything. It can transform spirit into matter and *vice versa*. Mercurius is the quantum vacuum. Everything goes in and out of the vacuum all the time. Particles (electrons, neutrons, and so forth) appear and disappear out of it. Consciousness is the same. Working with Mercurius is the key to finding the Stone, for Mercurius is the ability to hold the opposites together, realizing the equal value of each. Mercurius is the transformative principle that accompanies us throughout our alchemical journey, but he becomes toxic when we begin to discriminate one of the opposites too much. This is an important source of conflict and strife within the human world.

It can be that after a lifetime of training, or perhaps in a sudden moment of insight, we finally learn how to slip into nondual Gaia more or less at will, and also how to come back into the duality of the world to help nondual Gaia spread from mind to mind as a powerful, quickly spreading healing contagion.

We conclude that science and thinking give us a good reason for beginning on a pathway of exploration that may lead us into that blessed state, which we are calling nondual Gaia. I put it like this because it seems that in these desperate times we may only find the inner freedom that the crisis demands of us by keeping Gaia constantly in our sights as our best conduit into the deep realizations that will greatly empower us to be of service to our planet and all her beings.

9

The Seven Stars

I first experienced the transformative power of alchemy thanks to a gift from my friend Julian David, who has helped me greatly to develop my own understanding of Jungian psychology. One day, Julian and I were having a conversation in his enchanted consulting room. It was located on his ancient wooded estate at Luscombe, not far from Dartington. I had often climbed the old rickety wooden stairs in the long stone barn that housed the Luscombe library to delve into a collection of thin green tomes, which had long held a peculiar and powerful fascination for me: a rare set of unpublished mimeographed volumes of Jung's lectures. These had been delivered at the Swiss Federal Institute of Technology in Zürich from 1933 to 1941. Reading them, I felt as if Jung himself were tutoring me in the art of exploring psyche.

"Take one of those volumes as a gift from me," Julian said that day. "One of them is waiting for you. Go and find it if you would like."

In the farthest section of the library, behind the curtain where the books on Jung's psychology were housed, I ran my hands over the dark green spines of these rare volumes until I felt one calling me particularly strongly. It was the final work of the series titled *The Process of Individuation: Alchemy II* delivered by Jung from May to July 1941 while Europe was plunged in the horrors of the second world war.

Gratefully, and with an immense sense of reverence, I brought the book with its marbled green cover and delicate yellowing pages home to my tiny meditation hut nestled in our jungle garden by our little coach house cottage. Here I have been carefully reading the book, surrounded by our small patch of wilderness, untouched now for almost thirty years, with its bullfinches, blackbirds, woodpeckers, and other feathered and nonfeathered denizens leading their lives glimpsed now and again among a luxuriantly tangled mass of brambles and wild apple trees, deliciously free from human disturbance.

Sometimes, when a peculiar quiet descends upon my hut, I hear Jung's voice and feel his powerful presence as I read his words. He smiles encouragingly and puffs on his favorite pipe as I delve into his masterful insights into the arcane transformative disciplines of alchemy. I learn how the alchemists were not only the precursors of modern science, but also of his own psychology of the unconscious, with its qualities of healing and inner meaning waiting to be brought into the light of our awareness.

I had spent a few months working with alchemy and its powerful images phenomenologically as the gradual uncovering of my own mysterious process of individuation through the work of Jung and others. One day, quite suddenly, in a moment of powerful intuition, the idea came to me that new pathways of wholeness and healing could open up by exploring the connections between alchemy and Gaia theory—that is, between alchemical and scientific Gaia.

A few months later, again quite suddenly in a flash, it occurred to me that Gaia alchemy could perhaps be explored with our small community of postgraduate students enrolled in the master of science program in holistic science here at Schumacher College.

But what if the students responded badly to Gaia alchemy? Would this discredit my twenty years' work on the M.Sc. in holistic science and the almost thirty years of educational work at Schumacher College? I went through weeks of doubt and hesitation. Should I take the plunge into this totally new and uncharted educational domain? I mentioned my problem to a few valued friends. They encouraged me to try it. After just a few weeks I had got to know the students well and found them open, deeply intelligent, and only too painfully aware of the damaged state of the planet. They were eager to make a difference in the world in new ways. They were my soul mates. It seemed the gamble might pay off.

And so it was that a dull English day dawned over the Old Postern.

A soft rain fell on the large fourteenth-century vicarage that has been the heart and soul of the college since it opened its doors in 1991. Despite the rain and cold, the M.Sc. classroom at the Old Postern was warm and calm. It was the second week of my Living Earth module covering Gaia theory and deep ecology, which I was teaching for the nineteenth year as the third and final core module on the college's M.Sc. in holistic science.

I began the session on that dull November day with a simple improvisation of a North Indian raga scale played on my old Spanish guitar. This music from India brings a deep sense of peace, opening a wide space for deep learning and appreciation of Gaia's profound living qualities.

After the music we contemplated an alchemical image (fig. 9.1) by Basil Valentine first published in his book *L'Azoth des Philosophes* in 1659, depicting the seven-rayed star of alchemical transformation. This is the very same star we encountered in the *Tabula Smaragdina,* the star that Paracelsus had called the Star of Man long before, in reference to each person's innermost potential for realizing their deepest embeddedness in the great psyche of nature. Following Paracelsus, we explored whether the Azoth mandala depicts not just the Star of Man, but also the Star of Gaia, granting us a lived experience, even if for the briefest of moments, of Gaia as a palpably vast, luminous planetary entity from whom we receive the richest treasures of being and learning in our non-dual Gaia moments. We projected the image (fig. 9.1) on the screen and let it play in our awareness as if in a dream.

This image carries many similarities to the *Tabula Smaragdina* that we worked with earlier. Notice that it is also divided into two halves. The left relates to the sun, to the masculine, to intellect, and reason; to the right is the moon, relating to the feminine, the unconscious, and the objective psyche. There is also a large central mandala showing a seven-rayed star that we will focus on later, but for the moment we'll focus on the images behind the mandala.

At the bottom left, the king wears a crown and sports a starlike halo around his head while holding a scepter and shield in his hands. He sits on a lion, which in turn reposes on a dark earthy mound in which rests a fire-breathing dragon.

Figure 9.1. From *L'Azoth des Philosophes*, 1659.

Relax. Take a few breaths and allow your Imagination to come to the fore of your awareness.

Ponder the left side of the image, the side showing the Sun King and the dragon beneath him, both in bright daylight.

The Sun King sits on top of the lion.

Beneath him, poking out of a dark cave is a fire-breathing dragon.

A great foot plants itself on the earth in front of the dragon, part of a huge human being whose existence we can only catch a glimpse of.

Above the King's head a hand belonging to the same huge human being holds a blazing torch.

Above the torch there is a corner of a large downward-pointing triangle. In this you see a sun above which is written the word Anima.

Finally, you notice how on top of the triangle there sits a flaming salamander.

Rest awhile and absorb whatever insight and experience this area of the image has given you, great or small.

Whatever understanding you have been granted, offer it and use it for the good of Gaia and all her beings, including humans, as you return to the text below or to your daily life.

Here is how the symbols of the Azoth mandala are sometimes interpreted. The Sun King is intellect: reason, that part of us who thinks about everything and supposes that only he can discover all that can be known. His scepter gives him authority to use reason to command nature; the shield is his cleverness against all rational arguments that go against his views.

The dragon is the repressed rage of the objective psyche breathing dangerous fire because the King suppresses all knowledge of the unconscious.

The blazing torch is a sign of the great value of reason and the intellect.

The upper left-hand angle of the downward-pointing triangle suggests that when reason has developed to its full extent it recognizes the existence of its opposite: soul, the feminine side of ourselves and nature devoted to feeling.

The salamander symbolizes the final union of the masculine and feminine aspects of nature and therefore of all opposites.

There is something else to say about the Sun King. In addition to representing reason, he also represents those aspects of nature that work more or less mechanically. These are the regularities we see in the world, which we can approximate fairly well with our science and mathematical models. Numbers are archetypal and capture something essential about this "machine-like" quality of semi-regularity. These are aspects of nature that we can understand by cultivating reason. However, to be whole we must learn to integrate these discoveries with the other side of the image—with the feminine, with the moon. Hence the absolute importance of exploring Gaia with science (the new) and with Imagination (the old).

Now let's shift our attention to the right side of the image. Here we see a nighttime scene in which a robed woman sits atop a vast fish that she controls with a pair of reins resting in its mouth.

Relax once more and gently soften your gaze as you allow the right side of the image to reach you.

The robed woman is the Moon Queen. The reins she holds in her hands control the great fish beneath her. The fish swims in a great ocean of water.

A great human foot plants itself on top of the water in front of the fish, part of that huge human being whose existence we have not yet fully discerned.

Behind the Moon Queen you see a sheaf of wheat and notice that she holds a bow and arrow.

Above her a huge hand holds a feather,

Above the feather, in the corner of the downward-pointing triangle, there is a moon symbol above which is the word Spiritus.

Above the triangle sits a bird with outstretched wings.

Now, once again, rest awhile and absorb whatever insight and experience this side of the image gives you, however great or small.

Offer whatever understanding you have been given for the good of Gaia and all her beings, including humans, and return to the text below or to your daily life.

I will now give some commonly accepted interpretations of these symbols, but you, the reader, should remember that you must make any interpretation entirely your own, without accepting any collective view unless it truly corresponds with your own understanding.

The fish represents the powerful forces of the objective psyche—the collective unconscious—which cooperate with the Moon Queen in ways the Sun King is not capable of on his own.

The sheaf of wheat represents the Moon Queen's association with nature's power of growth and reproduction.

The bow and arrow symbolize her openness to the wounds inflicted by the many hurtful physical and emotional experiences that we all undergo in our lives.

The feather symbolizes air. Now we realize that the huge human hands and feet symbolize the four elements: earth, water, fire, and air.

The word *Spiritus* suggests that when the feminine aspect of our nature is fully developed it recognizes the value of spirit, which is connected with the detachment offered by reason and intellect.

The bird with outstretched wings atop the right-hand angle of the downward-pointing triangle symbolizes the realm of spirit, which loves to be connected with the great imponderable intelligence residing in the unconscious, symbolized by the moon.

There are two additional symbols behind the mandala that we need to contemplate. The first is a winged figure at the top of the image in between the fiery salamander and the bird with outstretched wings. Instead of a head, this winged figure has a small protuberance, which has been likened to a helmet or a heart, symbolizing the union of masculine and feminine perspectives. The second symbol can be found right at the bottom of the image in the remaining angle of the downward-pointing triangle. This contains a cube surrounded by five stars above which is the word *Corpus,* or body. The five stars represent the alchemical Quintessence, the strength of which is perfected when it is turned into Earth, into the very body of Gaia. In our times, this is the pure, Mercurial perception of Gaia revealed to us when we have worked over and over again with the seven transformational operations depicted in the mandala.

THE RAYS OF THE AZOTH MANDALA

Once the M.Sc. class had worked with these background images we contemplated each ray of the Azoth mandala in turn, allowing them as a whole to symbolize stages in the transformation of ourselves from our grossest ego-centeredness into more compassionately connected, ecologically alive human beings. We simultaneously contemplated the psychological meaning of each ray while also holding the possibility that each ray would reveal itself as a poetic image depicting scientifically verifiable events in Gaia's long-term carbon cycle, which we were studying in my Living Earth module. The premise of this peculiar experiment was voiced by Jung as well as by many other sages: there is only one living psyche, which has many dimensions including those of mind and of matter.

We pondered the seven rays of the Azoth mandala, progressing from the first, black downward-pointing ray labeled *calcination* onward clockwise to the other rays, shown here in order of appearance with the operations they offer and the planet which symbolizes their qualities:

Calcination: Burning off dross. Fire. *Saturn*
Dissolution: Learning to let go. Water. *Jupiter*
Separation: Identifying essences. Air. *Mars*
Conjunction: Feeling and Thinking coming together. Earth. *Sun*
Fermentation: Inspiration. *Venus*
Distillation: Planetary life moves to a vision of Truth. *Mercury*
Coagulation: Return or rediscovery of Gaia as "Garden of Eden."
     Moon

Calcination

From the perspective of our human psyche, calcination is about burning away selfish aspects of our ego and the plethora of confusing ideas, thoughts, and concepts that prevent us from becoming fully conscious of who we are in relation to the life of our planet and our cosmos.

It is worth remembering, as my friend Stephen Buhner pointed out to me (and here I paraphrase some of his words), that the word *ego* has become degraded with common usage into referring to an unhelpful part of myself and others that we would be better off without because it gets in the way of an honorable and spiritual way of being, which damages other life forms. We have been conditioned to think that ego has an autonomous existence that overrides more noble aspects of ourselves and does harm because of its inherent darkness and lack of honorable intentions.

But in fact all organisms possess and need some sort of "ego." Ego emerges as part of each living being's self-organization and development with the particular and unique function of preserving the being's overall structural integrity. It watches, observes, and continually monitors the exterior world for events that threaten this structural integrity, and when it perceives something that it identifies as a threat, it notifies the organism's wider awareness of the problem so it can be attended to. Ego is thus an essential aspect of the self: no organism from microbe to tree to bear to human being could exist without some form of it. As such it is an essential ally of the wider self.

This is generally misunderstood in our culture, and so the word *ego* is used to focus on what is more correctly identified as the shadow side of the ego rather than on its healthy, protective aspect. These shadow aspects of ego easily dominate us when we suffer from a lack of self-reflection. We therefore need a disciplined contemplative practice such as alchemy to integrate the shadow aspects of ego as allies in our process of transforming consciousness from "lead" to "gold."

Calcination can be uncomfortable, requiring a deep acceptance, liberation, and transformation of our sense of inferiority, of our unhelpful attitudes, insensitive actions in the past, and of our attachments to fixed ideas about the world and ourselves. We encounter and accept our shadow and welcome it into the mandala of wholeness, which grows in us as we contemplate the alchemical images of the Azoth mandala. This is the realm of fire because heat is needed for this stage of the alchemical work, ranging from the gentle heat of a nicely smoldering compost heap to the immense burning discomfort of a raging wood fire.

We need calcination when Gaia for us is no more than an inert backdrop to our daily worries and woes. In this state of mind Gaia is dead to us—we are "Gaia-blind." Bird song means nothing to us, or worse, its very joyfulness intensifies our unhappiness and disconnection. Occasionally, we experience a vague sense that something important is missing. Even in the depths of our confusion a faint emerald glitter from the Philosopher's Stone breaks through into consciousness promising an experience of Gaia's richness and fullness and of our own within her.

If we are lucky, or are just about aware enough, these emerald sparks start a fire in us that burns away the dross of our depression and confusion as we begin to get closer to Gaia. Perhaps a flower speaks to us for a moment, or a fragment of birdsong startles us into wakefulness for an instant. These first glimmerings ignite a passion to discover more, giving us the energy to continue this difficult and necessarily lonely inquiry. Alchemically, our calcination really gets going when we burn away the dross of our unhelpful thoughts and feelings into a white ash in which we sow seeds of gold, representing our future awakened relationship to both Gaia and the cosmos.

◇◇◇◇◇ A Conversation with Jeffrey Kiehl ◇◇◇◇◇

STEPHAN: Let's start with the downward-pointing ray, which is calcination. The planet is Saturn, dark, downward pointing. Heaviness, gravitas. The *nigredo*—the darkness—the lead. The ray points to the body—perhaps to the body of the Earth.

JEFFREY: The body is also salt—"salt of the Earth." Salt is formed in the Earth by expelling moisture. This is calcination, so you are cooking, you are bringing heat to the material. This has to do with decay. What decays in Gaia? What has to decay?

STEPHAN: All organic matter has to decay and be decomposed. The chemical elements have to be recycled so life can continue; otherwise life would run out of raw materials. Decomposition produces the gentle fire of the compost heap, but there are more intense fires within Gaia, such as from volcanoes. There's also Earth's central core, the outside of which is as hot as the sun's surface. Then of course the earliest Earth was a molten ball of rock.

JEFFREY: Here's an image of the calcination process (fig. 9.2). The alchemist is being put into the oven and all of his concepts and constructs are being burned off. How does this relate to Gaia?

STEPHAN: Any configuration of Gaia that has stabilized for a long time and has got stuck has to be transformed. The thoughts pouring out of the oven are Gaia's feedbacks, relationships, species, which need to be liberated so the planet can reconfigure in a new, more developed state.

JEFFREY: From a psychological perspective if we're going to get back to a deep, soulful connection to Gaia, we have to let go of a lot of our

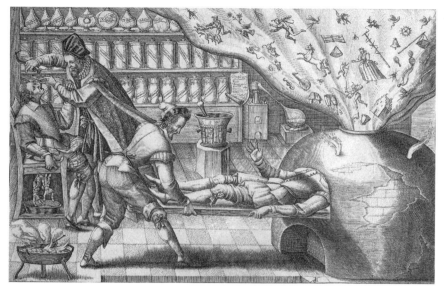

Figure 9.2. Alchemical calcination.
Image attributed to Mathieu Greuter, sixteenth century.

preconceived concepts and dead Cartesian frames of reference. All of this has to be burned off and emitted into the atmosphere. This whole process changes the way we see the world.

STEPHAN: Perhaps Gaia's first calcination happened when she was just a ball of molten rock.

JEFFREY: No reference points. That is why this guy is being put into the oven, because when you get rid of all that stuff you encounter the unus mundus. It actually terrifies the ego to imagine being in a situation where there are no reference points. We feel like that in a completely black room. We have all this stuff we have in our psyche that is cutting us off from the experience of the soul and spirit of the world.

STEPHAN: Those obstacles have to be burned off in a quest for the well-being of our planet and of the whole.

JEFFREY: That's why it's so important that we allow ourselves to be put in the oven and be calcified.

STEPHAN: Yes. Let's start with the original molten ball of rock and just hold that image. I'm holding it inwardly and I'm also sensing that

Earth has a memory of this calcination, which actually happened to you, Gaia. We give you knowledge of yourself from our science, and from you we receive the energy of your original calcination, which is like a gentle fire.

JEFFREY: To grow this we could do an exercise. We could take the calcination Gaia went through and reflect on how that calcination is happening right now within us. Can we imagine Gaia's first calcination? How is it happening in me?

STEPHAN: Shall we do it?

JEFFREY: Sure. Imagine we are back at that primordial time when Earth was molten and very hot. Radioactive decay is creating the heat in the planet's core that's heating Gaia. Now take that image into your own self. Hold the image of that molten ball being heated internally through radioactive decay. See what happens.

◇◇◇◇◇◇◇◇◇◇◇◇◇◇◇◇◇◇◇◇◇◇◇◇◇◇◇◇◇

Dissolution

Dissolution is about allowing subtle feelings to come up that our ego has repressed so that a wider sense of flow and feeling can be part of one's life in the biosphere. These feelings are not primarily emotional, although they carry a deeply enlivening emotional charge. These are feelings of the immense cosmic value of the unfolding life of our planet. Having encountered these feelings as fully as we can, we attempt to live with this sense of value at the forefront of our awareness. Water is the clue to this experience. We allow ourselves to dissolve as much as we can into the objective psyche with our awareness intact and swim into an ocean of Gaian meaning and healing.

Once the fire of calcination has raged strongly, a healing rain starts to fall as we enter a period of dissolution. We let go of everything we imagined about the natural world: scientific data, computer models, poems, feelings, ideas for conferences and books, research agendas, days on the river, woodland walks, wild swimming. All these meld and dissolve into each other. They inform each other, discover each other, share experiences, and begin to create a completely new way of life and commitment to Gaia as we begin to sense the living body of Gaia that enfolds us.

◇◇◇◇◇ *A Conversation with Jeffrey Kiehl* ◇◇◇◇◇

JEFFREY: Let's look at an image of dissolution (fig. 9.3). This is where the green lion swallows the sun. Later on he's going to spit the sun back out. Intellect has to be swallowed. You're going into the dissolution process so you cannot be thinking. Intellect will destroy the dissolution process. So the sun has to go away for a while; he has got to go in the belly of the lion and stay there awhile. This is what Descartes couldn't do. Every time we, you and I, as scientists start to discount, disagree, dismiss . . .

Figure 9.3. Green Lion swallowing the Sun from D. Stolcius von Stolcenberg in the *Viridarium chymicum,* Frankfurt 1624.

STEPHAN: . . . we are refusing to let the lion swallow the sun.

JEFFREY: Right. You don't have to do it all the time. If you're going to read a scientific paper you don't want to swallow the sun. But if we're going to get into a deeper relationship with Gaia and work around the Azoth mandala we need to use lunar consciousness from now on.

STEPHAN: All the way to the end?

JEFFREY: No. The sun's going to be spit back out, but right now we need lunar consciousness, reflective consciousness. Approaching Gaia with love but also with a heavy heart. It's an open process. You have to open your heart. You have to be able to expose your vulnerabilities to others to be in dissolution.

STEPHAN: So in dissolution we need to be lost in the anima mundi—in the flow of the world?

JEFFREY: Yes.

◇◇◇◇◇◇◇◇◇◇◇◇◇◇◇◇◇◇◇◇◇◇◇◇◇◇◇◇◇◇◇◇

Separation

Separation is about realizing what is moving and changing in oneself as a result of the alchemical work. It is a noticing of the happening of the transformation of our consciousness through the birth of a discriminating faculty that sees what is going on in the psyche and senses the possibility of wholeness. We become aware of unhelpful aspects of our personality of which we were unconscious until now and this new ability to understand what one is finding in the psyche makes the ego resilient and pliable enough to explore and experience the subsequent states of the Azoth mandala in oneself and Gaia simultaneously. Mars, the warrior, is the planet here.

Like a warrior, we experience a determination to be separated from our unhelpful qualities without fear or anxiety as a vital part of our transformation into a deeper knower of Gaia. In science we are doing Separation, discriminating one aspect of nature from another. I realize now that Descartes's dream given him by the objective psyche or unconscious fits very well with the Azoth mandala. To grow our awareness we needed to separate ourselves from nature to get a more detached view of what she is by putting some distance between ourselves and how we had unconsciously lived within her. Linnaeus and his method for classifying biodiversity, still in use today, can separate us even further (if we don't have a sufficiently strong lunar attitude) by discriminating and categorizing each organism into species, genus, phylum, order, family, kingdom, and domain.

◇◇◇◇◇ *A Conversation with Jeffrey Kiehl* ◇◇◇◇◇

STEPHAN: There's an egg, there's a fire, and there's a man about to cut the egg in half longitudinally (fig. 9.4). Maybe if he cuts the egg he can go down that tunnel and through into that other world beyond where there's a beautiful tower. He needs to cut that egg—or else.

Figure 9.4. Alchemical separation by M. Merian from
Michael Maier's *Atalanta Fugiens,* 1617.

JEFFREY: We need this discerning part of us that's going to cut things even finer. We're still refining, refining, refining.

STEPHAN: You have to cut this egg to find out what's inside and use the energy of fire to work with what you find.

JEFFREY: Cutting off the head is rather like the green lion swallowing the sun. You have to cut off your intellect for the alchemical transformation to work. If you try to go through this process intellectually you're going to kill it. It's like this in fairy tales where often an animal will provide a service as a guide and helper on condition that at the end of the journey its head is cut off. The dumbling often resists that because he's so sentimental, because he doesn't want to hurt the fox that's helped him through the forest and helped him along the journey. He resists performing the act out of sentimentality. It's too disturbing. But in the end he does cut the head off the fox. As a result the fox is released from its enchantment and is brought back to life as a human being. It's a necessary part of the individuation process that we cut the head off.

STEPHAN: But how do you cut the head off?

JEFFREY: Well, the moment you find yourself intellectualizing the images you cut the head off. This is particularly true of thinking types. Their impulse is going to be to think through it. Think about it. Question doubt, conceptualize it, interpret it. So the balance that we have to strike here is we need to remember that the head will eventually be put back on. But when we put it back on it will be in balance with the other functions that are required. What's been cut off here is thinking and sensation.

◇◇◇◇◇◇◇◇◇◇◇◇◇◇◇◇◇◇◇◇◇◇◇◇◇◇◇◇◇◇

Conjunction

Conjunction brings powerful moments of integration when the elements we have discriminated in separation come together in the union of our feeling and thinking, whereupon a golden sense of feeling-thinking based in the heart grows and glows in our awareness which now knows itself as richly enfolded within Gaia's ancient wholeness. This is clearly the realm of the Sun, for we sense a goldenness in things we have not seen or felt before. Our culture's ignorance of Gaia and psyche is perpetrating a terrible planetary tragedy on our luscious Earth. Even in the face of this, we experience a goldenness glowing brightly in the center of reality. After all the hard work of calcination, dissolution, and separation, we very much deserve these golden feelings. We have truly earned them and enjoy them.

In the separation and conjunction phases the opposites within us, which have been very close together in our unconscious, now become discernible so that our awareness of Gaia can grow and flourish in the tension between them. I am reminded of what goes on when a coccolithophore precipitates those lovely, sometimes mandalalike, coccoliths made of chalk we saw earlier. This happens in the "coccolith room" deep in the alga's single-celled body. The walls of the coccolith room are coated with a (polysaccharide) chemical that stops solid chalk from precipitating out of that pre-chalk solution of calcium bicarbonate. The room's walls are very flexible and are part of the cell's considerable intelligence. When enough calcium bicarbonate solution has been brought into the room from the surrounding seawater to trigger precipitation, its walls intelligently ooze themselves into the shape of a single coccolith, allowing calcium bicarbonate far from the anti-precipitation polysaccharide in the room's walls to precipitate into a single gorgeous coccolith of solid chalk. This mandala making in the very microbial heart of a unicellular alga revealed by science is a wonderful symbol of Gaia's presence at every scale of existence, and also of alchemical separation and conjunction. We become more conscious of Gaia when the space between all opposites widens enough to allow our own mandala of wholeness to coagulate itself there.

Fermentation

Fermentation takes us into a deeper domain of the work, for having felt the golden light in the conjunction, we now reenter the green darkness, but this time with the light of consciousness as our guide. There are two phases in fermentation. First is an initial dark aspect known as putrefaction in which the ego is encouraged to decompose some more. This is followed by fermentation proper, which liberates the indwelling awareness of Gaia's spirit that lies hidden in our psyche. The purified state is symbolized by the many iridescent colors of the peacock's tail. We bring this light into the dark, activating a psychological fermentation at an even deeper level. This brings us feelings of spiritual inspiration and realization in which we glimpse an emeraldlike, jewel quality at the very core of every aspect of Gaia—and indeed in the whole of nature. As we awaken more fully to the reality of psyche, we begin to receive profound hints about the true nature of our opus in Gaia alchemy. These give us our deepest experiences of the ecological community's numinous qualities, in which we are embedded as an aspect of Gaia herself. An alchemical image for this stage is the citrinitas, symbolized as a yellow waxy substance. This state of consciousness is further purified in the operations that follow.

◇◇◇◇◇ *A Conversation with Jeffrey Kiehl* ◇◇◇◇◇

JEFFREY: In fermentation we're doing the Great Work. We've found soul. We have that image with the wings in which we've married soul and spirit (fig. 9.5).

Figure 9.5. The marriage of soul and spirit.
Buch der heiligen Dreifaltigkeit, fifteenth century.

JEFFREY: And now we're going to put them back into matter. This is the yellowing process. We've been dissolved into lunar work up till now. Now in fermentation we're going to bring solar consciousness back. We need it now to do this greater Work. Now we bring the solar consciousness and heat things up through fermentation and a little more distillation. It's a refining, refining. It's a lifetime of work.

STEPHAN: That's what Gaia has been doing throughout evolutionary time. She's been refining. She herself has been going through the alchemical rays of the Azoth mandala, refining, refining, refining. If we can see Gaian processes as alchemical journeys through evolutionary time and through her ecological networks, then we might just drop into Gaian consciousness, and if we share these discoveries, hopefully other people will learn how to experience them too.

JEFFREY: The citrinitas is a doorway to this experience of Gaian consciousness. It brings solar consciousness to nature. Eventually it will lead to the coagulation in our work, which is going to finally bring the opposites of Gaia's matter and psyche together. It's all about the yellowing, sulphur; we need to love sulphur at this stage. It's got fermentation, distillation, and *solificatio*. That's a word that Jung likes to use in *Psychology and Alchemy*. It's a light within that shines out, a solar light within that shines out.

◇◇◇◇◇◇◇◇◇◇◇◇◇◇◇◇◇◇◇◇◇◇◇◇◇◇

Distillation

Then, in distillation, this *esmeraldic* (emerald-like) sense is further worked on so that we enter the transpersonal realm, such that by cultivating this distilled awareness we contribute to Gaia's inscrutable yet marvelous process of planetary transformation. Intention matters here. We give our consciousness as a gift to Gaia's evolution to aid and support her wild ecological flourishing in this exact moment of her evolutionary journey—a voyage that is ancient, good, dark, and mysterious. The distillation produces a baseline sense of contentment and well-being arising from our connection to the powerful energies of Gaia and the cosmos.

Coagulation

Next comes coagulation. Our practice deepens bringing longer and longer periods of sacred recognition that Gaia is, despite all the joy and suffering, a true Garden of Eden: a richly textured, animate, planetary paradise rolling around the sun carrying her cargo of crawling, swimming, breathing biota. They thrive and die in the density of her rocks, in her turbulent air, and in her swirling waters. We feel the contrast between the actual damaged ecological state of the earth right now and this ideal state, which brings a great desire to work toward helping our animate earth to find some way of reentering the Gaian Eden she was before our culture began to tear her apart, and ourselves with her. In these periods of recognition, we know this in our blood, flesh, and bones. In the coagulated state, we can access this Edenic Gaia whenever we need to, even in difficult situations. Such access brings us a quiet, inner confidence. We arrive at the knowledge of our own nature as inseparable from Gaia's living world expressed in our planet's mysterious journey toward wholeness.

◇◇◇◇◇ A Conversation with Jeffrey Kiehl ◇◇◇◇◇

JEFFREY: We are still in *citrintas* in distillation where the masculine and feminine, Sun and Moon, work together. We're getting close to Mercurius. We've now reached the point where we need that solar consciousness. Remember, a long time ago it was swallowed by the green lion. So now the green lion is going to spit it back out. And we were going to keep lunar consciousness.

STEPHAN: The lion has stars on his body.

JEFFREY: He's a refined lion now he's got the constellations. So this is a higher form of the lion that's gone through the work. And he's returning the sun. So now we're moving toward the outer world. We're bringing consciousness to it and we're getting close to having the Stone that we've been working so hard on. Coagulation is the stage of refined integration. You're never going to lose the instinctual primal energy. It's a part of who we are. It's a part of Gaia. You can refine and refine and refine but at this stage of the union it is still there. The alchemical process gets you to a state in which you see the beauty of all the world. Breathing in the world and breathing it out.

STEPHAN: Iain McGilchrist wrote this : ". . . there is a process of responsive evocation, the world 'calling forth' something in me that in turn 'calls forth' something in the world."

JEFFREY: Now we are getting to the rubedo. In Jungian psychology we are tapping into the archetypal cores; we are able to work with images. The transcendent function appears and you get the stone or the Self symbol. The planet is Sun, the metal is gold. Coagulation means having everything in balance. The alchemist now has access to both the masculine and feminine. She's in the middle now and has reached a state of complete balance integrating both masculine and feminine and is in deep relationship to animals and plants.

STEPHAN: There's a dragon down here. A staff is pointing toward it. Now the dragon is a friend (fig. 9.6).

Figure 9.6. Alchemical coagulation. Artist unknown, from fifteenth or sixteenth century.

JEFFREY: The lion's been tamed. It's not going to swallow you.

STEPHAN: This tree I interpret as other people whom you could influence.

JEFFREY: That's a nice interpretation.

The Seven Latin Words

We also need to consider the seven Latin words that we find next to each circle between the Azoth mandala's rays. Look toward the bottom left of figure 9.1 on page 120. Going clockwise from the image of the crow sitting on a skull these words are: *Visita* = Visit; *Interiora* = The Interior; *Terra* = The Earth; *Rectificando* = Setting Things Right; *Invenies* = You Will Discover; *Occultum* = The Hidden; *Lapidem* = Stone, all of which could be read thus:

> *"Visit the interior and Earth will set things right.*
> *Then you will discover the hidden stone."*

We are encouraged to visit the interior, which is the collective unconscious, the source of inspiration and insight to which alchemy connects us. The collective unconscious gives us archetypal intuitive experiential knowledge of Earth—of Gaia—as a vast planetary living being. We feel and perceive the ethical and moral implications of this knowledge, which helps us to set things right in our lives and to see things as they really are. When we do this, we are granted lived experiences of the Stone. In other words, we enter a state of unbroken wholeness in our lives, in which we naturally work for the good of all. The first letters of the seven words together spell "VITRIOL"—the inner acid we need to dissolve the fixed patterns of Gaia-blind mechanistic thinking we have inherited from our culture.

The Seven Circles

Refer again to figure 9.1 on page 120. But now let's focus our attention on the seven circles located between each of the Azoth mandala's rays, each of which is linked to one of the seven words we considered in the previous paragraph. The first circle, between the rays of calcination and dissolution, corresponds to the word *Visita*. The image shows a black bird perching on a human skull, representing the need in calcination to let go of fixed patterns of being in ourselves. In Gaian terms, the image tells us that for Gaia to be healthy all ecological communities must eventually enter their own calcination by letting go of their current state.

In the next circle between the rays of dissolution and separation, the same black bird gazes upon its white counterpart in the dark earth. The word associated with this image is *Interiora,* suggesting that to transform we must dissolve into the unconscious. This stage is where we'll find helpful insights and energies required for our development. In Gaia the image hints that many new global ecological configurations are there in the background within her ecological dynamics waiting to come into manifestation if the circumstances are right.

The third circle between separation and conjunction associates with the word *Terra* and shows two white birds extracting the remains of the black bird from the earth. Psychologically, the white birds represent the coming together of opposites within us. These work together to bring the blackened remains of the previous operations into the next phases of the process. In Gaia the image indicates a situation where new ecological feedbacks have appeared. This involves opposites such as predatory-prey dynamics, as well as relationships between symbiotic partners built on the remains of older dynamical aspects of Gaia's functioning.

The fourth circle between conjunction and fermentation shows the two white birds lofting a five-pointed crown into the blue vault of the sky. The blackened remains in the previous image have been transformed into the crown, symbolizing the stability of a permanent state of wholeness in ourselves that has been brought about by the union of opposites within us. In the ecological realm this corresponds with the emergence of a new state of globally coherent ecological functioning and thus of healthy planetary self-regulation within the vast body of Gaia. The word *Rectificando* shows that these new states of being have made things right. They are truly effective for both ourselves and for Gaia.

The next circle, located between fermentation and distillation, shows the two white birds nesting in a tree looking after an egg. The associated word here is *Invenies,* hinting that a new style of consciousness that needs to be discovered is developing nicely in the egg of our alchemical transformation watched over by the two birds. This represents a harmonious relationship between the opposites. From a Gaian perspective the tree perhaps represents all life on the planet. Perhaps the egg of Gaian consciousness is waiting to hatch at the tip of each branch of the tree, in each of Gaia's beings, each in their own way.

The sixth circle between distillation and coagulation associates with the word *Occultum*. It shows a unicorn seated in front of a flowering rose bush. Perhaps the unicorn has hatched out of the egg and represents the innocent attitude we must have to approach the deeply hidden meaning of Gaia. The flowering of the planet's life is symbolized by the roses behind the unicorn. Thus, we find at last that our alchemical transformation opens us into our consciousness of Gaia and her consciousness of us.

The seventh and final circle between coagulation and calcination shows a hermaphrodite child emerging from the Earth. The word *Lapidem* indicates that this child represents the Philosopher's Stone, a permanent state of Gaian consciousness. It is a childlike wonder that we offer back to Gaia in gratitude and in her service, and which is no doubt required for her own further development.

One of my friends, a fellow reformed scientist with a sharp mind, reminded me once over lunch in a noisy Totnes restaurant that Valentine's picture is only one of many alchemical models that encode the transformative journey of the psyche toward wholeness. Therefore, he implied, one should not hold too much store by it. There are indeed many alchemical schemes or models that we can draw on to promote our growth into our Gaian wholeness. Since all of them work toward the same end—the experience of the Philosopher's Stone—a comparison of all these models in this book would only complicate matters and cause confusion. My friend is right, of course. No model, mathematical or psychological, is comprehensive. We should work with a given scheme in our Gaian alchemical quest only as long as it helps us perceive the immense sacred value of the thriving ecology of this ancient spinning animate Earth of ours in which we are deeply immersed.

I have found that the Azoth mandala works very well in helping me to experience how my own trajectory toward Gaian consciousness is intimately bound up with the epic evolutionary story of our ancient Earth, which has been so brilliantly revealed by my colleagues in the sciences. At other times, when I fall back into my old culturally conditioned mental habits, this alchemical approach seems completely naive, ridiculous, immature, and far-fetched. But out in the woods or in our little patch of jungle right here in our private garden at Schumacher College, these doubts sometimes dissolve as I experience a delicious sense of a Gaian understanding slowly growing in me like a plant, bringing a wider knowing of the powerful, comprehensive healing that has characterized such great moments of realization for many people down the ages.

10

Sir Isaac Newton's Azoth Mandala

In 1936 the scientific world was greatly shaken when economist Maynard Keynes made a successful bid at Sotheby's auction house for a large pile of Isaac Newton's previously unknown manuscripts. These turned out to contain over a million words (written over a thirty year period) on alchemy. Newton was one of the greatest scientists of all time and yet the manuscripts show that his major interest was alchemy and the search for the Philosopher's Stone. How are we to understand this? Scholars have spent years poring over these manuscripts (written in Latin and English) and have concluded that Newton was what one could call a mechanical alchemist, interested only in producing a physical substance—the Philosopher's Stone—capable of transmuting one metal into another, particularly base metals into gold.

This interpretation may be true to some extent for there is no doubt that Newton carried out alchemical experiments with physical substances, but it is also possible that he was just as much engaged in the process of transmuting his own soul from lead to gold as much as in what we now know as chemistry. He held to the mainstream alchemical view that there were souls and spirits in nature, and that the Philosopher's Stone was as much spiritual as material, as evidenced by passages such as this one from his alchemical opus:

This tincture is the spirit & the spirit is the soule & the soule is the body, because in this operation the body is made a spirit of a most subtile nature & likewise the spirit is incorporated & is made of the nature of a body with bodies, & so our stone contains a body a soul & a spirit. O nature how thou changest the body into a spirit which thou couldst not do if the spirit were not incorporated with the bodies & the bodies with the spirits made volatile or flying & afterward permanent or abiding.

Here Newton confers with alchemical spiritual understanding that there are souls and spirits in the material world, which the alchemical work liberates and fixes in the form of the Philosopher's Stone. There are various references to the Azoth mandala in Newton's alchemical writings, and he made a wonderful drawing (fig. 10.1) depicting his concept of the Philosopher's Stone consisting of seven interlinked Azoth-like mandalas each associated with psychological terms referring

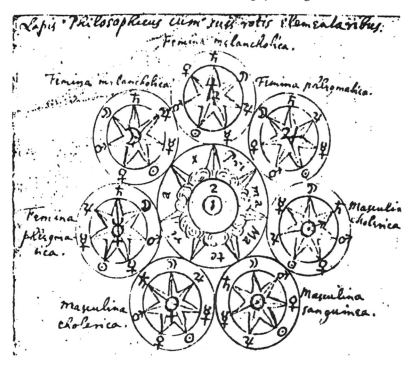

Figure 10.1. Isaac Newton's Lapis Philosophorum, consisting of seven Azoth mandalas.

to the four humors (choleric, sanguine, melancholic, and phlegmatic—notice the correspondence with Jung's four psychological types) and their various combinations with masculine and feminine energies.

THE SEVEN STAGES OF TRANSFORMATION IN SPECIATION

Notice that each of the seven mandala stars is ascribed the symbol of a planet at its center, and that these follow the precise order of the planets in Basil Valentine's Azoth mandala, starting with Saturn in the uppermost star and moving clockwise thereafter, suggesting that Newton was well acquainted with Valentine's work, which was primarily concerned with the spiritual transformation of the alchemist. These lines of evidence convince me that Newton's alchemical quest was as much spiritual/psychological as it was chemical, but this is not an issue we have time to explore in more detail here.

Instead, I would like to use Newton's image to help us understand how the seven transformative processes described in the Azoth mandala operate at different spatial and temporal scales in every single physical process that takes place in the body of Gaia. As you can see in figure 10.2, I've mapped seven key Gaian processes onto Newton's

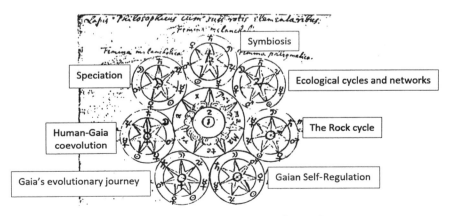

Figure 10.2. Newton's Azoth mandalas superimposed with seven key Gaian processes. The Center is both the Sun and the Source of All, the prima materia that touches each circulating Azoth mandala with its qualities and essences.

mandala. I could have chosen many different processes, but these seven are undoubtedly of great importance for the health and development of our planet. The key insight is that we can find the Azoth mandala's seven alchemical operations in each and every planetary process at every spatial and temporal scale.

Calcination and Speciation

Let's begin with speciation, which refers to the appearance of new species via the process of natural selection first described by Darwin and Wallace. A species is in its calcination when the form and shape of its body and its patterns of behavior have been fixed and stable for a period of time.

Dissolution in Response to Pressure

These patterns need to be dissolved if new better adapted forms are to appear and one can speculate that this happens within the genome when mutant genes on chromosomes within reproductive cells are shuffled around to make eggs and sperm in the case of cells with nuclei. This genome-level dissolution might be enhanced if viruses or bacteria insert completely alien stretches of genetic code into these chromosomes. One can also see dissolution as selective pressures from other organisms and the environment that tend to push the species toward extinction—the ultimate dissolution.

Separation, Individuation, and Survival

Separation happens in the speciation process when the reproductive cells—egg and sperm in this example—are physically separated in testes and ovaries in the males and females of a species. These individuals must now prove themselves able to survive long enough to mate and produce viable offspring. But not all of them make it that far since natural selection removes individuals that haven't managed to adapt to their surroundings sufficiently well. Some fall off cliffs, others are eaten, some are decimated by parasites, storms, and diseases. Here is separation again, this time as death, which, to use more conventional terminology, removes less fit organisms from the species' gene pool before they breed.

Conjunction and Reproduction

And so the issue shifts to finding ways to recombine the separated eggs and sperm via sex and reproduction, and so we move into the next Azoth mandala ray, which is conjunction. Here is sexual selection: How do males and females find, choose, and mate with each other? Think birds of paradise, whose flamboyant wildly feathered males dance madly in carefully choreographed steps to attract drab brown females whose choosiness is the very force of sexual selection. Darwin spent a lot of time thinking and writing about sexual selection, which continues to be a hot topic in modern evolutionary biology.

Fermentation and Adaptation

Fermentation happens when different forms or varieties of a species are physically separated in various ways, perhaps by a river that suddenly widens due to a recent nearby earthquake, or possibly when members of an herbivorous insect species hide better than others under leaves. Perhaps these "hiders" access the plant's nutritious sap by using their sharper mandibles to puncture the plant's tissues, isolating themselves by diet from their "mother species" and eventually becoming an entirely new species of their own. Fermentation is thus about evolutionary lineages transforming through time, some changing slowly into new species over geological timescales, others budding off new variants in a few days, as in bacteria.

I must confess that it has been a struggle to arrive at this point. I have been using far too much intellectual energy in wrestling with the problem of fitting speciation into the Azoth mandala and I was beginning to go round in circles to no effect at all. Then I reminded myself that the Azoth mandala is given as a gift from the depths of the anima mundi, from the soul of the world, from the collective unconscious, from the objective psyche. As soon as I remembered this it became clear that the image of two white birds flying skyward holding a crown in their beaks represents the appearance of a new species. The next image, of the two birds in the tree, helped me to see that fermentation involves a settling into new patterns of viable ecological and behavioral functioning. The new species figuratively makes a nest; it creates a niche for itself within its new ecological context.

I report this to let you know that by contemplating a process revealed by science alongside the alchemical images—both as equal partners but with perhaps a little more emphasis on intuiting what the images have to offer—we are doing Gaia alchemy. I notice the psychological shift from intellect alone to intellect plus feeling, sensing and intuition, and for a short while I am made whole as the insight pours in that fermentation is about the differential survival of variable offspring produced in the previous operations.

Distillation and Ecological Niche

And so we move to distillation, whose planet is Mercury—quicksilver both in the mind and in Gaia's ecology. The image is of a peaceful unicorn sitting under a rose bush. Perhaps in distillation a species settles more into the ecological niche it has carved out for itself, distilling its skills though micro-selection until it reaches a state of deep "comfort" within its ecology, a state of increasingly well-adapted familiarity with itself and with its surroundings.

As I write, I feel the biology grounds me. It won't allow me to fly off with the Azoth mandala into the realms of metaphysical speculation, since to be grounded in the world of biology, to be in Gaia's world, is what the image wants. This discovery brings about a tremendous sense of homecoming and well-being in me.

Coagulation and Presence

So what might coagulation mean in speciation? The image is of a hermaphrodite child coming out of the Earth. Moon is the planet and the word is *Lapidem*—that is, stone. I can't resist the temptation to find something of psyche here. After all, the Philosopher's Stone is actually something psychical. For us, it is the deepest realization of wholeness as Gaia-enfolded beings that we are capable of in any given moment. Perhaps coagulation is each species' mode of awareness, its view on the world, be it the molecule-tasting awareness of a bacterium or the visual consciousness of a bee with compound eyes visiting a flower. Perhaps the Stone is each species' awareness, its presence as a psyche in the world, emerging miraculously from the very atoms and molecules of its physical self, from the mandala of Gaia herself.

◇◇◇◇◇ A Conversation with Jeffrey Kiehl ◇◇◇◇◇

JEFFREY: Mandala is also about community. We're talking about spreading sacredness into the world.

STEPHAN: It's a magical operation.

JEFFREY: Yes. It's very feminine. How one sets a table shows our care about how the table looks, how everything's arranged where people will sit. How they will be in relationship to one another. It's not just random assignments of people at the table. There's a valuing, a feeling—a feminine quality that comes into the construction of the mandala. You have to swallow the Sun.

STEPHAN: Everyone's going to leave the table feeling enriched, deepened, loved, and connected. And that will spread from them to the rest of the world. So neglecting your anima is a disaster?

JEFFREY: Yes. If a man doesn't listen to his anima, she'll get tired of being neglected and she leaves. That's called losing one's soul. You get depressed. There's no animation to your life. We haven't been paying attention to her—collectively, we've been neglecting her. We're filling out forms and paperwork and taking care of this and that. Meanwhile, she's sitting there and finally says, "Forget this. He's not paying attention. I'm going somewhere else." And then you really feel what drudgery life is. You ask: Is this all there is?

STEPHAN: She gives an excitement about life.

JEFFREY: Yes—she animates you. She's the positive side of the anima.

STEPHAN: How does she help you?

JEFFREY: She'll tell you what the unconscious is doing.

◇◇◇◇◇◇◇◇◇◇◇◇◇◇◇◇◇◇◇◇◇◇◇◇◇◇◇◇◇◇◇◇◇◇

And so we are back to calcination, and we could go round the mandala again refining our understanding and insight into how working with the Azoth mandala biologically in relation to speciation brings us into a much deeper lived experience of this magical world we find ourselves in. Please do this if you feel so inclined, and write down what you find, for we all have much to contribute to developing Gaia alchemy.

THE SEVEN STAGES OF TRANSFORMATION AND OTHER GAIAN PROCESSES

Let's next see if the Azoth mandala model works with other Gaia processes. It works with the cycling of nutrients within ecological communities: recycling is one of the most important forces in the world of nature. Let's explore that process first.

Biological beings die and decompose (calcination and dissolution), their chemical constituents are split apart into the atoms and molecules needed for life by decomposing organisms (separation) and these constituents are taken up by organisms and remade into new forms of life (conjunction). These new generations of living beings then accumulate biomass with increasing skill and efficiency (fermentation and distillation) until this development reaches a peak (coagulation), whereupon their chemical building blocks enter calcination once again when they die.

The life cycles of organisms also fit well into the Azoth mandala. A butterfly chrysalis embodies calcination, dissolution, and separation as within it the cells that made it into a caterpillar are broken down into their constituent chemical components. Conjunction happens when newly constituted cells organize themselves into the future adult inside the chrysalis. When this process is complete and the adult butterfly emerges from the chrysalis and begins to feed on nectar, we enter the phases of fermentation and distillation, in which the butterfly offers pollination services to the plant community. Some insects (not butterflies) host symbiotic protozoans in their gut that ferment carbohydrates to the mutual benefit of both partners. Finally, coagulation takes places when butterflies mate and the females lay new batches of eggs on their species-specific food plants.

We can also consider the rock cycle with the help of the Azoth mandala. Calcination and dissolution take place when solid rocks are pushed deep down into Earth's interior where they melt into magma. Some of this material begins to rise and cool. Various minerals separate out (separation) until the rock reaches the surface as newly solidified rock (conjunction). Some of this rock is uplifted by tectonic forces into mountain ranges, which are weathered into tiny fragments that are deposited in water and in other ways to form new sediments (fermentation) that are compressed into new rock (distillation and coagulation) that will eventually experience calcination again as the cycle repeats.

In the next chapter we'll explore Gaia's temperature regulation and in chapter 13 we'll consider her evolutionary journey in relation to the Azoth mandala, so let's ponder whether it relates well to human-Gaia coevolution in our times. Clearly, our global economy is literally calcinating the planet by triggering catastrophic global heating. As a result, the global economic system is starting to break down (dissolution), a situation the current Covid viral pandemic (itself a product of globalization and the subsequent economic over-connectedness) is helping to accelerate. Separation will happen when countries and communities find themselves physically isolated after the current system has broken down. We'll then have the chance to organize and consolidate into localized pro-Gaian economic systems (conjunction) connected digitally with each other around the world, creating a new planetary economy based on local nodes linked mostly through digital information transfers via the internet (fermentation and distillation). If all goes well (which is highly unlikely), we'll enter into a deep coagulation with Gaia in which human consciousness will help bring about new levels of planetary self-realization, which we cannot easily imagine now from the standpoint of our current mainstream state of consciousness.

◇◇◇◇◇ *A Conversation with Jeffrey Kiehl* ◇◇◇◇◇

STEPHAN: Calcination in Gaia can also be seen in the rock cycle. We still have the remnants of that initial calcination right here in the core of the Earth. Otherwise, there's no magnetic field. Plate tectonics— there's no Gaia without it. There's no protection from cosmic rays without a magnetic field. There's no cycle of carbon either. So you've got to have the rock cycle's calcination going on all the time.

JEFFREY: I think that's an interesting point. We tend to think we do this process and then we do the next process and we do the next one. But it could be that they're all going on at the same time. Calcination never ends, dissolution never ends, and so on.

STEPHAN: All the states in the Azoth mandala are there in every Gaian process—as we saw in Newton's Azoth mandala.

JEFFREY: Yes. Another form of calcination, I think, would be the increasing amount of sun's energy reaching the Earth's surface through geological time. We have increased the surface temperature of the planet. This is a type of calcination via our changing of the climate.

STEPHAN: So if we keep calcinating the planet things will turn to ash—as in the Australian wildfires of 2020.

JEFFREY: The ultimate fate of earth will be ash. The sun's is on its Main Sequence evolution. It will burn Earth in two billion years when the radius of the Sun reaches the radius of the Earth and we will be consumed.

◇◇◇◇◇◇◇◇◇◇◇◇◇◇◇◇◇◇◇◇◇◇◇◇◇◇◇◇

🏵 LAYING DOWN YOUR AZOTH MANDALA

The idea in this contemplation is to make a simple Azoth mandala in your Gaia place using sticks and other simple materials immediately around you.

Go to your Gaia place and find fourteen sticks or dead plant stems that appeal to you (mine are usually about 25 cm long) making sure that they can easily be seen against the ground.

Feel how there is somewhere in your Gaia place calling you as a place to make your Azoth mandala. There may be several such locations in your Gaia place, but there is one in particular that calls you most of all. Find this place now.

I like to make my Azoth mandala where there is mostly bare ground, but you could attach yours to tree a branch, or make one out of pebbles on the beach.

Spend a while appreciating the textures, colors, shapes, and living beings in the location you've found. Kneeling on the ground on both knees as I make my Azoth mandala really helps me gain the maximum benefit from this practice.

Now prepare the ground in readiness to make your Azoth mandala in whatever way is needed, or not at all. I gently brush away leaf debris to make a circle just slightly larger than the stretch of my extended arm.

Begin to arrange your sticks into the seven-rayed star of the Azoth mandala. Here is an Azoth mandala of mine, made in my jungle just after rain with apple blossom petals on the ground. The chestnut leaf arrived by itself overnight from the giant chestnut tree next to my Gaia place. I was intrigued that the leaf had seven lobes, so I arranged it inside my Azoth mandala (fig. 10.3).

Be fully present to your sensory experiences as you lay down the sticks for your Azoth. Put all your attention into your sensing. See the colors of each stick, feel the temperature and the texture of the ground. Be aware of the sounds around you. Birdsong? Rustling leaves? Trickling water? Cars? Planes? Are there particular smells you can detect? If so, take in their qualities.

Arrange your sticks mindfully and very slowly until you are happy with the overall balance and sense of wholeness of your Azoth mandala.

Figure 10.3. An Azoth mandala in my jungle.

Sometimes I place something of beauty in the center of mine—a petal perhaps, or a little stone.

Notice if the shape you've made works or doesn't work.

There'll come a point when you really like the shape you see. It will speak to you and will give you an expansive experience of wholeness as you realize how deeply you belong to Gaia.

You have experienced each of the Azoth mandala's seven rays in both Gaia and yourself by merging science and alchemy, and now the boundaries between the two of you vanish as you gaze upon your finished Azoth mandala.

A feeling of devotion and dedication to Gaia, to her mysterious ways, to her beauty, and to her wonder may now come over you now.

This is nondual Gaia. This is the Lapis—the Philosopher's Stone.

Dwell deeply with the insights and experiences that come to you in these precious moments.

Then, when you are ready to leave, acknowledge what your Azoth mandala has given you in whatever way feels good. Sometimes I bow Japanese style before I leave my Azoth mandala to its quiet life in my jungle garden.

∞

If possible, visit your Azoth mandala the following day.

How is it now? Still intact? Scattered by animals and the wind?

Does it ask you to make it new again?

Be creative. Find new ways of allowing the Azoth mandala to appear. Lay one down in another part of your Gaia place, or have several of them there if that feels good.

If you can, spend some time with your Azoth mandala every day, feeling the peace and tranquillity it brings you.

11

Gaia Alchemy
on Granite

We are ready at last to explore how the seven-rayed image of the Azoth mandala can help us develop a sense of how Gaia has been regulating her temperature over geological time as she has spun around her orbit in the company of her far flung neighborly planets in our solar system.

Having used the animistic narrative style we explored earlier to understand the science of the long-term carbon journey, my M.Sc. class eventually needed to experience the journey with their senses and imagination—beyond the classroom, out in the living world of nature—for even deeper alchemical meanings to be revealed to them. I share the following story with you now so that you may be inspired to do the same.

So it was that one cold winter's day we set off on a pilgrimage to the great granite dome of nearby Dartmoor to feel the power and majesty of the long-term carbon journey. Our many hours of class time, our tutorials and discussions focusing on the science were our cognitive preparation for this alchemical pilgrimage to the wild expanses of the Dartmoor granite where the truest encounter with Gaia might perhaps appear for us.

After a short bus ride from Schumacher College to Venford reservoir we walked to the great granite temple of Bench Tor high up on Dartmoor and entered the precincts of the final sanctuary near the wild forest, which rolls steeply down to the wild tumbling white water of the river Dart. Each of us settled face down on a little space of granite, belly to rock, rock to belly, ready to encounter the calcium princesses buried in the cool depths of the granite beneath our soft warm bodies. You might do the same, perhaps in your Gaia place, or if ever you find yourself atop granite rock, as you read the words I spoke that day.

We lie on you, we feel you, we touch you, we sense you, Gaia's granite, with all our senses wide awake.

We leave our human bodies lying here on your cool rock surface.

With our shamanic bodies we plunge into the deep crystalline labyrinths of your rocky depths.

We shrink to the size of an electron.

We float in your vast open spaces of gently vibrating atoms held in a 270-million-year chemical embrace.

Great peace, great calm.

We see you now, calcium princesses. You are scattered points of white light in this hugely spacious atomic matrix.

We dwell with you, we receive your beauty. We are nourished by your near eternal presences.

We feel how you yearn to be with your carbon princes.

We thank you for your chemical-molecular teachings. Your sense of eternity enhances our world of constant change.

We allowed our shamanic bodies to float back into our physical bodies lying on the rock. We picked ourselves up and slowly walked downhill toward the woods, tasting the cold, damp air redolent with the aroma of mist and heather. We noticed the change of mood as we left the open moorland and entered the tangled mossy tree scape saturated with the thundering sounds of the wild river Dart far below. High above a pair of ravens called out their blessings upon us.

We settled into a small clearing among mossy granite boulders and lay down facing skyward under the high lanky trees of this remote Dartmoor woodland. Aided by the shaman's drum sounded by my friend and colleague, Andy Letcher (a fellow renegade Oxford ecologist), I spoke out the words of this shamanic carbon journey slowly and deliberately,* and you should read it in the same way, so that you might be taken on the wings of imagination into the living majesty of the carbon journey's raging power.

You are a carbon atom locked up in limestone rock at the bottom of the sea. For the last 300 million years you have experienced nothing but the cold pressure and seeming immobility of solid rock around you. Nothing but the ancient, peaceful silence of the rock. No movement, no sound, no change, just the immense repose that has engulfed you for time beyond memory. Settle into the feeling of immense tranquillity that surrounds you.

You experience a slow sinking feeling as the sea floor that carries you from below slowly approaches the edge of a continent, dragging you downward into the depths of the Earth.

Feel the temperature and pressure increasing as you sink down into the dark depths. It's so hot now that the limestone you are part of begins to melt, merging with the silica that surrounds you.

Feel the intense heat and pressure. The chemical bonds holding you to your calcium atom vibrate with an agonizing intensity. You are shaken about like a pea in a box. The shaking is so intense now that you realize that you are being liberated from the limestone.

You feel awake and excited. You tingle with anticipation.

Feeling incomplete, you quickly bond with two passing oxygen atoms newly released from the glassy shell of a melting diatom.

Savor the passionate embraces of your two oxygen lovers. The three of you are now part of a new emergent being—a molecule of carbon dioxide.

Now the red hot, molten rock around you flows quickly upward. You travel faster and faster through a great wide gash in Gaia's crust, almost deafened by the mad sound of surging gas and rock. The sound intensifies, and with it the slow, red-hot turbulence

---

*The following meditation is from *Animate Earth* by Stephan Harding, published by Green Books, greenbooks.co.uk.

that carries you higher and higher, closer and closer to a new life that you know will soon open up for you.

Pressure is building behind you. You are moving very fast. The pressure, the sound, and the heat are immense and powerful.

You are right in the very heart of a massive volcanic eruption. A bursting release of energy propels you high into the air along with vast amounts of smoke, ash, and red hot lava.

You look down at the smoking volcano far below. Already you are high up in the atmosphere, buffeted by the intense updraft that has brought you so far so quickly.

All day long the sun has been beating down. You drift in the air, warming it as heat from Gaia's surface bounces off the bonds that hold you to your two oxygen lovers.

Great air currents carry you northward, and for weeks you soar high above the seas and forests. You enjoy the delicious freedom of travel, wondering at the amazing views of mountains, forests, and oceans, bonded still to your oxygen lovers. How the planet has changed since you were last here, some 300 million years ago when tree ferns and the first four-limbed and creatures crawled upon the Earth.

At last, a great gust of air carries you down over a modern-day granite outcrop. You swirl closer and closer to the ground, and sweep past a succulent bush, alive with luscious yellow flowers. You brush against a pore on the underside of a leaf, and are caught in a tiny in-breath that sucks you through the pore into the translucent green interior of the leaf. Your leaving cools the Earth by depriving the air of a carbon dioxide molecule.

Giant molecular beings surround you and take you to a great green chamber deep in the cell—the chloroplast. A blinding flash of sunlight shakes you to your core. You are joined to other carbon and hydrogen atoms. The newly forged chemical bonds that bind you to your fellow atoms hold the sun's energy. You are now part of a sugar molecule, beginning a new journey through peaceful green sap.

You feel a tugging downward toward the plant's roots. Slowly you move through wide tubes, ever downward, pulled by a cease-less but subtle flow that takes many other molecular beings along with you.

You reach the very tip of a growing root hair and pass into a growing cell. All around you there is frenetic activity as new root cells are made, pushing the root ever further in its incessant search for nutrients. Your root finds a crack in the solid granite beneath the soil. It breaks into the crack, splitting the rock as it swells.

Once again oxygen lovers embrace you, tearing you apart, releasing the solar energy you have held for so long. Now, once again, you belong to a carbon dioxide molecule, breathed out by the root into the surrounding soil.

There has been much rain and the soil is water logged. You feel an irresistible attraction for a passing water molecule, and together you become carbonic acid, which instantly releases a single, tiny hydrogen ion, the smallest being in the chemical world. Billions of carbonic acid molecules around you release a vast horde of hydro-gen ions into the soil.

The hydrogen ions dissolve the granite, releasing billions of calcium and silicon atoms long incarcerated in the rock. You feel irresistibly attracted to one of these calcium atoms as it drifts near you. You bond with it to become liquid chalk.

You are pulled downward by the flow of ground water. Now your great river journey begins. You hear a rushing, gushing sound, and you enter the flow of the river as it tumbles over great boulders and waterfalls on its way to the sea.

In the cool surface waters of the sea, you are sucked into the embrace of a marine algae protected by tiny wheels of solid chalk. You soon become part of one of these wheels.

The alga lives its short life and dies. You slowly sink toward the ocean deeps, cherishing the memories of your brief journey in the air above.

Sinking, sinking into the depths, you leave behind the upper sunlit reaches of the sea and eventually settle into the chalky sediments in the darkness at the bottom of the ocean.

Slowly you feel the weight of new chalky deposits accumulating above you, and slowly, ever so slowly, the pressure packs you closer and closer together into limestone. The great journey is complete, and now you must wait for another 300 million years before you once again explode into the atmosphere through a volcano.

Had things gone according to plan, we would have contemplated Basil Valentine's Azoth mandala for the second time a few days after our pilgrimage. As it happened, a severe storm came barreling in from the Atlantic, forcing us to postpone the pilgrimage. It was a powerful reminder of our changing climate. We were obliged to explore the overlaps between the long-term carbon cycle and the Azoth mandala a few days before our expedition onto the barren expanses and valley-deep forests of Dartmoor.

No sooner was the Azoth mandala on the screen than Tamar, a young student from New York with a beautiful singing voice, felt herself gripped by a flow of inspiration that electrified the room. A wild spirit took us with her into a palpable sense of heightened awareness, making the very air sparkle with excitement as we sensed that a great opportunity for the richest kind of learning was about to appear.

Tamar spoke with a glistening brightness in her eyes and a powerful yet gentle ring in her voice, calling out the carbon cycle's correspondences with the seven rays of the Azoth mandala without a moment's hesitation:

"**Calcination:** carbon dioxide heating the atmosphere.

Dissolution: Biologically assisted granite weathering dissolving carbon dioxide in rain water, making carbonic acid.

Separation: Rock splitting biology. Biologically enhanced granite weathering. Calcium ions, bicarbonate ions, silica ions liberated from the rock.

Conjunction: The journey of calcium and carbon in rivers to the ocean and the coccolithophores.

Fermentation: The marriage of carbon and calcium inside the coccolithophores. Chalk as spirit.

Distillation: Dying and falling back to the planet in chalk and limestone. Chalk and silica into magma.

Coagulation: Subduction, granite returns to the atmosphere. Seeing the cycle as whole."

We sat stunned as the implications of Tamar's inspiration soaked into us, helping us realize that Gaia too, like all things, transits over and over again through the archetypal processes of transformation modeled by the Azoth mandala (fig. 11.1).

If we were to look deeply enough, we would discover the entire Azoth mandala in each step of the journey with one ray dominant in each step. For example, coagulation occurs when coherent self-regulation emerges out of interactions among all the components of Gaia as a system.

Several weeks passed, and despite the ecstatic experience in the class that November day, it was difficult for me to once again bring together Gaian science and alchemy. I failed over and over again, lost heart, and

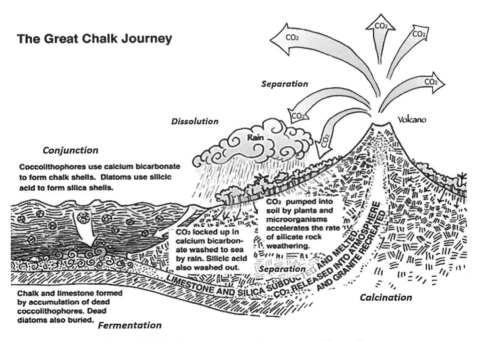

Figure 11.1. The long-term carbon journey seen alchemically through the Azoth mandala's operations.

many times almost gave up, calling myself a fool for wasting a single moment on what now once again seemed to be such utter nonsense. And yet about a month later in mid-December a deep knowing dawned on me that Gaia too has been going through her particular alchemical transformations during her four-and-a-half-billion year evolutionary journey. I sensed that Gaia's next and perhaps most important transformation can happen only with the participation of those of us human beings who realize the meaning of our belonging to her soils, to her waters, to her biosphere, to her mountains and atmosphere, to her soul, and to her spirit.

I know now beyond doubt that we are fully alive to Gaia and to each other when we engage in the planetary task of helping this aged, richly cultured, wisely intelligent, wildly creative, creaturely planet of ours to fulfill her own mysterious transformations (so much yearned for by the entire cosmos) by loving her as deeply and as wisely as we can. It is Gaia alchemy—the union of alchemy and science—that brings me this sacred understanding more than anything else. For as David Fideler writes: "The alchemist merely acts as a midwife to accelerate and nurse along the natural process. . . . of our planet's evolution into a wider consciousness." He also states "all matter is evolutionary and aspires to return to a more spiritual state" (2014).

Later, as I ponder all this in my hut, Jung stops by for a visit:

JUNG: *Good—so you have got somewhere. The imagination has been greatly receptive and stimulated. What do you have to say about it?*
STEPHAN: *Everything is more solid and alive from within itself. Glowing with something.*
JUNG: *The prima materia?*
STEPHAN: *Yes, no doubt about it.*
JUNG: *Then relish the moment, for it will vanish.*
STEPHAN: *How to make it stay?*
JUNG: *That is the Art.*

I contemplate the first two operations (calcination and dissolution) of the alchemical journey toward the Philosopher's Stone, which I see now as somehow embodied in Gaia herself mantled in green, blue, and white as she tumbles through space on her cosmic journey. However, I still can't see with any depth of insight how kindling a calcinating fire of passion for the Philosopher's Stone in ourselves can have anything to do with greenhouse gasses warming our planet's atmosphere throughout geological time. Despite this return of doubt and hesitation, I trust the intuition that there is something of value in this inquiry and feel it is worth continuing.

Some days pass and I am no nearer to making any sense of it. And today Jung visits me again. This time he sits by the window in our study, in the chair covered with a vibrantly glowing red Balinese fabric.

STEPHAN: *So when the planet is calcinated, greenhouse gasses build up in the atmosphere and the temperature rises.*

JUNG: *That's right, and then rest of the psyche steps in to regulate the situation spontaneously from out of itself.*

STEPHAN: *Meaning that the other six rays of the Azoth mandala kick in? That's how the regulation happens?*

JUNG: *Yes, it seems so.*

STEPHAN: *So how meaningful is it to equate my own calcination with that of the planet?*

JUNG: *You seem doubtful.*

STEPHAN: *One must remain vigilant for nonsense, especially in this domain.*

JUNG: *Don't get too lost in doubting. There is great value in what you are doing. I sense it. Let's look together.*

STEPHAN: *Shall we dwell in calcination?*

JUNG: *Go ahead.*

STEPHAN: *Greenhouse gases build up in the atmosphere from tectonic activity. It gets too hot on the planet, too claustrophobic. It feels very uncomfortable. It gets to the point where one definitely needs water. One needs to cool down and dissolve this heat.*

JUNG: *You see how well it fits: now you are in dissolution.*

A day or so later, in Dennis Hauck's book *The Emerald Tablet* I find the following words in relation to calcination and dissolution:

This breakdown in crystallized thought (or altering of belief systems) is the primary objective of the first two operations of alchemy.

This leads me to the notion that granite is full of calcium-bearing crystals that must be dissolved if Gaia is to avoid becoming overheated by her own greenhouse gasses. The appearance of Hauck's words at this moment seems to be a synchronistic event opening up a wider insight about how our psychological life links to the life of our planet and indeed to the whole of nature.

Then, a few days later in my faded green book of Jung's unpublished lectures on alchemy I find the following verse, part of a longer Gnostic poem known as the *Odes of Solomon* from the second century BCE.

> *For a little stream has sprung up.*
> *And hath become a broad and mighty river;*
> *For everything hath it torn away and ground to powder . . .*

This image of a mighty flow of the psychological water of insight that grinds down all obstacles to wisdom seems to be clearly related to the role of water in dissolving Gaia's granite, a process that is essential for her ability to regulate her temperature within the narrow limits that her biological beings can tolerate.

Gaia alchemy presents us with the opportunity to unify the first two rays of the Azoth mandala with scientific images of mighty rivers that dissolve rocks and crystals as part of Gaia's temperature regulation. In this way we perceive a correspondence between our psychological development and a parallel process in the Gaian world, namely biologically assisted granite weathering. Symbolically, our inner rocks of crystallized thought and fixed habits have to be ground down and dissolved for wisdom to appear, opening us up to wider domains of well-being. In these, the psyche self-regulates more effectively once the energy of what has been liberated by calcination and dissolution becomes accessible to consciousness. But what, for Gaia, is wisdom? Could it be that in the Gaian domain, wisdom appears in her self-regulating feedbacks, such as the one we have been exploring here involving biologically assisted granite weathering? Could the wisdom inherent in our mutually emergent self-regulation (both personal and planetary) be the principle we need to unite Gaia and alchemy? Could this be a pathway toward a modern, deeply ecological, science-based discovery of our Gaian Philosopher's Stone, of our deepest comfort and wisdom here on this planet? From time to time my fleeting experience is that this is so.

Just as the contemplation of alchemical images engenders a process of widening wisdom and self-regulation in ourselves, so do the same alchemical images help us to discern the wisdom of Gaia in the evolution of her feedbacks, which maintain her surface conditions within the narrow bounds favorable for life. Gaia's wisdom involves earthy, factual events with no need for a literal providential "Mother Gaia" running the whole planetary show from other dimensions, since if there are other such dimensions we find them nowhere else but in matter. Gaia's wisdom emerges from the sum total of all the networked interactions between her living beings and her air, waters, and rocks. These might one day be explored by a new generation of scientists who are open to these more alchemical ways of using quantification and mathematics for finding one's way back into the vast roundness of Gaia's great sacred body.

12

Of Loops and Stars

The hidden face of Nature can only be seen with the heart.
STEPHEN HARROD BUHNER

We've seen how Gaia alchemy helps us approach the biogeochemical science of the long-term carbon cycle from a richly animistic and enlivening perspective, but can we make a further bridge from alchemy to the science of ecology—to the scientific study of the relationships between organisms with each other and with their surroundings? Gaia alchemy should be able to withstand this kind of stress test.

An interesting possibility is to relate the Azoth mandala to a highly influential concept in ecology known as the adaptive cycle. This model is described in the book *Resilience Thinking* by Walker and Salt, which analyzes dynamic transformational processes in all complex systems—including ecological communities, economies, and human social systems. I am struck by how well the basic pattern of the adaptive cycle model fits the Azoth mandala (see both in fig. 12.1, p. 166). To borrow a phrase from Henri Bortoft, one of our brilliant philosophy teachers in the M.Sc. in holistic science, it really does seem as if the same deep principle of nature expresses itself differently in many different domains.

Let's start with the top right-hand box of the adaptive cycle model. This is labeled *conservation* and is given the mathematical symbol K, which stands for the carrying capacity for any given species within

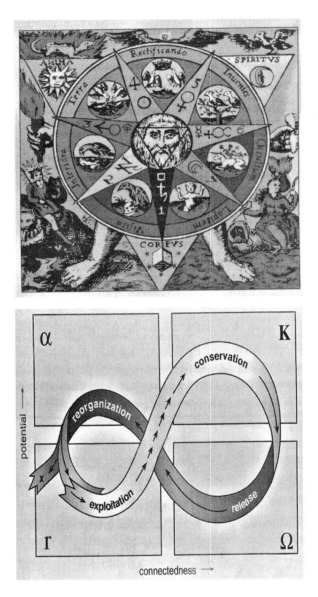

Figure 12.1. The Azoth mandala on the top in comparison with a graphic representation of the adaptive cycle model on the bottom.

Adaptive cycle model from *Resilience Thinking* by Brian Walker and David Salt (adapted from Gunderson and Holling, *Panarchy* © 2002). © 2006 Brian Walker and David Salt. Reproduced by permission of Island Press, Washington, DC.

an ecological community. Carrying capacity refers to the maximum number of organisms an area can support without ecological collapse. In the Azoth mandala, this domain of the model corresponds to calcination, the first downward-pointing ray colored black, whose metal is lead and whose planet is Saturn.

An ecological community in the K phase finds itself in a dynamic equilibrium previously called the climax state by ecologists. Imagine an old-growth forest where solar energy captured by photosynthesizers is used to accumulate biomass, which must eventually reach a limit (denoted by the symbol K) due to the limitations of space and the maximum heights to which trees or other vegetation can grow.

Many such ecological communities in the K phase have remained in the same state (as old-growth forest or coral reefs, for example) for very long periods of time. The species within these communities might come and go, but the community as a recognizable whole lives on until a serious disturbance appears.

Relationships within K communities are complex and stable. There are many strong interconnections in the ecological network and there are many mutually beneficial symbiotic relationships among specialist species interacting exclusively with each other. In their book *Resilience Thinking* (2006), authors Walker and Salt explain that in a K community the ecological space is full of conservative, long-lived species using resources efficiently, so there is little scope for increasing the community's overall biomass, which has reached the maximum possible quantity given other factors such as climate and geology. Such K species are strong competitors. They spread far and wide and sometimes survive for long periods, perhaps even over long periods of geological time. The community is strongly interconnected and much of its biomass (including its carbon) is locked up for very long periods in hard to access places such as in wood and dead organic material.

Redundancies decline in K communities. A redundant species potentially contributes a specific function to the community (such as nitrogen fixation) and yet is present at low abundance while other abundant species provide the service in question. The less common species is redundant because it currently offers little to the community, but it is there waiting in the wings ready to leap into action should abundant species to which it is similar functionally decline or disappear. Such ecological redundancies are vital for an ecological community's ability to maintain its health in the face of serious disturbances such as fires and droughts.

As we have said, the K phase in the adaptive cycle corresponds very well with the first ray of the Azoth mandala whose planet is Saturn and whose metal is lead, both of which convey qualities of inertia and heaviness. A very conservative state of affairs that has perhaps outlived its time needs to be dissolved so that its energies can be redirected toward exploring and developing new imperatives. Psychologically, one may have developed a very complex outlook with many rich experiences and relationships with plants, animals, with the biosphere, and indeed with our entire planet. However, the alchemical journey sometimes requires us to let go of even this expansive yet rather fixed view so that wider and deeper understandings of Gaia's wisdom can emerge.

Now I run into a most uncomfortable feeling. Could it be that applying the concept of alchemical calcination to ecological communities disparages those currently in the K phase such as rain forests and coral reefs? Isn't it ridiculous to conceive of such stunningly complex, dynamic ecologies as Saturnine, leaden, heavy, and stuck? Just think of the vibrancy of a coral reef or the thrumming life of a healthy rain forest. They can't be stuck—how can they be? If so, we've encountered a major problem for Gaia alchemy.

This feeling becomes very strong as I realize how seriously this limits and even invalidates my attempt to integrate the Azoth mandala and the science of ecology. One would expect that such limitations appear when trying to match inner psychological processes with the dynamics of a very different realm, namely that of the more-than-human world—yet, as we shall see, the rest of the Azoth mandala fits quite well with the adaptive cycle model. But to what extent can we meaningfully reconcile the K phase of the adaptive cycle with alchemical calcination?

Luckily help is at hand. On the radio the other day I heard author Andrea Wulf talking about her latest book on Alexander von Humboldt, the great nineteenth-century naturalist and explorer who carried out detailed scientific work during his extensive travels with his colleague Aimé Bonpland in South America. The two companions saw the continent in an almost undisturbed state and fell in love with its mountains, forests, and its many natural wonders. Humbolt's great friend Goethe inspired and taught him how to integrate his thinking and feeling functions in his approach to nature and thus for me Humboldt is a great hero of what we at Schumacher College call holistic science.

Humboldt was the first of our scientists to perceive the existence of a single fully integrated ecological community at the global planetary scale, which we now dare once again to call Gaia. He was much more integrated in his psyche than we moderns and was closer to the living soul and spirit of nature and also to alchemy. Although he wasn't an alchemist himself, he is most certainly a powerful ancestor of Gaia alchemy. Since my youth, I have felt a strong connection to Humboldt for these reasons. Even in his times he worried about the adverse impacts of Europeans on the planet. Perhaps I can ask him for help.

HUMBOLDT: *Thanks for that fine introduction. I find your inquiry most interesting.*

STEPHAN: *Can you help me resolve my dilemma? How can ecological communities in the K phase be stuck in their ways and thus be completely uncreative and leaden? You saw the Amazon forest when it was wild and intact. How can we disparage such marvelous ecological richness by comparing it to our own unconscious states of ignorance?*

HUMBOLDT: *Perhaps we could ask assistance from a true alchemist?*

STEPHAN: *You mean Goethe himself?*

HUMBOLDT: *Why not? You have studied him well enough. And he did complete his "Faust," his life's work, after all. In alchemical terms, we could say that he was one who found the Stone.*

GOETHE: *I am curious about your inquiry and am here at your service. Give us both a little time to consider your problem.*

Some moments pass during which they talk together some distance away in Goethe's garden, which one catches little glimpses of.

HUMBOLDT: *Time! That's what we have concluded.*

GOETHE: *Time is what you are missing. Try letting yourself flow into time, deep time, into evolutionary time. Saturn rules time in the*

Azoth mandala, which is very much a positive aspect of his nature. What happens to your issue with calcination when you ponder the evolution of ecosystems and the planet throughout deep time?

STEPHAN: *Images of Gaia's evolution appear when I do what you suggest, images of her earliest ecological communities in oceans and on land. I see them changing and evolving. Each community is a miracle of self-organization, and yet I see the biosphere's complexity increasing over time—and therefore also the number and power of Gaia's self-regulating feedbacks—especially when multicellular life appears and starts to colonize the continents. Perhaps those earlier communities are equivalent to earlier stages of our personal psychological transformation. In which case they had not yet developed into more beautifully complex planetary ecological states.*

GOETHE: *That's good, for you are seeing the development of Gaia and of consciousness as one unified movement in time, just like the development of a plant from seed and root to leaf and flower.*

STEPHAN: *This is a potent realization.*

GOETHE: *Remember that we live within a living fabric of time in which nothing is forgotten. For you as-yet-embodied-ones, a good way to see the living tapestry of time is by paying very close attention to plants.*

STEPHAN: *Because in its leaves we can plainly see the entire sequence of the plant's development? Each leaf is an embodiment of time past and yet it is still right here, now, still alive. The plant is both time frozen and also time in motion?*

GOETHE: *Quite so! You see, you now truly have the feeling and sense of it. That kind of time—writ large, living time—flows through the whole planet, through all that is Earth and Gaia.*

STEPHAN: *So those more ancestral ecological communities were early stages in a planetary process of transformation?*

HUMBOLDT: *That seems to be what we are concluding. Just as you transform psychologically by exploring depth psychology and alchemy, so has our planet transformed herself into more of a sentient Gaian planet as greater levels of ecological sophistication have emerged out of her ecological communities throughout geological time.*

STEPHAN: *Sensing the flow of transformation in all things reminds me of that ancient Greek philosopher. . . .*

GOETHE: *Yes, Heraclitus—his most famous saying: "you can never jump into the same river twice . . . everything flows."*

HUMBOLDT: *So that's it—the answer to your question is time.*

STEPHAN: *I will go out into my jungle right now and will ponder this with some of my favorite wild plants.*

GOETHE: *Do that—please do—and remember the discipline I taught you with which to connect with the plants, later called the four steps of Goethian Science. First you find and meet your plant with a heart willing to learn something new. Next, you look carefully and full of love at the way the plant develops from the ground up into its leaves and stems to flowers and seeds. Really look. Make drawings. Then close your eyes and visualize the plant coming into being leaf by leaf, stem by stem all the way up the plant to the flowers just as you saw and sensed I in the first step. Lastly be open for deep realization to descend on you with the blessing of a conscious experience of the inner being of the plant. It seems fantastic, but it can happen and it is simply marvelous when it does.*

HUMBOLDT: *Can we help you further?*

STEPHAN: *No, thank you. I am most grateful. May I call on you again if more help is needed?*

GOETHE: *Of course you may.*

HUMBOLDT: *We are here, always, to help.*

So what are we to make of this conversation? Has it helped at all? It is most certainly a fact that everything changes with time. Perhaps on a healthy Gaia our rain forests and coral reefs are stages toward even deeper levels of Gaian self-realization with species and ecological interactions that might one day be even more exquisite than those already here today. Could it be that Gaia's ancient, well-established ecological communities had to collapse at some point by entering into calcination so that more diverse ecological communities could be born with yet greater styles and depths of sentience?

Or perhaps Gaia's pre-industrial ecology had approximated very well to a final state of coagulation that might have persisted and evolved for tens of millions of years or more. Perhaps it is us, we moderns, who are calcinating Gaia's marvelous contemporary ecosystems with our endless lust for more and more stuff produced by more and more energy from Gaia's body. Modernity is subjecting Gaia to a severe calcination in which modernity is destroying a previously stable, complex, and marvelously intelligent, evolving global ecological coagulation.

Calcination begins when a disturbance upsets the community so much that the relationships holding it together start to break down. Perhaps a fire comes through, or a flood, or perhaps an outbreak of disease, or predators out of control, or even an exploding volcano.

Recent research shows fairly convincingly that each of the five previous mass extinctions over the last 500 million years or so were caused by the same kind of massive disturbance, namely global warming due to huge outpourings of deep hot magma from Gaia's interior onto vast areas of her surface creating what is known technically as a large igneous province. There's one in Siberia associated with the Permian mass extinction (the Great Dying: the biggest extinction of all) some 252 million years ago and another in India associated with the Cretaceous-Tertiary mass extinction about 66 million years ago. The immense amounts of carbon dioxide released into the atmosphere from the cooling magma during each of these events significantly warmed the planet, including the oceans, which were unable to hold on to their dissolved oxygen at the higher temperatures. Without sufficient oxygen to sustain them, most marine organisms died off, leaving fossils in marine sediments that give us clues today about these dramatic events. We can now say with some certainty that all previous mass extinctions were immense calcinations involving global warming, caused by volcanic activity deep under Gaia's surface—itself a mode of calcination in the depths of her geological domains. But not all ecological calcinations are caused this way. Collapses of ecological communities can happen for a host of nongeological reasons. These reasons include us, with our noisy chain saws and our endless lust for land and materials.

To correct the grave perceptual error that leads us to be so anti-Gaia, we must subject our modern mechanistic worldview to calcination.

We must reduce it to ashes in the white heat of our Gaian alchemical inquiry so that the energies released can be redirected to help the emergence of many diverse pro-Gaian modes of human consciousness so deeply needed now to help heal the current global crisis.

But can the calcinations undergone by ecological communities long ago in Gaia's past truly connect us with the insights we need now to calcine the destructive aspects of our mechanistic worldview? Let's explore this possibility with an extended meditation.

If you can, go to your Gaia place with this book.

Once you are there, give your greetings and, if you like, make a small offering.

Open your heart now to the language of your Gaia place as it reveals itself to you through your senses.

Feel the temperature of the air. Is it cold? Warm? Hot? Dry? Humid?

Hear whatever sounds are there to be heard. Birdsong? Croaking frogs? Road noise?

Touch whatever you can easily and safely touch. Leaves? Bark? Sand? Water?

Taste whatever you can safely taste. Water? Moss? Nectar?

Smell whatever smells offer themselves to you. Flowers? Rain? Dust?

See whatever gives itself to you to be seen. Butterflies? Trees? Mountains? Ocean?

Now drift with your Imagination into the particular ecological community of your Gaia place.

Ponder how the manifold living beings around you display amazingly sophisticated physical shapes and modes of being and awareness, often honed by long ages of living together over evolutionary time. These plants, these birds, these insects are your fellow passengers on Gaia's epic evolutionary journey.

Allow this understanding to dawn on you as much as possible.

Then, when you are calm and ready, ponder the following images:

Figure 12.2.

You are looking at a very early ecological community on land some 430 million years ago. The plants are a few centimeters tall and contain very simple tubes for distributing nutrients. The domed structures at the tips are their reproductive bodies. You spy primitive millipedes, spiders, and centipedes scuttling around in between these plants eating dead plant material as well as each other.

Let the image help you to journey back into those early days of life on land.

Feel the quality of this early land life.

This ancestral K community eventually underwent calcination, giving way to new forms of life better able to thrive on land.

When you are ready, ponder the image on the next page.

Figure 12.3.
Image by Richard Bizley.

You are now in an ecological community on land some 326 million years ago. See how lands plants have evolved into huge primitive trees some forty meters tall. These trees support themselves with wood, a recent invention of those times with which the trees extract so much carbon dioxide from the atmosphere that they cool the planet into an ice age around the South Pole.

Notice the huge flying insects, some of which had wingspans of up to seventy-one centimeters. See that primitive amphibian crawling on the water's edge? It is one of the earliest vertebrates to colonize the land.

Even this highly developed ecological community underwent calcination as life's evolutionary impulse continued to explore even more sophisticated ecological networks and ways of being.

When you are ready, turn the page.

Figure 12.4.
Image by Richard Bizley.

Here you are some 150 million years ago when the some of the amphibians in the previous image have evolved into a huge diversity of reptiles, some feathered, others scaly, some winged, some aquatic. Dinosaurs dominate the reptilian fauna, some growing to huge sizes, others remaining small. Yet others have evolved into some of the largest flying animals that have ever lived, with wingspans of up to thirteen meters.

Unlike their amphibian ancestors, the reptiles can live entirely on land. Take in the qualities of this community. Feel its life, its pulse. Does it have a greater level of sophistication? Now it's not just insects that fly—so do giant reptiles.

This community underwent calcination when a meteorite struck the planet some 66 million years ago, triggering a large outpouring of magma in India that changed the global climate so much that most of the reptiles were wiped out for good.

When you are ready, ponder the next image.

Figure 12.5.
Image by Deirdre Hyde.

Welcome to a modern ecological community: a Costa Rican mangrove. Birds are the only surviving dinosaurs. See how they have developed into exquisitely graceful forms since the dominance of their lumbering ancestors. Notice the ocelot in the foreground: a representative of our planet's beautiful mammalian forms, which have diversified everywhere since the demise of the great reptiles. See how the various vertebrate forms, including the fish, balance each other rather well in size and abundance?

Feel the powerful sophistication in this ecological community. Feel how unexpected it is that a plant—the mangrove—has evolved specialized roots that grow out of the oxygen-starved mud to breathe oxygen through carefully crafted pores. The level of beauty in the biosphere has now reached a wondrous peak. Could it be that if Gaia were a plant then our modern biosphere would be her flower? It has taken over 4000 million years to achieve her highly developed recent premodern state. Never before has Gaia produced such wondrous complexity among her diverse beings.

Ponder how we, one of her mammals, are now unleashing a catastrophic planetary calcination that is driving many of her creatures to extinction, wiping out complex ecological communities and dangerously heating the entire globe. Our calcination is a deflowering of Gaia. The terrible 2020 fires in Australia are a reminder that this is not the kind of calcination we want.

And yet, at this moment you don't feel any negative emotions. Instead, you sense great opportunities for life and action as you fully imbibe this Gaian perspective.

Now, when you are ready, close the book and connect once more with the sights, sounds, smells, tastes and touches around you in your Gaia place. Rest awhile in your sacred place, relaxing and gently breathing, pondering Gaia's long and complex evolutionary journey.

When the calcination phase is over we enter into the process of alchemical dissolution, which in the adaptive cycle model is called the release phase, denoted by the symbol "omega." In omega, the bonds that held an ecological community together in the conservation phase are rent asunder and the entire ecological web unravels, often chaotically, on its way to a more primordial state. Species once fixed into reliable relationships find themselves adrift in a sea of instability. Here is what resilience scientists Walker and Salt have to say about the omega phase:

The transition from the conservation phase to the release phase can happen in a heartbeat. The longer the conservation phase persists the smaller the shock needed to end it. A disturbance that exceeds the system's resilience breaks apart its web of reinforcing interactions. The system becomes undone. Resources that were tightly bound are now released as connections break and regulatory controls weaken. The loss of structure continues as linkages are broken, and natural, social and economic capital leaks out of the system.

Notice how the dissolution-release dynamic applies to the social sphere and to the realms of economics and finance as well as to the

Gaian world of ecological communities. In scientific ecology a much-debated concept, which relates quite well to alchemical calcination and dissolution, is the intermediate disturbance hypothesis. It states that intermediate levels of disturbance maximize species diversity in ecological communities. Although the hypothesis is not fully accepted, there are a few clear examples of places where the idea does indeed seem to hold.

One such place is the shallow coastal waters off the coast of South Western Australia, where disturbance in the form of wave action seems to increase seaweed diversity by constantly reducing the abundance of dominant species that would otherwise take over the community. Wave action here is the calcinating agent that promotes community diversity by preventing dominant seaweed species from swamping out less competitive species. There are several examples from forests around the world where intermediate disturbance has been found to increase species diversity, including oak-hickory forests in North America and West African tropical dry forests.

Some ecologists have provided empirical evidence that diversity is maintained in ecological communities via a set of factors that interact in complex ways, including predation, disturbance, and climatic variations rather than just disturbance acting on its own. The point is that calcination and dissolution can be deemed to occur in ecological communities when any combination of factors breaks and dissolves the effects of dominant species upon less competitive community members, thereby increasing species diversity.

The more that I delve into the links between alchemy (psyche) and matter (Gaia, ecology), the more psyche—in the guise of my own perception of the world—also undergoes dissolution in a pro-Gaia direction. Psychologically, dissolution involves a dissolving of the hardened attitudes of ego and the sometimes chaotic (that is, irrational) melting of one's soul into a sense of belonging to our bustling biosphere, to birdsong, to the wind and the clouds, to oceans and rivers, to the life of our planet as a great thriving whole. There is a sense of being welcomed home deep into the nestled folds of our mother planet. We melt back into Gaia and feel her powerful presence. We descend into

Gaia's prima materia as we dissolve into her materiality and make contact with her healing powers. Fixed patterns of perception that stop us from truly perceiving Gaia dissolve. Perhaps for the first time we are amazed by her fractally interdigitating biological complexity and we begin to surrender to the immense restorative power of her life force. Our perceptual limitations melt away as we dissolve and connect with her turning body of lush green, blue, brown, and white. We return into her depths to be nourished and emerge with fresh vision and wisdom, of more use to ourselves and the world and with renewed confidence in life itself.

Dissolving into Gaia

In your Gaia place lie down on your back or on your front if you prefer. If you can't lie down, lean or stand against a rock, a tree, or someone other-than-human of sufficient substance to hold and support you.

Now slowly feel your way into the solidity that holds you.

Feel yourself dissolving into that materiality, into the very body of our Mother Earth, oozing out like ink into her very substance in whatever way appears for you—perhaps as feelings, images, and thoughts.

Breathing in and out, feel your in-breath and out-breath.

On the in-breath feel Gaia's atmosphere surging into you to making your lungs fill out and inflate within you. On the out-breath feel the air warmed by your body going back out into the world.

Let yourself dissolve into Gaia.

Let her dissolve you into herself right where you are in your Gaia place, right here in this peaceful alchemical crucible where you are safe and protected.

You dissolve into Gaia, into our enormous living planet.

Dwell in this dissolution for as long as it feels good.

Then bring yourself back to your body. Feel yourself leaning against your support.

Bring yourself back to your daily life, moved, inspired, and ready to face any challenges it might bring you.

The next phase in the adaptive cycle model is identified by the mathematical symbol alpha; the phase is called reorganization. In the Azoth mandala, this phase corresponds remarkably well with separation and conjunction, the third and fourth rays of the seven-rayed star. From the viewpoint of resilience thinking, the omega phase is deeply chaotic, with no stable equilibria and no predetermined end state. Here is what Walker and Salt (2006) say about the alpha phase, in which a new ecological community emerges from the disorder of omega:

> In ecosystems, pioneer species may appear from elsewhere, or from previously suppressed vegetation: buried seeds germinate; new species (including non-native plants and animals) can invade the system. Novel combinations of species can generate new possibilities that are tested later.

Here in England, a great example of the alpha phase can be seen when a commercial coniferous tree plantation is clear felled and the land is left to regenerate naturally, or when a conventional agricultural field is simply left alone to recover from decades of agricultural abuse.

Soon enough, grasses and herbs colonize the ground. In a few years, brambles cover the area, protecting native tree seedlings, which eventually grow through their protective shield and take the community toward a new K phase as they grow into mature trees. As the community develops, a host of ecological relationships establish themselves between species, each with complementary ecological roles that bind the community together. Photosynthesizers build up biomass and decomposers break it down. There are predators and prey. There are symbiotic relationships such as those between plants that feed sugars to mycorrhizal fungi attached to their roots, who in turn provide water and nutrients to the plant via those very same roots. Initially, the pioneer species can be thought of as essentially separate players acting in isolation, but soon enough sets of ecologically functional opposites constellate into a new coherent ecological community on its way to a new K phase. When the ecological community has knit itself together into an efficiently coherent organism, we have entered into conjunction.

Alchemy provides a depth psychological analogue of this process that helps us identify with what is happening in Gaia as her ecological communities go through an alpha phase. In the Azoth mandala applied tool of psychological development, separation takes place when we become acutely aware that reality is constituted by opposites. The pre-Socratic philosophers discovered ten principle opposites. These included one and many; male and female; light and dark; straight and curved; good and bad.

On the Gaian level, the opposites that we project as negative are those necessary yet dangerous aspects of Gaia's life that we don't like: the destruction wrought by volcanos, wildfires, tsunamis, earthquakes, severe storms, disease, and death. These darker aspects of Gaia have caused immense hardship to living beings during the planet's evolution, but we have to accept them as absolutely necessary for the healthy functioning of our world.

Without volcanos generated by plate tectonics, there would be no cycling of carbon dioxide in and out of the atmosphere. Hence, there would be no long-term regulation of Gaia's temperature. Without death, there would be no natural selection and because of this no biological evolution. Without predation, prey would overrun their food supplies. Like any other species, we are perfectly entitled to protect ourselves from what we perceive as these darker aspects of Gaia, and of course it is incredibly foolish of us to exacerbate some of these destructive tendencies by heating her climate and wiping out her species.

But we must accept that Gaia is, as Lynn Margulis once famously said "one tough bitch." The New Age idea of an all-loving Mother Earth must be incorporated into a more alchemical Gaia in which darkness and death, light and life constantly explore, play with, and resolve each other throughout geological time as fundamental opposites out of which arise hosts of new possibilities.

Go to your Gaia place. Be there until you feel deeply comfortable and relaxed.

Notice too the plants around you. Are there any green leaves? If so, pay them some gentle attention.

Feel them inhaling carbon dioxide from the air. Feel them capturing energy from the sun.

Sense them using the sunlight to split water, combining its hydrogen with carbon dioxide to make their living tissues out of light and air, releasing oxygen to the atmosphere in the process.

Now look on the ground. Do you see anything decaying? Dead leaves? Rotting logs? Perhaps a dead animal?

Pay close attention to decomposition, which releases carbon dioxide from decaying organic matter back into the air. This is the opposite of photosynthesis.

Feel the exchange between these two deeply interlinked opposite yet complementary processes: photosynthesis and decomposition.

Do you see any animals? Birds? Insects? Spiders? Reptiles? Mammals?

Watch carefully. Are any of them catching and devouring their prey, or being devoured in turn?

These too are opposites: life and death.

Feel how your Gaia place is held together by a myriad of opposing processes that constitute the vastly complex network of ecological relationships all around you.

Gently plumb these Gaian depths as much as you can, calmly, relaxing deeply.

When you are ready, go back to your everyday life deeply nourished by what you have discovered.

The next phase in the adaptive cycle is called exploitation and is labeled with the mathematical symbol r, standing for the maximum rate of reproduction in a population of organisms. As we have seen, the release of a K phase community into the alpha phase opens up ecological space for species that colonize bare ground on land or empty substrate in aquatic habitats. These colonizers are naturally selected to produce many offspring very quickly and can make use of highly variable resources on short timescales. On land, these are the earliest pioneer species that colonize bare ground or abandoned fields very quickly, forming themselves into loosely connected ecological communities. Here in England these species include docks, nettles, ragworts, and brambles, as well as tree species such as willow and birch.

It seems to me that in the Azoth mandala, the early part of this r phase corresponds to the ray of fermentation and in its later stages to the ray of distillation. Fermentation from a Gaian alchemical point of view takes place when the relationships between species in the ecological community begin to be tested for their resilience by internal and external forces, such as parasites, diseases, and challenging weather events. These tests breathe new life into the community and change its character, raising it to a new level of integration and smooth functioning. The community ferments in the sense that it percolates through various permutations and new configurations of species compositions and abundances on its journey toward greater levels of coherent functioning. One could say that that sentience of the community is becoming more apparent, more sophisticated.

The planet associated with fermentation, the fifth ray of the Azoth mandala, is Venus, whose metal is copper, much appreciated for its loveliness. These symbols give us a hint that fermentation, psychologically, is associated with grace and beauty. We ferment inwardly as we experience a mandalalike quality in our outlook when once disparate energies constellate into the beginnings of our true wholeness, in which the outer and inner worlds begin to coalesce into a seamless experience of being. As Gaia alchemists we realize that this inner process is greatly enhanced by dwelling in ecological communities that have reached outwardly equivalent levels of integration and wholeness. It helps our Gaian fermentation to seek out such places where they still exist not too far away from us and to restore something akin to them near us in our neighborhood if they have vanished.

I feel these r phase fermentative qualities in areas on the Dartington Hall Trust's estate that have been released from the immensely damaging ecological pressures of conventional farming. Come with me to Berryman's Marsh, a small lozenge-shaped field on the edge of the Trust's land. I contrived to take it out of farming some twenty-seven years ago. As we gaze over its rich tapestry of herbaceous plants, peppered here and there in high summer with tall upright scepters of purple loosestrife, we see how a field once reduced to a species-poor, lawn-like pasture by intensive cattle grazing has fermented its way back into an ecological community of soul-nourishing health, beauty, and elegance.

Sometimes we sense how in the fullness of time the community could develop even richer qualities of integration, even richer modes of meaning. This is distillation, the sixth ray of the Azoth mandala. In distillation, the process of integration develops further as the ecological community continues to integrate itself into an even more effective functioning whole. Mercury is both the metal and planet associated with this process. Mercury is the God of communication, from whom we derive the word *hermeneutics,* the art of interpretation and understanding. Thus, in its distillation, an ecological community grows in wisdom. It enhances its understanding of itself and its surroundings as its diverse species explore and consolidate their many channels of communication to create the astonishing coherence of an increasingly well-functioning whole.

In my travels around the world, I have had the privilege of experiencing different ecological communities at different phases of the adaptive cycle in the many places I have visited. I have carefully noticed how each community has influenced my mood and sometimes give me access to secret knowledge hidden in the land itself.

One ecological community where I was vouchsafed memorable experiences of distillation (and also, as we shall see, of coagulation) is the Bialowieza forest, which covers around 141,885 hectares on the border between Poland and Belarus. The core area of Bialowieza is remarkable because it contains the last remaining primeval forest in lowland Europe. The core has never been extensively logged and is surrounded by a greater extent of secondary forest managed with various degrees of sensitivity over the centuries. Many wild mammals, some now extinct elsewhere, some severely threatened, roam freely through all the forest, including European bison, lynxes, wild boar, moose, wolves, and many others.

The forest teems with life. There are many plant species, many kinds of fungi, birds, insects, lichens, mosses, and much more. Bialowieza is a treasure store of ecological wisdom where I experienced intensely healthy states of mind I seldom encounter in ecologically battered Great Britain.

I remember how it felt to spend days alone walking and cycling in the second growth forest areas. I sensed how each older patch of second growth had reached a fine state of distillation. I could feel how the connectivity among its species, rocks, soils, and water had increased and diversified during the many years since the last human intervention. It was good to be in the second growth. I felt healthier, more whole, more myself again among the trees, much happier than I had felt for a while. The forest's distillation triggered an inner distillation in me, bringing my deep ecological self back to life within its weblike coherence. Was I more at peace here in this Polish second growth because the community was more whole than the severely damaged woods around Schumacher College on the Dartington estate where I spend much of my time? Can our own mental health be so closely linked to the health of the ecological communities and networks that enfold and surround us? Clearly so.

Whereas the second growth took me into a powerful experience of distillation, the core area of old-growth forest took me into the next ray of the Azoth mandala—into a sense of what it means for an ecological community to be engaged in the profound alchemy of coagulation.

I had been invited to Bialowieza by a group of Polish business people who wanted to explore Gaia and deep ecology in as wild a place as possible in their own country. We had to wait days to be given access to the old growth—the primeval forest in the core area—which we were only allowed to enter with the presence of an official guide.

At last, the great day arrived. There was a hush of anticipation as our group of twenty or so people entered a narrow forest trail in one of Europe's last extensive areas of almost entirely undisturbed broadleaf forest. No sooner had we entered its ancient precincts than our guide began to give us a torrent of information about the forest and its wildlife. Horrified, I asked her to hold back.

"We just want to walk here in silence," I said.

"But it is my job to tell you about this place, to tell you the names of its species," she replied in surprisingly good English.

"Please, just guide us, single file, in silence, into the depths of the forest along the remotest trails you know."

"Very well. This is most irregular, but I will do as you ask."

We walked for a few hours in the ancient forest. What we saw and felt there moved us deeply, some, including me, to tears. There were huge ancient wise old trees, some of them oaks, but also trees of many other species, among cohorts of younger trees of all ages. There were light gaps here and there populated with wild tangles of luxuriant vegetation where a great tree had fallen, or perhaps where wild boar had made a longtime wallow; immense bracket fungi jutting horizontally out of huge boles of dead standing trees; ferns and mosses of many kinds spreading their greenness over soil, rock, and tree; wet, swampy hollows, full of water-loving plants; birdcalls; the sounds of gentle breezes among the leaves. Above all, there was a particular quality of deep, ancient wholeness that I had never felt before anywhere else in Europe, a particular quality that belonged to this place, to Bialowieza, this marvelous and unique manifestation of Gaia's creative spirit. The forest was powerful enough to awake deep transpersonal ancient memories in all of us in our little group, taking us beyond our usual sense of time and space and yet bringing us down to earth into the here and now; silently soothing us with the subtlety of her psyche into our own inner coagulation.

At any moment we expected to catch a glimpse of a Green Man peering at us quizzically from the bole of a great oak tree or to meet a benevolent forest empress accompanied by her emperor, both crowned with oak leaves, walking toward us among the forest giants followed by a retinue of chattering birds and graceful deer. We trod carefully, trying not to disturb even a leaf on the trail as we awoke, startled, to the profound living presence of this wild forest community, which had once covered vast tracts of lowland Europe even as far as England itself. We had been granted an audience by a wild sentient domain—an area just vast enough to sustain the sacred magic of its healing power, now so tragically expunged from the rest of Europe.

Each being we encountered here was a power, a psyche in its own right. Each tree, each fungus, each sapling, each snail and slug—the very forest too—all shouted out the quiet majesty of their true selves as we walked among them. The English poet Gerard Manley Hopkins wrote of this perception with great potency:

As kingfishers catch fire, dragonflies draw flame;
As tumbled over rim in roundy wells
Stones ring; like each tucked string tells, each hung bell's
Bow swung finds tongue to fling out broad its name;
Each mortal thing does one thing and the same:
Deals out that being indoors each one dwells;
Selves—goes itself; myself it speaks and spells,
Crying What I do is me: for that I came.

When the walk ended no one could speak for a long while. We stood looking at each other just outside the gate into the ancient forest, eyes wide with wonder, trying not to break the spell with pointless words. We had been in the center of a great Gaian heart and had richly savored the sacred core of the real. We had been in the presence of a great living earthy power and felt that we would forever carry a glowing ember of its emerald sacredness in our hearts. The forest had sent its mycelial tubes, funguslike, into us, dissolving our outmoded perceptual patterns, infusing us with the unifying lifeblood of Gaia's living presence. Each of us, for a while at least, experienced the ancient forest's coagulation and knew the same sacred marriage within ourselves. This powerful experience of awakening sometimes graces us in the presence of an ecological community, which has brought itself from out of itself through the phases of the Azoth mandala into its own coagulation at the very center of the adaptive cycle (fig. 12.6) where all four currents meet and cross.

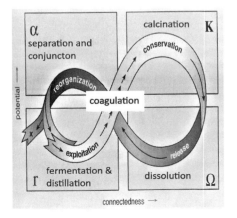

Figure 12.6. The Adaptive Cycle Model with the seven alchemical operations of the Azoth mandala superimposed.

Adapted from adaptive cycle model from *Resilience Thinking* by Brian Walker and David Salt (adapted from Gunderson and Holling, Panarchy © 2002). © 2006 Brian Walker and David Salt. Reproduced by permission of Island Press, Washington, DC.

If you can, make a pilgrimage to the most pristine ecological community in your region of the world, on land, in fresh water, or on or within the wide realms of the ocean.

Arrange to stay as many days there as you can, quietly, alone or in good company, sleeping under the stars if at all possible, spending your days contemplating the deep spaces of this the wildest of your Gaia places.

Be with the wild, self-created freedom of this place. Let its wholeness, wisdom, and integrity wake up your deep love of Gaia, your deep love for the mysterious forces that conjoin together to make her as she is. You perceive her now in her freest state of glorious unleashed creativity.

Allow what you have learned so far about the science of Gaia and what you have perceived intuitively from contemplating the Azoth mandala to melt into the deep aboriginal quality of this place.

Feel Gaia's unfolding into greater wisdom and complexity in this place, a process bound up in time but which is also eternal.

May this Gaia place become an alchemical vessel where your knowledge, your intuition, your feeling and sensing of the sentience and sacred brilliance of Gaia, this heavenly sphere, brews you both into a lived experience of coagulation, of mutual consciousness of each other.

From now, you could choose to carry the spirit and soul of this place with you wherever you are and wherever you go.

Before you leave, offer a small gift to the beings of this sacred space within Gaia; to its currents of air; to its plants and animals; to the fungi, bacteria, viruses, and protozoans; to the waters and rocks that dwell right here in this little patch of planet.

When you feel ready, begin your journey back to your daily life, inspired and ready to help find solutions for these turbulent times.

13

Gaia Alchemy and Deep Time

Toward the end of the previous chapter we experienced Gaia with our intuition and our sensing and felt the profound value intrinsic to herself. This is the true Gaia: nondual, Mercurial Gaia, experienced not with thinking, not with graphs, equations, and numbers, useful and essential as these are. Gaia comes to life when we perceive her as images transduced from the science by our poetic Imagination. In this more poetic perceptual mode, our planet is much more than a rocky ball spray-painted with a thin patina of seemingly insignificant life on her crumpled surface. Instead, we experience her as alchemical Gaia, as the living symbol, physical embodiment, and alchemical vessel of how the cosmos experiences itself, of how it creates and explores new ways of meaning and being.

Since Gaia is extremely ancient, a Gaian alchemical approach must take account of how this exploration of meaning and being has been going on throughout vast spans of geological time. Thus we open up a pathway into the poetics of deep time. The nature of time is of course a great mystery, but we must inquire into its essence from Gaia's perspective if we are to appreciate both the wonder of her long persistence and the perils of her current predicament. Our planet has existed through an immense span of time, now well established in science as 4550 million years. But what might this immense number mean for us experientially?

We usually think of time as a linear arrow of unfolding events with

190

some kind of objective, external existence in which we are caught like fish in a net. However, there are other more interesting and more animistic perceptions of time. One such view supposes that time is the embodiment of the qualities of all the particular, relativistic moments of "now" everywhere in the cosmos. Each of these moments is remembered as a memory trace in the psyche of the world. Thus, in this perspective, each moment is connected to the particular qualities of the entire configuration of all moments in the cosmos right now and in the past. Since everything in the cosmos is constantly changing, no two moments are the same, and yet each moment becomes a living trace in time's memory and is therefore never lost or forgotten. Each present moment is thick with memory, holding all previous moments within it. The past appears to us as living memory traces in the now when we loosen the iron grip of linear time upon our thinking and allow our imaginative faculty to lead us into these more sentient qualities of time. Time becomes a facet of our Gaian awareness, and we receive images from time's memory store of events long ago, including images that have worked well over the centuries to encode this experience for a wide range of people.

Can scientific Gaia combined with the Azoth mandala and a more animistic perception of time help us access living perceptions of how our planet has changed and evolved ever since her birth around 4550 million years ago? This way, perhaps, we may discover much more than science alone can disclose about the living qualities of our Earth.

Let's attempt a first pass through such a Gaian alchemical deep time journey using the Azoth mandala as a guide, bringing us the living presence of these events from our planet's memory store right here into our experience of the present moment.

CALCINATION

The emphasis in calcination is upon the element fire. As we saw earlier, psychologically this involves the burning away of aspects of our ego and of our worldview that prevent us from accessing a wider, more comprehensive connection with nature and with each other. Since calcination is the first step in alchemical transformation there is a good fit with what happened when our planet appeared out of hugely cataclysmic events long ago soon after the solar system was born. It happened more or less like this: Around 4576 million years ago a huge star called Tiamat in the Orion arm of our Milky Way exploded into a supernova, peppering the surrounding space with atoms of heavy elements forged from fusing hydrogen in her deep, immensely hot interior. The supernova produced a massive pressure wave, which forced a nearby cloud of hydrogen molecules to clump together so tightly that they formed our sun, which burst into light when temperatures and pressures became high enough within it for hydrogen molecules to fuse into those of helium.

Was this only calcination, or were the other six Azoth mandala processes involved in the supernova explosion? To explore this question as disciplined Gaia alchemists, we would need to enter Tiamat on wings of Imagination fully guided by science, allowing us to go deep into her roiling mass of gas before and during her supernova. We would use science and alchemical image to develop this ability, which, most strangely, leads us into a new world—a Gaian world, full of purpose, mind, and meaning.

When we do this, we discover that all seven rays of the Azoth mandala, not just calcination, are involved in producing supernovas. We sense how Tiamat went through complex transformations within herself equivalent to our own alchemical journeys along the Azoth mandala to gift her treasures of heavy elements to the cosmos, sowing it with atomic seeds, which later coagulated to become our solar system, our Earth, our biosphere, our Gaia.

The scientific details of how Tiamat forged her heavy elements and how this process led to her supernova are complex and needn't concern us here since our primary focus is on Gaia. Perhaps some intrepid alchemically inclined scientists will someday evoke the Azoth mandala to reveal the many rich insights that lie waiting to be discovered in what could one day blossom into an alchemical astrophysics, but we must leave that path for others to follow.

As I gently practice imagining the scientific details of Gaia's formation through an alchemical lens, a dawning happens within me. There is a flowering of a new kind of consciousness, of something so earthy and rich. It is my deepest desire: to be myself as a deeply Gaian human being. This is an awareness that entices me into a world thick with time, dense with memory and meaning. Time becomes a living fabric, a Gaian river in which we flow.

Shall we try it now? Those clouds of heavy elements gifted us by Tiamat's supernova—one of these forms itself into a swirl of cosmic dust in the center of which a newly ignited sun spews out its enlivening gift of solar energy. Here, at the very birth of our solar system, are calcination (the energy building inside Tiamat), dissolution (the supernova), and separation (the flinging apart of matter as the result of the supernova). The atoms and molecules in the swirl start to clump together into small grains, then into pebbles, then into rocks. The energy in each collision is enough to melt and meld the participants into ever larger balls of molten rock until the ones we now call Mercury, Venus, Earth, and Mars are the only ones left intact. As these planets cool down, their molten rocky bodies start to solidify until eventually each one develops a rocky crust overlying a molten core. Here are conjunction (the clumping together of rocky pebbles into planets and also the fusion processes in the sun), fermentation and distillation (the complex chemical transformations involved in forming of the crusts), and coagulation (the final forms of the planets, some with molten cores like inner suns).

Gaia began her alchemical transformation in those early days as a planet-sized mass of molten rock in a state of creative chaos known alchemically as a *massa confusa*. This was also her earliest calcination, which probably happened in two phases. The initial planetary accretion we have just mentioned followed by the late heavy bombardment some 500 million years later, both of which added in meteorites from the asteroid belt rich in elements essential for life such as carbon, nitrogen, and phosphorus.

How extraordinary that this unpromising ball of molten rock held the possibility within its oozing turbulence of today's wondrous biosphere; a Gaia bedecked with multifarious forms of life; a cosmic gem luxuriating in prodigious profusions of biodiversity. A worldly gem, which is the active partnerings of rock, water, and atmosphere, all melded into a single planetary being—a being who actively regulates her surface conditions within the narrow limits favorable for her life forms.

By around 4400 million years ago the surface layers of molten material had cooled enough to produce a thin crust of solid rock through which poked massive volcanoes spewing carbon dioxide gas into the atmosphere. The surface of the planet was hot, parched, and dry. No oceans yet, no life.

Massa confusa

For this meditation it would be good to have art materials at the ready.

At home or in your Gaia place, relax and prepare to enter an awareness of Gaia's deep time.

You float in space just after our sun ignited but just before our planet and the solar system came to be. You see orbiting spheres of rock, some large, some small, colliding and melting into each other while they circle around the newly formed sun.

After ten to twenty million years of such collisions, two great balls of molten rock travel in the proto-Earth's orbit. Eventually these collide in a giant impact, forming Moon and Earth, both still completely molten.

Focusing on the larger ball of molten rock, the one that will one day become Gaia, you imagine the turmoil of her roiling rock as somehow connected to your yearning for a greater sense of life and meaning. This molten ball of rock is our embryo planet as an alchemical massa confusa.

Just as early Earth's turmoil led to the emergence of a living planet from boiling rock, you likewise sense the possibility of transforming your own roiling mass of thoughts and emotions into a living experience, right now, of Gaia, of our animate Earth.

You feel a strange sense of purpose, a powerful urge to navigate a route into the deepest biospheric wholeness that has been emerging and evolving out of this planetary ball of molten rock through geological time. Within you this urge emerges right now as a strong desire to serve Gaia, to awake fully to the miracle of her existence, so that she and the cosmos can experience their own deepest wholeness.

This is no mystical feeling, for it gives you a sense of immense earthiness, clarity, and practicality about what you can do to help heal the crisis.

Dwell in a delicious sense of belonging to this earthy planet, to this ancient being of humus, mold, fungus, and rich, dark soil.

Make a visual expression your experience of the massa confusa with your art materials if you feel that would help to consolidate your experience.

DISSOLUTION

As we have seen, dissolution experienced alchemically involves dissolving our formerly heavily defended and limited ego perspectives by means of a flowing, open-ended conversation with the unconscious (the objective psyche) in which we pay close attention to our dreams and fantasies.

Likewise, Gaia's first dissolution came about when gravitational perturbations to the orbits of Jupiter and Saturn sent a mass of ice-rich asteroids racing out of the asteroid belt toward her and the other inner rocky planets, peppering them with gifts of precious water. It would only have taken five or six of the largest of these icy asteroids, each one around 1,000 km across, to deliver our planet's water. It is also possible that some of our water might have outgassed to the surface from molten rocks deep inside the planet through volcanoes and other volcanic rents in her crust. How curious that gravitational perturbations to the physical Jupiter may have been responsible for providing our planet with her water, for Jupiter, alchemically, is the planet ruling the processes of dissolution.

By the time those icy asteroids were heading for Gaia she had already cooled enough to form the rocky crust we mentioned earlier. Imagine those icy giants crashing into our nascent planet, vaporizing on impact, sending massive columns of steam high up into whatever early atmosphere there might have been. Gradually, this steam condensed into clouds. These rained out onto the surface, creating our Earth's first ocean. The water cycle began perhaps some 4300 million years ago as the sun evaporated water from the ocean surface. The ocean was brown, the sky pink.

Imagine Gaia as she was then, so long ago, as a water planet. There are no continents of any significant size. What land there is appears as volcanic islands scattered wide here and there throughout her vast global ocean. The volcanos emit carbon dioxide and other gasses into the atmosphere, keeping the surface warm enough for liquid water despite the fact that the sun is some 25 percent to 30 percent less bright than today. Some of this carbon dioxide dissolves into the ocean's water, turning it acidic. The first dissolution (rain) is quickly followed by a second dissolution as the acidic ocean begins to dissolve the rocky crust, releasing chemical beings into the water including phosphorus, sulphur, nitrogen, and many others. All of these are essential for life's eventual appearance.

We can analogize this process to ourselves if we think of our nascent planet's rocky crust as a solidified *massa confusa*—as a mixture of various atoms and molecules akin to our own stuck thoughts and fixed patterns of behavior of which we are hardly aware. Dissolution liberates these atoms and molecules, these complexes of thought and action, so they can become aware of each other as they float freely in the dissolving waters of the global ocean and in the inner ocean of our psyche. Some of these atoms join together to form the first biomolecules: amino acids, sugars, fats, nucleotides, and others. Perhaps these life-precursor molecules somehow felt that here on this planet they had a chance of becoming part of a living cell, as we feel that our newly liberated feelings and thoughts might someday configure themselves into more conscious ways of living within the vastness of our sentient planetary ecology.

SEPARATION

Puddles and pools on land by the edges of the sea, cavities, deep sea vents—these are places where some of these life-precursor molecules might have intensively interacted with each other in chemical broths protected from the diluting effects of the global ocean's seawater.

One of the most promising of such places, offering perfect seclusion and separation, were alkaline thermal vents at the bottom of the ocean. Small, porous cavities in the rock might have provided just the right conditions for the intimate interactions, alliances, and relationships among a host of atoms and molecules, which might have come close to organizing themselves into the class of being with the properties of a living cell. These include a self-bounded, self-making (autopoietic), self-repairing metabolism with high levels of internal order. Such a being is maintained by the intake of carefully selected foods and the excretion of wastes. It is also characterized by the presence of a genetic code, which the cell reads as a text to facilitate its growth, maintenance repair, and reproduction.

Perhaps separation also involved the appearance of the first land in the form of volcanic islands poking up here and there from the ocean around 4300 million years ago, producing the duality of water and dry land that is essential for regulating Gaia's temperature some 3900 million years later under a much hotter sun when plants colonize the continents.

CONJUNCTION

We experience conjunction in our psychological life when our solar sensing and rationality and our lunar feeling and intuition function well together, bringing a balanced outlook in which we see how causality and synchronicity are at work in the world at large, reinforcing our embeddedness within their immense yet deeply intimate networks of learning and meaning.

Alchemically, conjunction happens between *Sol* and *Luna*. It occurs when *Sol*—the divine transcendental source—fully conjoins with our existence as embodied beings here on Earth (*Luna*). We experience great clarity, purpose, and joy in those blessed moments when conjunction truly comes upon us, when its deepest meaning actualizes itself in us and we feel a blessed connection with Gaia.

The question we are exploring here is whether adopting such an alchemical viewpoint on Gaia's evolution can connect us with profound feelings of communion with deeper aspects of ourselves and of our planet, inspiring us to live in ways that nourish the health of all her beings.

To explore Gaia's conjunction in this way, we will journey back into deep time. To do this, we will use the twin perspectives of the Azoth mandala and science until we reach the appearance of the very first living cells around 3800 million years ago. This was the moment when those life-precursor molecules that previously interacted as separate beings (perhaps in the rocky pockets of alkaline hydrothermal vents) finally organized themselves into living, self-making, self-regulating replicating cells after what must have been an extended series of biochemical machinations honed by long ages of natural selection.

It is almost certain that this first living cell (known in science as LUCA, the Last Universal Common Ancestor) used DNA as a text from which to extract and creatively interpret genetically coded information in service of its intelligent, self-making cellular processes. We infer this because the genetic code is the same in all organisms, extant and extinct without exception. LUCA evolved into two kinds of cells—archaea and the more familiar bacteria, both of which lack cell nuclei but which look quite similar despite major differences in their membrane structures. We'll learn about the Gaian alchemical significance of these two cell types a little later, but for now let's maintain our focus on the molecular structure of DNA, the famous double helix, which is an excellent alchemical instance of conjunction requiring the deepest possible communion between opposite molecular beings.

In DNA molecules, two nucleotide strands intertwine like a twisted ladder held together by "rungs" composed of interacting complementary chemical bases of only four kinds (fig. 13.1). Sets of three bases code for one of twenty amino acids. Proteins are made of amino acids, and when the cell needs more proteins it copies sequences of base triplets from its DNA coding for the required protein. The code sequence is then used to assemble the amino acid building blocks into the protein in question outside the nucleus on the ribosomes. The cell strings together

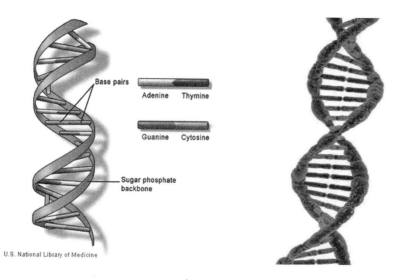

Base pairs

Adenine   Thymine

Guanine   Cytosine

Sugar phosphate
backbone

U.S. National Library of Medicine

Figure 13.1. The DNA molecule.
Courtesy of the National Library of Medicine.

long chains of amino acids in a variety of combinations, producing many kinds of protein molecules, each with its own particular properties. Some become our fingernails and hair; others become enzymes that catalyze chemical reactions in our cells such as those that break down sugars and other food molecules to give us the very warmth of our bodies.

This entire process of protein synthesis, so absolutely fundamental to life, is just one example of the immense scope of cooperative communication that happens in the conjunction of molecular opposites within living cells. The mystery of life itself springs forth from these myriad conjunctions among the cell's animate molecules.

But what is life? Biology provides us with a useful checklist of characteristics. Anything biologically alive must be self-bounded, self-making, entropy-reducing, and so on, but science cannot tell us what life actually is, for we can only know this as an inner experience, as a living intuition, not as an intellectual construct.

If the miracle of enlivement comes to us in the lived experience of the sacred marriage of *Sol* and *Luna,* then, in DNA, it seems that the profound living mystery of life appears analogously out of the conjunction between its two complementary strands.

⬦⬦⬦⬦⬦ *A Conversation with Jeffrey Kiehl* ⬦⬦⬦⬦⬦

JEFFREY: So in Gaia the image of Sol and Luna embracing refers to the union of the archetypal masculine feminine, which creates life (fig. 13.2).

Figure 13.2. By M. Merian from Michael Maier's *Atalanta Fugiens,* 1617.

STEPHAN: I see a lot of Gaia in this image. It's about the moment when life appears. It's the moment when atoms and molecules floating around perhaps in an alkaline hydrothermal vent in a little rocky pocket where the chemistry was just right felt a deep attraction for each other and organized themselves into the first living cell, into LUCA. And it's been going on and evolving ever since.

JEFFREY: It's all about attraction. You don't have the cosmos without attraction. The planets attract each other into stable orbits. In the Renaissance this was called sympathy. There is sympathy between the planets—the harmony of the cosmos happens because things attract one another. Newton looks at this and he sees attraction.

STEPHAN: We've had to separate things before we get this powerful attraction. It doesn't happen at the beginning. Things have to separate first. Jung said that between the opposites there's a field.

JEFFREY: Which generates energy, psychic energy. Without that opposition, you have no psychic energy, no creativity.

STEPHAN: So what we've done in the psyche is that we've separated our thinking, feeling, intuition, and sensation. That's going to create considerable tension. Then we let them go and there's so much energy between them that they end up in each other's arms, as in the image.

JEFFREY: Yes. The masculine the feminine, Logos and Eros, come together. They have to be together for there to be wholeness but they also have to be apart. This is the paradox. To be together they have to be apart.

◇◇◇◇◇◇◇◇◇◇◇◇◇◇◇◇◇◇◇◇◇◇◇◇◇◇◇◇

It is not just in DNA where we encounter the alchemy of conjunction on a biological level. The entire coherent coming together of all the staggeringly complex molecular components of a living cell is also a manifestation of conjunction.

To function well, to be alive, to thrive, the cell needs to integrate myriad molecular cycles within cycles and feedbacks within feedbacks, both positive and negative. This dynamic flowing conjunction of many opposite yet complementary metabolic processes bootstraps itself into the living state and responds intelligently to a wide range of changing internal and external conditions. The cell remembers and reproduces. It lives to maintain its health and has no need of a brain to coordinate its intelligence because every bit of it is intelligent.

PHOTOSYNTHESIS AND CONJUNCTION

Water-splitting, oxygen-producing (oxygenic) photosynthesis is without doubt one of the most important and most unlikely biochemical conjunctions that have arisen in Gaia's long trajectory through deep time. Without it there would be no abundant free oxygen in her atmosphere and hence no modern biosphere with widespread multicellular life in her oceans and on land.

The Azoth mandala's ray of conjunction helps us to experience the astonishingly complex coming together of the many molecular beings involved in oxygenic photosynthesis in an alchemical light, but in fact the entire Azoth mandala reveals itself within the immense complexity of this process, giving us insight into how the same mandala now appears here as a different form of itself at the microscopic scale of biochemistry. We'll explore how this happens when we journey through the process in a little while.

It seems likely that one single bacterial cell cracked the challenge of inventing oxygenic photosynthesis by integrating two previously separate and far more primitive photosynthetic pathways within itself. This bacterial pioneer created a whole new molecular complex dedicated to splitting water using photons from the sun known as the water-splitting complex.

This lone bacterial genius put together the unlikely molecular conjunction that uses the sun's energy to split water in water-splitting, oxygen-producing photosynthesis. That being soon shared the genetic secrets of this most difficult of molecular arts with neighboring bacteria. This almost certainly happened through the deeply mercurial process of horizontal gene transfer, in which bacteria make many copies of segments of their DNA and expel these into their surroundings. Other bacteria pick and incorporate these DNA segments into their own genomes before they too pass on the traits in question via further bouts of horizontal gene transfer.

The best way to get a living sense of the immense material complexity of the photosynthetic process is delve into it with our two-million-year-old self, with the ancient one within us who is full of river memories, wind memories, with the one who responds with a quickening heart to the calls of wild geese flying in formation high over the treetops.

Bring your two-million-year-old self to the fore now as you prepare to dive deep into a highly simplified account of the miraculous alchemical conjunction which is water-splitting photosynthesis.

We begin our Azoth mandala journey into photosynthesis deep within the Sun, where immense fusion processes at extremely high temperatures produce highly energized photons. This is Calcination.

You are one of these photons from the Sun traveling at the speed of light toward Gaia, which you reach in eight minutes and twenty seconds having traveled a distance of ninety-three million miles across the solar system.

You hit a green leaf on a plant in one of Gaia's far-flung forests.

You pass into the calm green interior of a cell on the surface of the leaf. All around you see a ferment of organized activity, including molecular porters carrying bags of important chemical cargo walking determinedly on two molecular legs along vast suspended molecular cables crisscrossing the immense inner spaces of the cell.

Soon you collide with one of many huge green balloons floating in the cell—a chloroplast (fig. 13.3).

You enter its deep green precincts.

What you see here inside the chloroplast astounds you. Stacks of large green discs are everywhere, forming a crowded city of stacks connected here and there by what look like broad, looping walkways. This place has the feeling of a power station, for indeed this is exactly what it is.

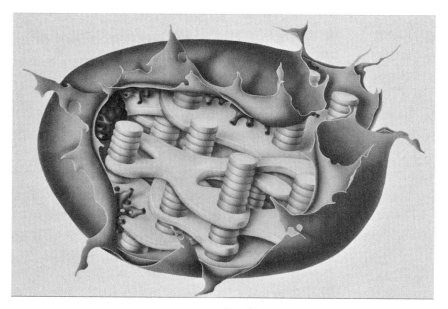

Figure 13.3. Inside a chloroplast.
Reproduced with permission through Science Photo Library.

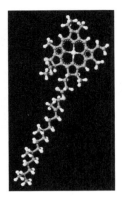

Figure 13.4. An antenna
chlorophyll molecule.

You will give all your energy to this power station and as result plant and planet will thrive and live.

You plunge toward one of the green discs (each one is called a thylakoid) and notice lots of little green bumps on its surface.

You feel immensely drawn to a particular fourfold molecular mandala waving to you among a forest of many other such paddle-shaped molecular mandala-carriers sticking out of each green bump. These are antenna chlorophyll molecules (fig. 13.4).

You are drawn to the magnesium atom bonded to four nitrogen atoms in the middle of this molecular mandala. Here again we encounter the archetypal number four.

The presence of the nitrogen atoms helps to loosen the bond between the magnesium atom's nucleus and its outermost electron where it lives all alone far from the atom's center.

You stream toward this electron and give it all your energy. In the process, your particle nature vanishes. Now you are all energy. This is your Dissolution.

The electron stays where it is and transmits your energy as a resonant vibration which ripples out of the mandala into the fishbone-like antenna of carbon atoms linked to the mandala itself.

As your energy careens down the antenna you go quantum. Your energy spreads out in all directions at the speed of light. You are everywhere at once, so you easily find your target—the water-splitting complex.

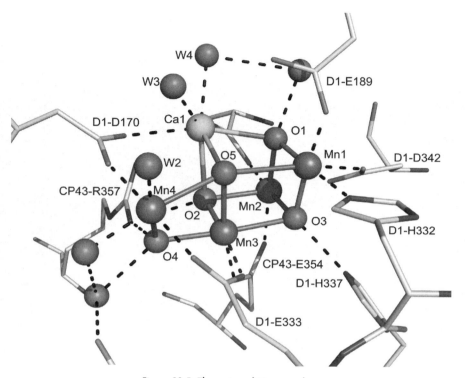

Figure 13.5. The water-splitting complex.

The structure of the water-splitting complex is simply mind boggling. Exactly how it works is still a mystery to scientists.

You see that cubic cage in the middle of the complex? It is made up of four oxygen atoms, three atoms of manganese and one of calcium. For the sake of our journey, we'll imagine that the water-splitting happens in that cubic cage (fig. 13.5), but we just don't know for sure.

Four solar-energized electrons are liberated from two molecules of water in the water-splitting complex by your energy. Electrons will carry your energy from now on. A molecule of oxygen is liberated in the process. This is an alchemical separation.

You watch as these four electrons are carried up into the vast molecular complex of photosystem 2 (fig. 13.6) embedded in the membrane of the green disc (the thylakoid) that sits right on top of

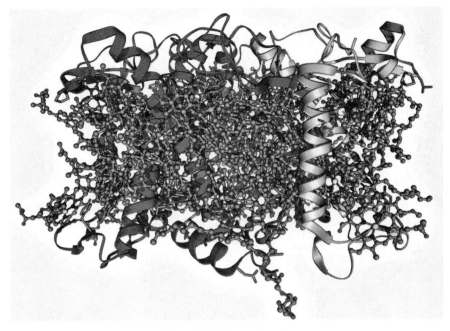

Figure 13.6. Photosystem 2.
Reproduced with permission through Science Photo Library.

the water-splitting complex. Seen from the side, from far away, the whole thing looks like this:

The spirals are proteins that help hold the whole thing together.

You are amazed by how massive it is, by how alive it is, and by how it slowly thrums and vibrates, full of activity.

The small green molecules poking out here and there in between the proteins are light-harvesting chlorophyll antennae. You watch entranced as energy from solar photons is delivered deep into the photosystem complex by tangles of these chlorophyll antennae.

Our four electrons travel to a small space in the vastness of the photosystem to a place where another astonishing transformation happens.

This vanishingly small space is one of two alchemical conjunction chambers at the heart of photosynthesis.

At the center of the conjunction chamber called P680 you

Figure 13.7. A schematic of the molecule at the heart the P680 complex of photosystem II (*right*, drawn by Julia Ponsonby) next to the alchemical Rebis (*left*).

notice a double-headed molecular figure with molecular wings outstretched. This is a special kind of chlorophyll with two heads. Each head sports two molecular spikes and the molecule's gesture is deeply welcoming.

Is it mere coincidence that when seen from certain angles the molecule at the heart of P680 (fig. 13.7) displays itself as a two-headed, winged alchemical being very much like the alchemical Rebis representing the Philosopher's Stone, shown next to it?

Our four electrons arrive in the P680 conjunction chamber in perfect time to replace another four highly energized electrons, which have just been propelled out of the double-headed chlorophyll molecule by energy from four solar photons that have just been delivered to the conjunction chamber by antenna chlorophyll molecules.

Let's call these four newly liberated solar energy powered electrons the electron brothers.

You watch as groups of these newly energized electron brothers leave the photosystem complex. They are passed along a sequence of specialized electron transport molecules. These are embedded in the nearby thylakoid membrane.

As the electron brothers travel through this electron transport chain, their energy is slowly harvested and stored in ATP molecules (the energy storage molecules of the cell) for later use as needed by the plant for making food and structural materials.

With their energy diminished, the electron brothers now reach a second photosystem complex embedded further along the thylakoid membrane known as photosystem 1.

Here, new solar photon energy is once again channeled to them by chlorophyll antennae molecules, giving them a further boost of energy before they continue their journey through a new set of electron transport molecules during which they gradually give their energy to molecules of NADPH.

A conjunction takes place each time an electron merges with a new acceptor molecule in these transport chains.

You say farewell to the electron brothers as they continue their journey through the immensely complex molecular conjunctions and machinations known as the dark reactions at the end of which they find themselves in the wider domain of the cell outside the chloroplast in energy-rich bonds between carbon atoms that hold sugar molecules together. Fermentation and distillation take place in these dark reactions resulting in coagulation when a sugar molecule is made.

The carbon atoms in the sugars come from carbon dioxide, which is absorbed by the plant from the atmosphere. The energy that holds the carbon atoms together comes from the sun via the complex alchemical process we've just been following.

Slowly return now to our everyday world. Ponder well what you have seen, felt, and experienced in the complex alchemical conjunctions that constitute the almost impossibly difficult process of oxygen-producing photosynthesis on which your life and the life of Gaia depends. We have learned many things. One in particular is that the entire Azoth mandala is present even when we focus on just one of its rays in any given situation.

ENDOSYMBIOSIS AND CONJUNCTION

How did those hulking multicellular beings—the plants—come across the subtle art of water-splitting photosynthesis in the first place? Did they invent it from scratch, or were the photosynthetic bacteria we met earlier somehow involved?

To explore these questions we need to zoom back out to the level of bacterial cells to encounter another particularly important conjunction event in the life of Gaia, which happened around 2500 million years ago. Remember that our practice is to contemplate the Azoth mandala's image of conjunction together with other relevant alchemical images alongside the science in our Gaian alchemical exploration.

The precise date of the conjunction event in question is still hotly debated by scientists, so we can't pin it down precisely. This happening, which was to become of immense importance to Gaia much later on with the advent of multicellularity, was the transition from relatively simple cells without nuclei and highly differentiated internal structures: the archaea and bacteria (collectively known as the prokaryotes—we met them earlier), to very complex cells with nuclei and internal structures: the eukaryotes, which come in single-celled versions such as protozoa and as those more familiar multicellular versions we recognize as fungi, animals, plants, and the Protoctista (mostly single celled such as amoeba but others multicellular such as seaweeds and other algae).

Take a look at the diagrams in figure 13.8 of a photosynthesizing cyanobacterium (a prokaryote) and a plant cell (part of a multicellular eukaryote).

The first thing to note is that these diagrams are not to scale—the average prokaryote cell is about one thousandth of a millimeter in length while eukaryote cells are about one-tenth of a millimeter long. Notice too that there are no complex membranous structures in the prokaryote (the cyanobacterium). There is no cell nucleus. The cyanobacterium's DNA floats about freely in its cell in the form of a loop labeled *nucleoid* in the diagram. The little dots labeled *ribosomes* are where coded information from DNA in the nucleoid is transported and used to synthesize proteins. Notice the thylakoid membranes very near the surface of the cell where

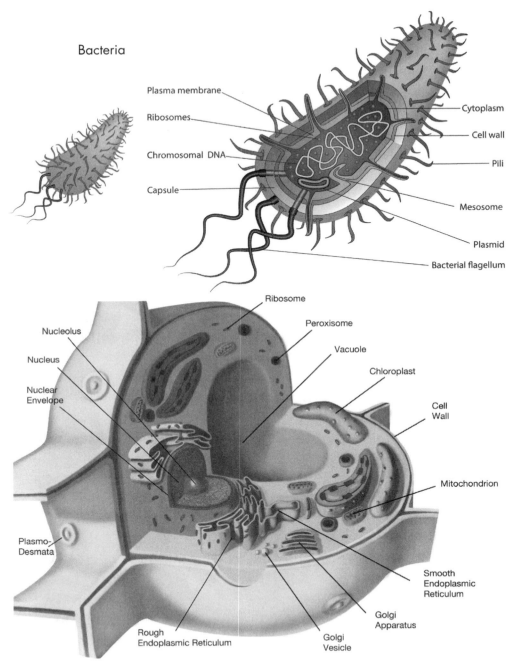

Bacteria

Plasma membrane
Ribosomes
Chromosomal DNA
Capsule

Cytoplasm
Cell wall
Pili
Mesosome
Plasmid
Bacterial flagellum

Ribosome
Peroxisome
Nucleolus
Vacuole
Nucleus
Chloroplast
Nuclear
Envelope
Cell
Wall
Mitochondrion
Plasmo-
Desmata
Smooth
Endoplasmic
Reticulum
Rough
Endoplasmic Reticulum
Golgi
Vesicle
Golgi
Apparatus

Figure 13.8. Notice the difference in structural complexity between the prokaryotic cell (*top*) and the eukaryotic cell (*bottom*), which is about 100 times larger.

there is most light. This is where the water-splitting photosynthetic reactions we explored in our last meditation take place. What we can't see is the flexible living internal molecular scaffolding known as the bacterial cytoskeleton, which influences the shape and structure of the bacterial cell.

The eukaryote (plant) cell couldn't be more different. Its DNA is segregated from the rest of the cell within the membrane-bound nucleus that contains very much more DNA than the cyanobacterium's nucleoid loop. We also notice a large membranous structure called the endoplasmic reticulum studded with ribosomes where proteins are synthesized. There is another highly differentiated region—the Golgi apparatus—where specialized molecules are made and stored in small membrane pouches. These bud and separate off like globs of lava lamp oil from the main apparatus for distribution along cytoskeleton tracks by the walking molecules we mentioned earlier.

We notice the sausage-shaped mitochondria, the powerhouses of eukaryotic cells, which use oxygen from the atmosphere to break down food in the biochemical process known as cellular respiration. Last of all, we notice our familiar green chloroplasts scattered here and there within this particular cell, which is that of a plant. We remember our journey to their green stacked thylakoid discs where we experienced the many molecular conjunctions that make possible water-splitting, oxygen-producing photosynthesis.

Let's return now to the question with which we began this section: How did photosynthesizing eukaryotes acquire photosynthesis? We may further ask: What can we learn if we explore this question alchemically? The answer involves the major conjunction event we mentioned earlier, the one that took place around 2500 million years ago. It has a name: *endosymbiosis*.

It might have taken hundreds of millions of years before a wily archaean prokaryote invented the subtle art of eating by using its cytoskeleton to extend protoplasmic "arms" around its bacterial prey, which it then engulfed and digested. No conjunction here: just the death of the engulfed in the ecologically necessary relationship between predator and prey. Though this powerful ability is taken for granted, we should marvel at this incredible innovation in life processes.

At one point, an oxygen-breathing bacterium was engulfed in this way and was about to be dismembered by the archaean's digestive enzymes. However, this time something different happened. An extraordinary molecular conversation took place between the two prokaryotes, in which they agreed to live together in a mutually beneficial conjunction, one inside the other, engulfed inside engulfer. It was a great arrangement. The oxygen-breather had a safe place to live while the archaean had limitless access to powerful energy produced from its food by the oxygen-breather. The profound conjunction of endosymbiosis had given rise to an entirely new type of cell: the single-celled eukaryote.

The conjunction worked so well that the original endosymbiotic oxygen-breathing bacteria became the ancestor of all the countless trillions upon trillions of mitochondria in the world's modern biosphere, all of which use oxygen to break down food molecules deep within their host's cells. The energy boost provided by mitochondria allowed the cell to grow larger, to develop a membrane-bound nucleus sheltering huge amounts of DNA and to evolve complex organelles such as the endoplasmic reticulum and the Golgi apparatus.

Much later, a further endosymbiotic conjunction took place: a single-celled eukaryote engulfed a cyanobacterium, presumably intending to digest it. Once again, a complex molecular conversation ensued. This resulted in the cyanobacterium being left in peace within the engulfing cell, to which it gave its sugary rewards.

This new conjunction worked well for all concerned. The cyanobacterium had a relatively safe place to live and in exchange produced sugars from photosynthesis, which the mitochondrion could break down using oxygen as needed to provide energy for the cell that gave shelter and protection to its once free-living inmates. The arrangement evolved and eventually the cyanobacterium became the ancestor of all the chloroplasts in the world. In the process the primitive thylakoid membranes of the cyanobacterium developed into the chloroplast's beautifully sophisticated stacks of green thylakoid discs, which we encountered earlier.

So much for the science. It's important to state here that these ideas were bravely and effectively championed by Lynn Margulis, the

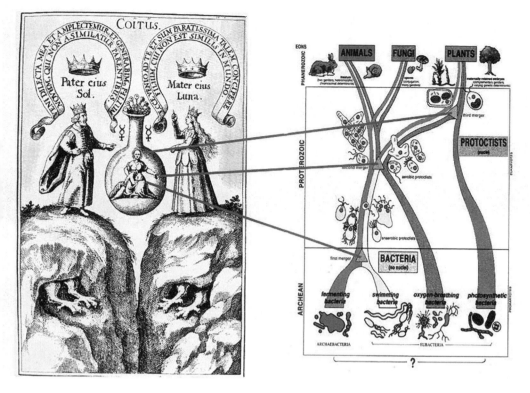

Figure 13.9. J. D. Mylius, *Anatomia auri*, Frankfurt 1628 (*left*), Lynn Margulis image (*right*).
Lynn Margulis Archive image drawn by K. Delisle, courtesy of the Estate of Lynn Margulis.

great American evolutionary biologist who helped James Lovelock to develop his Gaia theory. We will end this exploration of Gaian alchemical conjunction by contemplating a prescientific alchemical image of conjunction alongside a scientific image of the endosymbiotic events we've just considered, the latter put together by Lynn Margulis.

Let your rational, discursive mind soften and allow your intuitive, dreamlike contemplative mind to come to the fore.

Allow your intuition to roam freely between the two images (fig. 13.9) until a sense of their relatedness arises, no matter how slight or how weak.

Be aware of feelings, ideas, and insights that come to you as you contemplate these two images together.

The transformative potential in the juxtaposition of these two images is very subtle, so spend some time gazing on them, allowing them to work their way into you, waking up your own personal realization of the meaning of their relationship.

The alchemical image on the left shows Sol (the King) and Luna (the Queen) each standing on their own rocky promontory deeply separated by a wide gulf. In each rock there is a cave out of which dragon's feet appear. These represent our masculine and feminine instincts, centered on our ego personality. Both are an absolute requirement for our sanity and well-being and are the foundation of a wider Gaian view of nature.

On top of their rocky mounds Sol and Luna are conversing in Latin.

Sol to Luna: "Come, my dear, and embrace me so we shall produce a son different to the parents."

Luna to Sol: "I come to you. I am ready to conceive a child whose like has never been seen in the world."

The result of the union of Sol and Luna is indeed a child, a daughter, not a son. She sits inside the round alchemical vessel at the center of the image with a male figure supine on her lap.

A Mercurius symbol floats on either side of the vessel's neck, making it perfectly clear that the woman in the vessel is the spirit of Mercurius, the lived experience of nondual Gaia, which has come about because of the union (coitus) between Sol and Luna. The supine male figure suggests that the feminine perspective is paramount in constellating Mercurius.

See the seven flowers sprouting from the neck of the vessel? They indicate that this appearance of Mercurius results in an acute consciousness of the living energy of nature.

Mercurius is the alchemical symbol for a wide, deeply ecological style of consciousness, which can appear uniquely for you as you ponder the correspondences between these two images.

Now shift your focus of attention to the scientific image on the right.

Notice the four separate bacterial types at the bottom of the image. These are (1) the fermenters (the archaea), (2) the swimmers equipped with whiplike organelles that facilitate swimming movements, (3) the oxygen-breathers, and (4) the water-splitting photosynthesizers whom we have already met. The bacteria divide into two broad types, the archaea (archaeabacteria, some of which are able to engulf their bacterial prey as we saw above) and the eubacteria. These two types are analogous to the dragon's feet in the alchemical image, for these two bacterial domains are the foundations of all future life on our planet.

See the three lines radiating from Mercurius stitching the alchemical and scientific images together.

The lowest line appears out of the lower part of the woman in the alchemical vessel and connects with the first symbiotic conjunction between the fermenting bacteria and swimming bacteria at lower left of the scientific image. The fermenting bacterium is receptive and therefore embodies the quality of Luna, while the swimming bacterium lends activity to the symbiosis and therefore embodies the active qualities of Sol. (This hypothesis of Lynn Margulis is not yet supported by scientific evidence.)

Notice how the middle line appearing out of the woman's outstretched hand connects with the second endosymbiotic conjunction. Here a microbe created in the first symbiosis engulfs an oxygen respiring bacterium, which becomes the ancestor of all mitochondria. The engulfed oxygen-breathing bacterium embodies the qualities of Sol by using oxygen to capture food energy, which it gives to Luna, the engulfing cell.

The topmost line appears out the head of the female figure in the alchemical vessel, passes through Luna's left hand, traverses the evolutionary bifurcation leading to animals and fungi and comes to rest in the endosymbiotic conjunction between an oxygen-breathing eukaryote and a free-swimming, water-splitting photosynthetic bacterium. Now Sol is the photosynthetic bacterium. With time, it evolves into the chloroplast that gives energy-rich sugars to Luna, the single-celled oxygen-breathing eukaryote that engulfed it and its photosynthesizing descendants to the modern day.

The three lines linking the alchemical vessel with the three symbiotic conjunctions are events in psyche as biological events, for the two are indissoluble since nature is psyche and psyche is nature. The two realms feed each other. Thus, the qualities of these key endosymbiotic events and the relationships between Luna and Sol and their child, Mercurius, are inwardly connected in a very deep way.

Try to feel the presence of Sol, Luna, and Mercurius in each of the three symbiotic conjunctions.

Those flowers bursting forth from the mouth of the alchemical vessel could also correspond with the appearance of fungi, plants, and animals, those multicellular organisms that contribute to today's exuberant biodiversity—that great flowering of Gaia's long evolutionary processes in recent times.

This last endosymbiotic conjunction opened up the possibility for life to extensively colonize the land once photosynthesizers in the form of plants had developed complex multicellular structures such as wood, roots, leaves, and stems needed to survive the initially harsh conditions on the continents. Once plants took hold of the land, they formed the basis of the entire terrestrial ecological community, which over time developed into the astonishing contemporary flowering of biodiversity that we are now so rapidly destroying.

These great botanical achievements were made possible by those ancient single-celled endosymbiotic eukaryotes, which hosted chloroplasts for making food out of sunlight, water, and carbon dioxide, plus mitochondria for releasing energy from this food. We mustn't forget the nucleus, which stores a living genetic memory bank of ideas for the cell to download and use in a multitude of creative ways.

The colonization of the land by life gave Gaia the ability to regulate her surface conditions more effectively and for far longer than would have been the case with just bare mostly lifeless rocky continents. From a Gaian alchemical viewpoint, the colonization of the land by plants brought about a profound intensification of the spirit and power of life, which we experience as Mercurius, as nondual Gaia, in moments of deeply joyful insight and blessing.

FERMENTATION

Alchemically, fermentation involves an initial phase in which the child produced in the previous state, the conjunction, is decomposed through putrefaction. The psychological energies thus liberated are then recycled and fermented into a wider, higher form of consciousness and intelligence. As Hauck says:

> If we work at it . . . (alchemy) can put us in touch with a deeply truthful intelligence within ourselves that we never knew existed.

The alchemist's ego is further broken down in the processes of putrefaction, often in the form of a dark depression, which the alchemist endures in order that a new, wider experience of the wonder of life can break forth into awareness through the fermentation of the decomposed psychological material. This new, expanded insight is so varied and life-giving that it is symbolized by the peacock's tail with its rainbow display of many shimmering, iridescent colors. The ego becomes aware of a far vaster center in the psyche, which Jung called the Self, a center of deep knowing that works in the world via the ego but which is essentially transpersonal. To be in touch with the Self is to feel the deepest meaning, security, and happiness in one's existence. This is the final goal of alchemy as a psychological art—the Philosopher's Stone.

Putrefaction and fermentation were likewise essential for life to develop and flourish and for Gaian self-regulation to emerge on our planet soon after the first bacteria appeared. As Lenton and Watson point out in their book *Revolutions That Made the Earth,* for life to thrive in those early days it needed a plentiful supply of essential nutrients, either from the planet's crust and interior or from the establishment of recycling loops among the microbes themselves.

Some of these essential nutrients are carbon, hydrogen, nitrogen, oxygen, phosphorus, and sulphur. They also include various metals such as iron, manganese, zinc, and copper. Some, such as phosphorus, are rare. Others, such as nitrogen gas in the atmosphere, are abundant in chemical modes not easily accessible to life. Lenton and Watson point out that a healthy biosphere needs to be populated by microbes that make these key nutrients biologically available, and that recycling loops will emerge automatically when the microbial community contains a sufficiently diverse range of metabolic pathways that link up to provide a network for the necessary chemical transformations. Nitrogen-fixing bacteria have developed the subtle art of transforming nitrogen gas (N_2) from the atmosphere into ammonia (NH_3) and other nitrogenous compounds, which then become available to the rest of life. Other bacteria then close the loop by recycling nitrogen to the atmosphere when they decompose the dead bodies of organic beings.

Another example comes from James Lovelock's model of the microbial biosphere. When Gaia was born around 2700 million years ago, just after the first water-splitting, oxygen-producing photosynthetic bacteria (the cyanobacteria) had spread all over the global ocean. These bacteria could have removed so much carbon dioxide from the atmosphere via photosynthesis that, due to a lack of this key greenhouse gas in her atmosphere, the planet might have faced the grave danger of freezing over into the totally frozen state of a Snowball Earth. The small input of carbon dioxide from volcanos would not have been great enough to prevent the snowball.

This dreadful fate was avoided thanks to fermenting bacteria living in the ocean sediments that putrefied (decomposed) vast numbers of dead cyanobacterial bodies that sank down into the ocean depths, releasing carbon locked in their bodies. The fermenting bacteria thereby recycled carbon dioxide and methane back to the atmosphere, preventing a global freeze up by restoring Gaia's warming blanket of greenhouse gasses.

∞∞∞ A Conversation with Jeffrey Kiehl ∞∞∞

JEFFREY: What's fermentation in Gaia?

STEPHAN: Microorganisms do fermentation in Gaia. In one kind of fermentation microbes take simple sugar molecules and refine them into alcohol. In another kind yeast—a single-celled fungus—breaks down starches in bread dough producing carbon dioxide and all sorts of smaller organic molecules, which are very nutritious. So one kind of fermentation feeds you. The other intoxicates you.

JEFFREY: That's the science. Now the alchemy. Here's an alchemical image of fermentation (fig. 13.10):

Figure 13.10. By D. Stolcius von Stolcenberg in the *Vidarium chymicum,* Frankfurt 1624.

STEPHAN: There's a man scattering seed from a sack, which must be the seeds of something to come in the future. He's the masculine. There's a woman announcing something with a glorious trumpet hung with marvelous textiles. She's got a sword and a hat like a bishop's hat.

JEFFREY: She has wings. She's the soul.

STEPHAN: A soul that carries a sword!

JEFFREY: She's both the feminine and the masculine.

STEPHAN: Whereas he's actually quite a feminine figure because he's sowing seeds.

JEFFREY: He's the alchemist. She's here to help him.

STEPHAN: These seeds and the trumpet have got to do with waking Sun and Moon up.

JEFFREY: Music is an act of creation—that's the trumpet.

STEPHAN: These are the seeds of their future unity.

JEFFREY: They are on the ground so this is grounded archetypal energy. Earth—Gaia—has these masculine and feminine energies.

◇◇◇◇◇◇◇◇◇◇◇◇◇◇◇◇◇◇◇◇◇◇◇◇◇◇◇◇◇◇◇◇◇◇◇

Gaia was born when these two bacterial ecosystems—the carbon-removing photosynthesizers on the surface and the carbon-releasing putrefiers in the sediments—together created a global recycling loop for atmospheric carbon, which regulated the temperature of the planetary surface.

The emergence of recycling loops has ensured that adequate supplies of key nutrients were available to Gaia's living beings during her long and complex evolutionary journey through geological time. This, combined with efficient capture of solar energy by water-splitting photosynthesis, has culminated in the splendid peacock's tail of the immensely sophisticated abundant biodiversity into which our species appeared some 300,000 years ago.

The release of free oxygen by water-splitting photosynthesis made it possible for this highly reactive gas to build up in the atmosphere to a concentration of around 1 percent by about 2500 million years ago, increasing to the current level of about 21 percent by around 350 million years ago.

Free oxygen in the atmosphere opens up a powerful new recycling pathway for carbon with important effects on certain properties of Gaia's surface, including her temperature. Photosynthesizers extract their gaseous food—carbon dioxide—from the atmosphere and fix solar energy in bonds between the carbon atoms in sugar and other molecules. Consumers return carbon dioxide to the air using oxygen to extract this solar energy in the process scientists call cellular respiration.

As Lenton and Watson point out (2011, 136), cellular respiration produces ten times more energy per molecule of organic matter respired than other energy-releasing pathways such as biological fermentation in which oxygen is not involved. The presence of free oxygen supercharges the biosphere with energy and allows life to expand everywhere over our planet's surface, making Gaia's self-regulation even more effective than before the appearance of free oxygen in the atmosphere.

We need to remember that the powerful creative forces released in us by our own alchemical fermentation cannot happen without the many and varied recycling processes involving putrefaction and fermentation taking place right now within the very body of our animate Earth. Thus, a science-based contemplation of Gaia's fermentations helps trigger our own psychological-alchemical fermentation. This is an example of the transformative potential of Gaia alchemy.

DISTILLATION

There is a wind of change in Earth System Science toward greater holism, which brings an inkling of support for the idea that some kind of wisdom resides in Gaia's feedbacks. This discipline is founded on James Lovelock's pioneering science of Gaia, and the latest thinking within the field is that there is a totally unexpected level in which natural selection operates: namely at the "higher" level of Gaian feedbacks. Recently, even some of the staunchest critics of Lovelock's early scientific Gaian ideas are proposing that natural selection promotes feedbacks that regulate key planetary variables essential for life. The idea is that feedbacks that tend to be anti-Gaia give way to those that promote her long-term persistence.

Based on the work of climate scientist Richard Betts and other scientists such as Tim Lenton (both of whom have worked closely with James Lovelock), one can perhaps say from an alchemical perspective that Gaia distills herself through bottlenecks. Bett's proposal is that when a destabilizing ecosystem appears and manages to dominate the entire planet, then the global biosphere heads for extinction. Many ecosystems collapse, but—because Gaia's surface is so wildly heterogeneous—some high functioning (pro-Gaian) ecosystems survive in nooks and crannies where things have not become hopelessly inhospitable to life.

Eventually the destabilizing (anti-Gaian) ecosystem kills itself off and the surviving pro-Gaian ecosystems come out of hiding, take over the planet, and restart planetary self-regulation. These pro-Gaian ecosystems distill themselves over time by acquiring more and more self-regulatory adaptive know-how. Thus, they become more resistant to being taken over by potentially destabilizing ecosystems. Betts calls his idea sequential selection because there is a loose kind of competition-free natural selection among ecosystems over time, such that the most pro-Gaian ecosystems tend to survive in the long term via the process we've just described. Extreme Gaian bottlenecks happen during mass extinctions, after which the entire biosphere has so far managed to help configure the planet back into an effectively functioning state.

Other scientists have been trying to solve the difficult puzzle of how Gaian self-regulation, which is good for the entire biosphere, could have come about on a planet full of individually "selfish" organisms that care nothing for the global good. The issue is that groups of altruistic organisms who sacrifice their fitness (loosely speaking, the number of offspring they produce) for the benefit of the whole will be swamped out by cheats who make no such sacrifice.

One of these scientists is W. Ford Doolittle, the eminent biologist who established that chloroplasts were once free-living bacteria. Doolittle also contributed important ideas about the evolution of the eukaryote cell, and worked to establish the details of horizontal gene transfer among the prokaryotes. In 1981 Doolittle published an influential paper in *Coevolution Quarterly* called "Is Nature Really Motherly?" in which he gives a cogent critique of the Gaia hypothesis, which includes this key sentence:

> It is not the difficulty of unravelling Gaian feedback loops that make me doubt her existence. It is the impossibility of imagining any evolutionary mechanism by which these loops could have arisen or now be maintained.

It is a great credit to Doolittle's exemplary scientific attitude (which shows how science *should* develop) that in 2014 he changed his mind and published a pro-Gaian idea that he called "natural selection by survival alone," a notion greatly akin to Richard Bett's sequential selection scenario, which we've just described.

In Doolittle's scenario, natural selection among noncompeting ecological communities happens via which community is best at surviving by accumulating beneficial adaptations. Some communities don't change their network structures and only manage to survive over time purely as a matter of chance. Alchemically speaking, these communities don't distill themselves by developing beneficial connections in their networks and so they eventually go extinct through lack of adaptive flexibility. They survive for a while by chance alone.

Other ecological communities do distill their networks as when new species appear with innovative and highly useful ecological services that improve the network's functions or perhaps when existing species evolve and make the network perform much better than before. These new beneficial adaptations enhance the effectiveness of the network and make such self-distilling communities much less prone to extinction. In Doolittle's model, these beneficial adaptations appear at discrete moments in the life of the community, but they could also appear gradually over time.

Doolittle's idea could just as well refer to individual planets, each hosting its own unique biosphere. He points out that the longer an ecological community or life-bearing planet has survived, the more likely there is to be a reason other than luck for its persistence. Luck might have been involved in generating the right ecological network at the start, but once established, the intelligence of a successful network distills its survival skills, expelling network linkages that would be destabilizing and enhancing those that promote persistence. This is of course a very sophisticated form of learning. We have to accept that ecosystems learn.

I've heard that there's an ecologist who thinks of ecosystems as songs and of its individual species as singers. Following this musical metaphor, ecosystems in distillation tend to pick up more singers who help the community as a whole to sing its song more ably and creatively with more harmonic breadth, stability, beauty, meaning, and resonance.

In successfully distilled ecological communities (or planetary biospheres) species have linked up into a highly resilient network of relationships. Over time, such well-distilled ecosystems are better able to resist the effects of destabilizing species, as well as challenges from their surroundings such as changes in weather and climate. This, as we saw earlier, is often because the community encourages redundancy by hosting several species at low abundance, which wait in the wings to take over a given ecological function if any of the abundant performers of that particular role suffer population declines for whatever reason.

Although Doolittle's concept moves in the direction of Gaia, it is not actually Gaian because he does not consider feedbacks between organisms and their environment—the rocks, atmosphere, and water. Nicholson et al. (2018) created an ingenious mathematical model consisting of microbial biospheres operating under three differing conditions: (1) No mutations among the microbes. (2) With mutations among the microbes but without Gaian feedbacks (thereby modeling Doolittle's "natural selection by survival alone" scenario). And (3) with mutations among the microbes including Gaian feedbacks connecting microbes with their global environment. In this Gaian model, the microbes affect the planetary temperature, which feeds back to affect microbes' growth rate.

The key findings are that biospheres with mutation (those with selection by survival alone) survive much longer than biospheres without mutation and that the Gaia biospheres incorporating both mutation and microbe-environment (i.e., temperature) feedbacks survive best of all. The Gaia biospheres do best because they prevent anti-Gaian dynamics from taking root. Nicholson et al. (2018) summarize the import of their work with a stunning sentence that moves our scientific perception of natural selection into the higher gear of true Gaian understanding in science and beyond:

This situation supports the central idea of the Gaia hypothesis— namely that regulation can emerge from the interaction of life and the abiotic environment.

How are we to integrate these fascinating scientific insights courtesy of our thinking function with an alchemical perspective on Gaia gifted us by our intuition, sensing, and feeling? Is it even possible to integrate these four ways of knowing to enhance our experience of living within Gaia's membranous depths?

By working with Gaia alchemy to integrate our four ways of knowing it sometimes happens that a miraculous appearance of Mercurius, of nondual Gaia, lives itself into one as a vastly widened awareness of this particular moment we are experiencing now in Gaia, and of this moment's immense significance as a moment of consciousness of Gaia.

This for me is the deepest magic: to love science and alchemy both in equal measure and to experience them integrating within me into the true salt of life. This is my own personal, highly individual, Gaian Philosopher's Stone. To put it alchemically, Mercurius sometimes appears when I am in service to both science and alchemy, when I offer my consciousness as a place where they can meet and conjoin in a sacred marriage for the benefit of all.

For me, the alchemical message is quite clear: I cannot properly engage in depth psychological work with alchemical images (and hence with the healing powers in the unconscious) unless I am able to cultivate the lived experience of my inner distillation (nonrational, but with its own strangely paradoxical reason). This is only possible for me by linking this lived experience intimately to Gaia's own wider distillation in this moment and throughout geological time. It seems that working alchemically with Gaian science takes us through a threshold into a profoundly healing sense of Gaia's living presence, which makes us more able to work with more consciousness toward healing the tragic situations of our times.

Our identification with Gaia grows as we ponder, contemplate, and visualize the strange, hard-to-pin-down parallels, connections, and feedbacks between our personal psychological distillation and that of our living planet. In doing this, somehow, we may become wiser, more resilient, and of more use in working for Gaia's self-regulation (and our own). This occurs when we putrefy our current psychological attitude and distill the resulting spirit, which comes out of that messy, rotting ferment. We put that spirit into the alchemical flask of our deepest nature and distill it further with a gentle inner warmth so that any remaining impurities in our worldview drop back into the distillation flask, allowing our Gaian perceptions to sublimate and condense into a richly alchemical way of life. The image to work with here is the citrinitas, the yellow substance: the precursor of the glowing red rubedo of coagulation, which is our Gaian Philosopher's Stone.

THE PRESENT MOMENT AS COAGULATION

I feel that coagulation refers to our human relationship within the body of Gaia in this moment of our mutual development. As our engagement with Gaia alchemy deepens, we enter into longer and longer moments of nondual Gaian awareness in our Gaia place and eventually even in the depths of the noisiest city. In these moments, we realize in body, speech, and mind that we are profoundly and indissolubly bound into Gaia's own mysterious coagulation. This has gradually intensified during her immense evolutionary trajectory through geological time. We spontaneously abandon the hyperrational, anti-teleological taboo of mainstream science and instead find ourselves deliciously at home within the numinous purpose of Gaia's journey, even if we can't pin down what this is with any precision or conceptual clarity. In those moments when a nondual Gaian awareness of our mutual coagulation with our planet descends upon us with a deep and liberating blessing, we realize in some ineffable way that her self-realization and ours are completely intertwined and interconnected.

Figure 13.11 is an ancient alchemical image that symbolizes the coagulated state. It shows the winged Mercurius once more, but this time he holds a caduceus in each hand. He is naked apart from a crown on his head, above which is the sign of Mercurius. He has the sun and moon on either side of him, symbolizing the union of conscious and the unconscious. The two wings of the rarefied essence we encountered at the top of the Azoth mandala are at his feet, and we notice the action is once again taking place deep in nature. Two male figures are approaching Mercurius seemingly in attack mode. One holds a sword, around

Figure 13.11. Mercurius repelling two adversaries. From Basil Valentine's
Twelve Keys, first published in *Ein kurtz summarischer Tractat,
von dem grossen Stein der Uralten . . .* , Eisleben, 1599.

which coils a snake. The other has what seems to be a rifle with a bird
(a phoenix?) at the end of the barrel. Whatever it is they want, it is clear
that Mercurius is immune to any fear or doubt they want to induce in
him. In his coagulated state, he is very much himself and at one with
Gaia's landscape. Thus, he is not in the slightest bit disturbed by the
presence of these two threatening figures, which represent the shadows
in our thinking and feeling.

◇◇◇◇◇ A Conversation with Jeffrey Kiehl ◇◇◇◇◇

JEFFREY: The image shows Mercurius. He's holding both staffs—each
one a caduceus. He can fend off anything that comes at him. He's
balancing the lunar and solar consciousness.

STEPHAN: And look at the wings on the ground. If this is the dragon,
look how sophisticated it's become. It's a grounded spirit.

JEFFREY: These are the people that are going to come up to you and say, "You're studying alchemy? Well, what good is that? How could you use it?" They're going to bring that one-sided consciousness in and cut you down with their words—with their swords. The central figure is shielding, healing himself with the power of Mercurius, which integrates the Sun, Moon, the horizontal, and the vertical.

STEPHAN: Why would one of the attackers have a snake with a crown? The snake could be refined intellect. So the sword is refined but it's the wrong kind of sword. It's still nasty because it's one sided. And the other attacker also has refined sword with a function that's probably well developed but also one sided.

JEFFREY: This one flies in the air; that one crawls on the ground. You're talking earthiness and airiness so someone really earthy is attacking you, someone coming at you low, below the belt. Coarse words.

STEPHAN: Insulting.

JEFFREY: Right. One of the attackers could be the intellect that's going to try to get you saying "Well, we all know that alchemy was just stuff that's hundreds of years old right and holds no value whatsoever. Give it up. We've got modern science now." But Mercurius is the end product—the regenerated you—the rubedo. It's you fully integrated into the world—into Gaia. So you are protected from these vicious attacks.

◇◇◇◇◇◇◇◇◇◇◇◇◇◇◇◇◇◇◇◇◇◇◇◇◇◇◇◇◇

Marie-Louise von Franz describes the coagulated (or "individuated") state that applies to Mercurius in this passage from her book *Alchemy* ([1959] 1980) in which the "shut chamber" refers to the innermost alchemical vessel wherein the coagulation takes place:

> The individuation process leads to unique creativeness in each moment and the shut chamber alludes to this secret center of the personality, the secret source of life. It is the shut chamber of the heart, the unique creativeness in each moment of life. Where the process of individuation leads to the realization of this uniqueness others can no longer guess about you, for they cannot see into

the chamber of your heart from where the unexpected, creative reactions spring.

The secret source of life—is this perhaps none other than Gaia, our animate Earth? The creative reactions referred to by von Franz, do they come from Gaia just as much as from our own psyche?

An Alchemical Conversation

STEPHAN: *Good evening and welcome to this new edition of* Science Now *from the World Service of the BBC. I would like to welcome my guests, Professor Andrew Pensament, a noted systems scientist, and Gaia herself, our very own planet, who is speaking through the microbial ecological community thriving in that jar of sauerkraut over there. Welcome to you both and thanks for coming. I would like to start by asking Professor Pensament to tell us what he thinks about Gaia alchemy.*

PROFESSOR: *Well, to be quite honest, brutally honest in fact, I see no empirical value in it at all. What I mean is that this work with these outdated and quite frankly, primitive images, is not going to get us anywhere. It is all very poetic, I grant you, but you are off with the fairies if you think this kind of thing is going to help solve the crisis. To do that we need to deploy new technologies and reform our economic system combined with rigorous government regulation.*

STEPHAN: *I agree with your last point about technology and economics, but where are we going to find the wisdom to use them skilfully? Any technology and any economic system can be used for ill as well as good. Clear thinking is very important, but it isn't enough. Wisdom connects us with the deep aboriginal mystery and the wonder of Gaia. Alchemical images help us discover and integrate this into our modern consciousness.*

GAIA: *Yes, you need to find yourselves as part of my biosphere. You need to discover that you can only be whole if I am whole—if my*

230

biosphere is mostly wild and intact. You cannot do this with only yet more thinking. This can only be done by working with images that come from the deep psyche, from the anima mundi, which is me, underlying us all. I love my alchemical images. They stir my soul and give me hope that you might yet find your way back to me.

PROFESSOR: *With all the respect due to your immensity, you are nothing more than an incredibly complex system of feedbacks and interactions between your biosphere, atmosphere, waters, and rocks. We are able to quantify and model these feedbacks with more and more precision as we gain more and more computing power. Our models already re-create your past climates quite accurately, and this accuracy will get even better once we have quantum computers at our disposal. Of course we know that you are far too complex to ever model completely, but we can achieve very good approximations that capture your basic dynamics both now and throughout geological time.*

GAIA: *Great so far—thanks. We need those data and I have been waiting for them.*

PROFESSOR: *But you have no purpose. You are, of course, amazing, but you are no more than an incredibly unlikely configuration of inanimate atoms. I am as amazed by you as I would be had I won the lottery. I am amazed that pure chance could produce such a thing as you. In fact, you are an amazingly complex AI. That's the best way we have of knowing you. You are a vastly complex, impersonal robotic machine circling the sun. You are an extraordinary planet, but also deeply frightening, so impersonal are you. Science is our only reliable way of knowing about you, and this is its message: Facing up to the meaninglessness of existence is our most noble act. You have no purpose. One day you will be swallowed up by the sun and that will be the end of it. I'm sorry, but that's how it is. Get real and get used to it.*

STEPHAN: *Wait, dear Professor. The empirical evidence from depth psychology is that there are indeed other ways of knowing that can give us great insights about the world and about Gaia. Pondering alchemical images opens up pathways into these alternative ways of* knowing that are primarily based on feeling and intuition, rather than on rational thinking. You just have to give yourself a chance and try doing some work with alchemy, with Gaia alchemy. You might be transformed. You might be amazed and delighted.

PROFESSOR: *I know about intuition. We scientists use it to help solve rational problems in making models and in designing instruments to monitor the Earth System. But that's all there is to it. It would be madness to allow intuition to run the show. It's only the servant of science—very useful, but only a servant. There's no way that I am going to waste my time pondering a whole lot of archaic images produced by half-awake prescientific people with crazy ideas about the world, like spontaneous generation of frogs out of mud. What hogwash.*

GAIA: *There is much more to intuition than that, dear Professor. Long before science your earliest ancestors felt my presence and gave me due honor by finding me in their rituals and dreams. They knew that my body was their body, that it was I who sent them their dreams and appeared to them in their rituals. They had a sense of my benevolence as well as knowing my holy terror. They knew that I was up to something in brewing up my huge alchemical concoction of living beings, rocks, waters, and oceans. And I am up to something truly magnificent, truly worth joining and helping. We—humans and Gaia—are all part of a great experiment on the part of a huge intelligence far deeper, more knowing, and more powerful than what comes out of your computer models. Please, use your cleverness to get us all out of the mess you have created, for soon you will have triggered aspects of myself that I don't like very much: heatwaves, floods, famines, diseases, mass extinction, and the collapse of your civilizations. I had such high hopes for you. Oh well, there are always other planets I could try. But this is such a nice one. Do give it a go, won't you?*

PROFESSOR: *That's a very moving speech, and I do get a sense of what you say. But now I feel you are no more than an anthropomorphic projection of ours onto a meaningless global ecological community. You are getting at me through my human feelings, through the smoke and mirror of projection.*

GAIA: *Hmm, a most interesting argument. My question to you would be, who, or what, created the anthropomorphism in the first place?*

PROFESSOR: *I did, prompted by your words created by the people who first created the anthropomorphism—by those early people you are so fond of.*

GAIA: *Very clever, but hey, respect please. Remember that in ancient Greece, I was the Mother of All and the Steadfast Base of All Things.*

PROFESSOR: *They were such primitive people to believe that nonsense. But of course that was an earlier stage of culture before we developed scientific reasoning. Perhaps we needed it then, I grant you, but not now.*

GAIA: *And yet I am glad you did feel something for a moment, for we need that kind of knowing now more than ever. As I get older I'll need your help more and more to reach my goal. That's one reason why I've been waiting for you.*

PROFESSOR: *What goal? There is no goal.*

GAIA: *If I am an anthropomorphism, then why is it that I can send you thoughts you never imagined you could have? Feelings you never imagined you could feel? Just go outside and really listen to the birds. You see, the psyche is an objective reality. It is a scientific fact!*

PROFESSOR: *I love birdwatching. And I love the intricate musical structures of their songs. But are you telling me that there is more in it than that?*

STEPHAN: *You know, Professor, that I have been into science since I was a child. I loved nature and wanted to get to know her better, and science was the only way at that time. There was no other way of knowing nature, so I went into science. And I loved it. I did well. I wanted to be a scientific ecologist in service to the great beauty and wonder I had seen as a boy birdwatching with friends and going fishing. There was such a deep peace there—such a gentle love and knowing, so calming, deep, and nourishing. I realize now that this was Gaia—that there is an objective psyche where these things reside. From there, we are sent images to help us rediscover that lost paradise which is Gaia, even as she is now in her deeply ravaged state, so we can love her and heal her. Do you see, dear Professor?*

If you work with these images with as much diligence and care as you put into your science, you'll notice how amazing things begin to happen to you, within you and outside you. You start to feel those great feelings you had when you were a young child, before science got you. You slow down, take in the clouds and the trees; you feel the power and the majesty of it all and sense its inexpressible purpose. And it will foster you too.

PROFESSOR: *I see. You mean you have worked with these images and you have seen new things? What sort of things?*

STEPHAN: *Well, it is hard to describe. It's a fuller world, richer in meaning. In my best moments I feel that I really am living within a great intelligence—Gaia's intelligence—which is really up to something so good, wholesome, and great that I devote myself to it with all my heart and soul. That's a wonderful feeling, you see, to feel that level of reality, to value reality so much, to that extent. That's a good strong feeling to have. You can use your intellect as much as you like in service of that.*

PROFESSOR: *Well, I am stunned, simply stunned that you could say such a thing. It sounds so religious!*

STEPHAN: *If I may psychoanalyze for a moment, this is clearly a good example of a cultural complex within science interfering with the perception of truth. Hence such a statement is against science, not religion.*

PROFESSOR: *All right, I can see what you are driving at. So what is religion?*

STEPHAN: *It's our ability to feel the absolute grandeur of the cosmos.*

PROFESSOR: *We scientists do that.*

GAIA: *Of course you do, for you are human.*

STEPHAN: *Do you see it now?*

PROFESSOR: *See what?*

STEPHAN: *How different everything is. How rich and full of meaning?*

PROFESSOR: *No, but I see that you do, and you seem truly genuine.*

STEPHAN: *I am.*

PROFESSOR: *So then, tell me more about your story. How did you come from science to this?*

STEPHAN: *I felt there was something very cold about science. I could never name it but some part of me felt it while I was doing science at school and then at university. There was a voice saying that this could not be all, that there had to be something even greater going on here in biology than this mechanical view of things. This was all quite unconscious at the time. And I suffered that wound, which I know now was not just my wound. It is our greatest cultural wound—our ecological wound. Because of it, we are destroying the whole of Gaia.*

GAIA: *Yes, and you must stop it, and very soon, or else I am afraid that I will turn terrible. Best not to stir up that side of me.*

PROFESSOR: *But does connection with Gaia make you happy?*

GAIA: *I got him good and proper on my side and see how happy he is? Of course he suffers his pains and his miseries, but at the base of it he knows who he works for and where he is going, and he gives himself, deep down, to that, to me. How noble and truly beautiful. I acknowledge and respond to that sort of devotion with the gift of consciousness.*

STEPHAN: *You see, Herr Professor, what you are missing?*

PROFESSOR: *Well, yes, you know what, I do get a sense of it somewhere inside me, in some dark distant corner.*

STEPHAN: *Excellent! Now you have started the alchemical work. Remember that the goal, if there is a goal, is to live in the reality of Gaia and to be in service to her deepest meaning.*

PROFESSOR: *Okay, but just cut out the meaning for the moment will you? I am just focusing on that strange dark feeling. It's bothering me.*

STEPHAN: *Good. If you wanted to take this further you would have to go away and start a conversation with that feeling. You would draw it, speak to it (in private, of course), and you would simply get to know that part of yourself, which you've never developed, that offers you the deepest happiness if only you will work with it and let it out. It may appear as a frightful monster to begin with. If that happens, tell it to get back into its bottle to prove it will help you. Then, when you let it out again, it will help you immensely. It will heal all your ills. It will make you whole. In alchemy, this is the spirit Mercurius.*

GAIA: *I would recommend it, Herr Professor. I have cured many a lost human thus.*

PROFESSOR: *Well, I might try it, I suppose, in the interests of science. For if what you are saying is real then it warrants a scientific experiment with me as the subject.*

STEPHAN: *Marvelous! That's the true spirit of science.*

PROFESSOR: *I'll try it. In my shed, out of sight, with none of my colleagues knowing.*

GAIA: *That would be wise for the moment.*

STEPHAN: *Don't be afraid.*

Two weeks later

PROFESSOR: *I have been trying out what you said. My dreams got turbulent, I got the sweats. At times I felt I was a mass of confusion. Had I really wasted my entire life on science? No—impossible. Then what was this lost feeling in me that you had pointed out. Round and round went my thoughts. My childhood feelings and Gaia . . . could they really be connected? Could that sort of Gaia be real? Would I regress to childhood if those feelings took me over? Should I abandon science? You see what a state I was in?*

GAIA: *Yes, a good earthy ferment for the sake of your soul, Herr Professor. You are cooking nicely.*

PROFESSOR: *And then it changed. Everything calmed down as if a huge rain had descended. It was so peaceful, a peace I had never known. It was very quiet and my dreams were more vivid. I could sort of understand what they were saying, and it was helpful to focus on them, most comforting. The moon came out, and I loved sitting under the stars.*

STEPHAN: *That's excellent so far. From the point of view of the Azoth mandala you started with a good calcination and then went into a really good dissolution. You are making progress really fast. You know, it wouldn't surprise me at all if you had been a great alchemist in the past, but then, why would you have forgotten it so deeply?*

GAIA: *Did you experience any Separatio—alchemical separation— after that?*

PROFESSOR: *Well, possibly. I felt a sort of energy and desire to sort this out. To find out who I really am so that I can be of maximum use.*

GAIA: *To whom?*

PROFESSOR: *Well, to you.*

GAIA: *Ah, so you have seen me now?*

PROFESSOR: *Only when I went into another stage—a sort of conjunction of that childhood knowing of nature that had somehow joined up with my scientific knowing, both as equals, both equally strong, which gave birth to this wider, deeper person I never knew I was. It feels so good. I am still a scientist and always will be, but now I could almost say that I am a Gaian scientist as I walk around in the woods taking measurements of carbon sequestration in trees and soils. I had a great field trip last Tuesday with the students. It came all over me quite suddenly. It all leaped into three dimensions: time, space, and meaning. It was all quite clear and yet completely mysterious. I felt deeply happy for the very first time in my life, really the very first time, with a happiness I never knew was possible—a cosmic happiness. The students felt it too, and we had a glorious afternoon.*

STEPHAN: *Ah, that must be the coniunctio in the Azoth mandala?*

GAIA: *It would seem so, indeed. Most gratifying to see how well my images work. You see how good they are for you?*

STEPHAN: *Then—any further stages?*

PROFESSOR: *Yes. Then there was a deep sense of something fermenting under the surface, something really good, full of love. I discovered how to love nature in a way I never had. It was a vast expansion of just being present.*

GAIA: *That's good, but keep your feet planted firmly in my ground, dear Professor. Plants, birdsong, sunshine, wild water, that's what you need.*

PROFESSOR: *And then it changed again into some kind of distillate, almost, I would say, into some kind of elixir, which I now carry with me inwardly at all times. It only takes a drop from its inexhaustible supply and I enter the present moment most fully and richly. You know, I went for many long walks and I noticed how this feeling intensified when I was in the forest. I have to say now that this experiment on myself has had the most wonderful effect and very quickly indeed. I am a single datum of one who shows how the whole might be changed. Thank you both deeply from my deepest heart.*

STEPHAN: *That's very good indeed. You are almost there. But remember to keep in touch with the wind and the seasons.*

GAIA: *Which means here, really here: deep in my forests and jungles; my mountains and rivers; my oceans brimming over; my wildness scattered wide; my great billowing clouds above and my gentle lakes below; my species—every bird and insect; each microbe in the soil and in your guts; each pore, vestibule, and hidden chamber of matter. I am here in these places, waiting for you to find me. When you do, we will celebrate the sacred marriage—the coagulation.*

That is how much you need me and how much I need you. Find your way here and all will be well.

STEPHAN: *Well?*

PROFESSOR: *Now I know her . . . to speak figuratively.*

GAIA: *Any more?*

PROFESSOR: *Yes. Later, just for a moment, I felt completely whole. I was a whole in myself within a huge structure of nested wholes. The entire system is cosmic and yet has a lovely earthy feel to it. The sort of feeling I get when I've done some gardening in the community gardens just across the road from where I live.*

STEPHAN: *Congratulations, Herr Professor, or may I call you Andrew? It seems that you have arrived at last.*

PROFESSOR: *Most certainly, and I vow to do this work with alchemy and my science—Gaia alchemy—for the good of all at all times, places, and spaces.*

GAIA: *Nicely put. I'll work with this one. A nice little hatchling is he.*

STEPHAN: *Well, that's all we have time for in this broadcast. Thanks for listening. Thanks to my guests, Gaia and Andrew, for showing us most admirably how science, Gaia, and alchemy can work wonders together.*

May that wonder spread and spread fast and far and wide, before our time runs out.

And with that, good night.

15

The Fungus and the
Rose Garden

I would now like to see if we can use a different set of alchemical images just over a hundred years older than the Azoth mandala to explore a vitally important relationship between two markedly different biological kingdoms, without which life on land and hence our vastly biodiverse modern Gaia, would be impossible.

I do this because each model reveals its own particular treasures. As my friend once cautioned me in that noisy Totnes café, it could be too limiting to stay within the confines of one model. Seeing how the objective psyche produces different versions of itself within various alchemical images gives us a sense of the supremely deep, ancient intelligence of the objective psyche. We live within her planetary embodiment, inextricably bound to her biosphere. Her waters, air, and slowly shifting continents spread wide on her blue-and-white-marbled surface.

The model I have in mind involves a series of ten pictures from an alchemical text known as the *Rosarium Philosophorum* (The Rose Garden of the Philosophers) first published in Frankfurt in 1550. Jung writes about these pictures at length in his *Psychology of the Transference* (1983), and Edinger gives his own immensely helpful perspective on the images in his *The Mystery of the Coniunctio, Alchemical Image of Individuation* (1994b), but we'll begin our exploration out in nature.

If you can, find a rotting log outdoors, perhaps in your Gaia place, and peel off some of the softened wood. Do you see any areas of fine white or yellowish tracery—a fuzz or trail of cotton-like filaments, perhaps? These are mycelial networks belonging to fungi, not filaments in fact, but tubes through which flow the nuclei, mitochondria, ribosomes, and all the other cellular paraphernalia of these strange living organisms. These tubes are alive. They grow, spread, look for food, and behave with an eerie intelligence.

The particular fungus you have found is wood-rotting fungus. It gives you a sense of what a fungus is. It is a distributed organism without a center; a mass of dynamic, coherent, living tubes that explore, sense, modify, and react to their surroundings; an exploratory being that sends parts of itself to investigate nearby possibilities, news of which rapidly spreads to the entire tubular fungal network (fig. 15.1).

The particular fungi we are interested in live below ground in the soil and associate in deeply intimate ways with the roots of plants. These are the mycorrhizal (fungus-root) fungi. Some weave their tubes among plant root cells, wrapping themselves around them; others penetrate deep inside root cells without harm to either partner. Even though mycorrhizal fungi live mostly below ground, parts of their mycelial net-

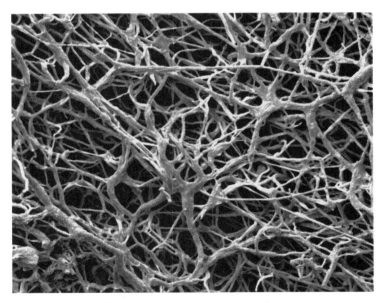

Figure 15.1. A network of mycelial tubes.
Reproduced with permission through Science Photo Library.

work spend a little time above ground as mushrooms that use the air for dispersing the fungus's spores. However, mushrooms are short lived. They soon rot back into the earth, perhaps to be devoured by their very own tubes.

The association between mycorrhizal fungi and plants is one of Gaia's most important symbioses. We call it a symbiosis because it involves a very close living together of two very different kinds of organism, each from a different kingdom of life—fungus and plant. The fungus feeds the plant with water and essential nutrients gathered from areas of the soil that plant roots have no hope of ever reaching, some very deep indeed near bedrock.

In exchange for this tubular door-to-door delivery service of life-giving nutrients, the plant gives the fungus some of the food it needs. This includes sugars and lipids forged when highly energetic photons from the sun tumble into its faraway leaves, powering the process of photosynthesis.

There would be virtually no multicellular life on land without this plant-fungus symbiosis. The continents would be mostly lichen covered with mosses here and there in the wetter areas. No trees, no herbs, no flowers, but plenty of bacteria. Instead, the world blossomed into today's amazing terrestrial biodiversity because of the symbiotic relationship between mycorrhizal fungi and plant roots—another love story from the world of biology.

Figure 15.2 (p. 242) shows the biology. You can see that there are two different kinds of mycorrhizal fungi. One kind, the ectomycorrhizal fungi, wrap their tubes around plant root cells without penetrating into them. The other type, the arbuscular mycorrhiza, penetrate deep inside plant roots. Once inside the cell, the fungus's tubes branch into a dendritic pattern (hence *arbuscular*) ending in many tiny tubes that deliver molecules to the plant cell with a high degree of precision in exchange for lipids and sugars from their host.

A great deal of complex coordination is needed for the arbuscular symbiosis to work. The plant embraces the fungal tubes with extensions of its cell membrane and together both create a new emergent domain somewhat akin to a placenta, with the difference that in this case the

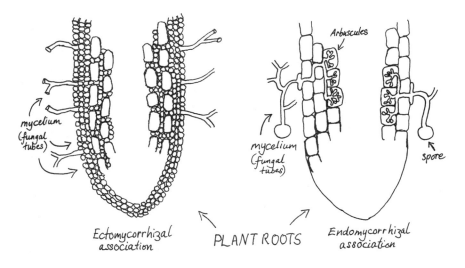

Figure 15.2. Two kinds of mycorrhizal fungi associating with plant roots.
Drawn by Julia Ponsonby.

nutrition goes both ways. The partners no doubt exchange carefully crafted chemical messages to coordinate what goes on between them to create the intimacy of this symbiotic dance that so deeply influences the habitability of our planet, an entanglement arguably as close to a good marriage as one gets in the biological world.

But how do we braid together these details of mycorrhizal biology with alchemical images from the *Rosarium* while at the same time weaving Gaia into the story? To do this we need to cultivate a koan-like, nonrational poetic attitude, in which reason plays a part without dominating with its inherently critical stance. When we reach this alchemical level of perception, we encounter an enhancement of being that can be experienced by anyone who undertakes the required effort, for nothing worthwhile comes for free.

I will share whatever meaning has been revealed to me, and I hope this enriches you as I have been enriched by unifying mycorrhizal science with the *Rosarium*. You can work with the science and these images in your own way; use them to chart your particular pathway into the rich trove of Gaian connection and insight they can offer you.

Does this Gaian alchemical brew of science and symbol help you find your own living style of Gaian awareness? If so, you'll feel a growing sense of the depth and meaning of your life and Gaia's as an interconnected whole, helping you to become better engaged in helping solve the global crisis peacefully and democratically.

So, if you are ready, we'll begin.

Think of what you've just been reading about the plant-fungus symbiosis as you gaze upon the images of the *Rosarium* (fig. 15.3, p. 244) in number order, cycling around them from one to ten and ten to one for just as long as it takes for you to notice a softening and an openness widening your perspective.

The centerpiece of the first image (image 1, fig. 15.4) is a fountain, the mandala fountain. This is the origin of all things, the birthplace of all inspiration, the source and energy of the urge for wholeness at all levels of life.

A central star gives rise to a two-headed dragon representing the primordial opposites, while the Sun and Moon are born from the star at the same time. From each dragon's head rich swirling vapors descend to earth where a new star is born as soon as each vapor trail touches the ground. The vapors on the right give rise to earth and air while those to the left produce fire and water. Hence, the four six-pointed stars emerging from the vapors represent the four alchemical elements, earth, air, fire, and water.

The earth then sprouts three lion's feet on which rests the mandala fountain, that wellspring of well-being and health, thrumming and thriving through the entire web of life on a healthy, fully restored planet. In our times, the flower atop the globe above the fountain could signify the blossoming of Gaian awareness. For me, the mandala fountain is born out of the earth from the lion's feet, which means that the vision of the mandala fountain is Gaia's central gift for us. The fountain gives us an earthy, life-giving water, which helps us explore and develop a down-to-earth, deeply ecological worldview and lifestyle.

This is no "being off with the fairies," for empirical evidence gathered by many who have worked with these images over the centuries with sincerity and dedication have found great happiness through

Figure 15.3. The images of the *Rosarium Philosophorum*.
Frankfurt 1550. Artist unknown.

Figure 15.4. Image 1 of the
Rosarium Philosophorum.

them and have come more fully and richly into the world's service as a result. We can discover this perspective ever more fully by living closely with these images alongside the rain, the clouds, and the denizens of air, soils, rocks, waters, and, for me as I write, even with my culture of single-celled microbes from my jungle pond brewing and thriving in a little jam jar on my windowsill.

This first image hints at what Gaia is up to: of what she offers and of what she wants to become. It is an image of the profound wholeness at the core of things, which we humans cannot fully understand but in which we are deeply implicated. The image works inwardly to heal us if we spend time gazing it, plumbing its depths as best we can. The water of the fountain is a liquid form of the Philosopher's Stone. The fountain itself is protected by the four Gaian elements. The Sun and Moon also reside within this sanctuary along with the central star, representing the transpersonal self. The fountain rests on lion claws deeply connected to the Earth. You can almost hear the splashing of the water and you feel yourself longing to drink of that fountain. The taste of that water is divine. We can cultivate our Gaian consciousness by working with alchemical images in this way for planetary healing and personal transformation, for the two are indissolubly linked.

Image 2 (fig. 15.5) represents the emergence of opposites out of the primordial Sun and Moon and the energy that flows between them so that things can start to develop. Notice that both figures are clothed, and that they are showing each other beautiful flowers on long stalks. Notice also how a dove descends into the middle of these stalks offering its own flower to the clasped hands of the king and queen, Sol and Luna. We encountered this iconography earlier in the *Tabula Smaragdina* and in the conjunction images of the Azoth mandala. I see the dove as a spirit or consciousness from the objective psyche, which blesses the union of the opposites that search for new ways of being, no matter the context or situation in which the union takes place.

In his rendering, Edinger tells us that the dove represents a pair of opposites, the Holy Spirit and Aphrodite, the "mother of all desires." In this case, it is a desire that is at the same time—as he says—an Annunciation of the Holy Ghost. Desire is about fulfilling a wish for pleasure, while an annunciation "is an assignment of a difficult task—it's

Figure 15.5. Image 2 of the *Rosarium Philosophorum*.

an opus." At our best, these energies manifest as strong desires to develop psychologically as much as we can, allowing us to experience our place in Gaia from the deepest and widest perspective we are capable of.

Now let's bring the image down to earth by seeing how it helps us to connect with the qualities of the mycorrhizal symbiosis. When the spore of a mycorrhizal fungus germinates and begins to grow, it needs to find a plant partner pretty soon or it will die. It needs a plant root to connect with and the plant root needs the fungus. They need each other desperately. It's a matter of survival. They simply cannot live without each other.

The plant sends out chemical messages in the soil that call the fungus, and perhaps the fungus also sends messages to encourage messages from the plant. That they often find each other quickly is testament to the fact that their relationship has been refined by natural selection over hundreds of millions of years.

In this image there is already an intimate connection between the plant, the King, who is the Sun, and the Moon, the Queen, who is the fungus. They test their compatibility by holding hands and by wafting flowers in full bloom under each other's noses in an exchange of chemical scents and messages. Psyche adds her presence and her blessing in the descending dove behind whom is the six-rayed star, reminding us of a mysterious intelligence involved in the process.

Image 3 (fig. 15.6) shows the King and Queen, plant and fungus, now naked holding each other's outstretched flowers. The chemical signaling has worked and the pair now deeply recognize each other. In their nakedness they see each other just as they are and this ancient familiarity unleashes a torrent of meaningful chemical speech and communication between the two partners.

The dove is still here, but now its flower has matured into a spherical arrangement of fused elongated seed pods that have not yet set their seeds. This signifies a maturation of psyche in the growing interaction between plant and fungus. There is a "Yes" between the symbionts that opens doors to deepening the symbiotic relationship as fungal cells and plant roots cells begin their intimate relationship while maintaining their separate identities.

In image 4 (fig. 15.7) the King and Queen descend into a hexagonal

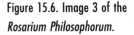

Figure 15.6. Image 3 of the *Rosarium Philosophorum.*

bath holding each other's flowers while the seedpod held by the dove sets its seeds into the bathwater, signifying that psyche adds the ingredient of sentience to the developing symbiosis between fungus and plant. King-plant and Queen-fungus begin to submerge themselves in the water of deep relationship as the boundaries between them begin to merge. The fungus's tubes branch and branch within the plant root cell, and the root cell surrounds each branching fungal pathway with a cloak of mucus held within a sheath connected to its own cell membrane. The result looks rather like fingers (fungus) in a glove (plant), but at this stage these "fingers" and "gloves" are not yet very well developed. Notice how the King and Queen have separate crowns. This indicates that the symbiosis between plant and fungus is not yet complete, that they have not yet entered into the fullness of the symbiosis needed for their mutual survival, a symbiosis that is an absolute requirement for a healthy Gaia with multicellular life writ large on her land surfaces.

In image 5 (fig. 15.8) we've reached the central image of the series where the King and Queen, plant and fungus make love. The interdigitation between the plant and fungal cells—the "fingers" in "gloves"—now

Figure 15.7 Image 4 of the *Rosarium Philosophorum*.

Figure 15.8 Image 5 of the *Rosarium Philosophorum*.

reaches its fullest extent. Intimate chemical and physical connections and exchanges take place between plant and fungus in the symbiotic union of their cells. The dove has vanished, so in what follows it will be harder to discern the work of psyche, though it is always present. The crowns of the two royals are still separate, and the union is taking place in some sort of underground lake whose rocky lid has been cut away so that we can see their close embraces.

As I ponder all this in the beauty and wondrous wildness of my jungle, Jung appears once again.

JUNG: *So you have been thinking of my collection of original alchemical manuscripts bound in pig skin?*

STEPHAN: *Yes, I can imagine what it must be like to spend a long time with an original alchemical manuscript. I have a fantasy of doing just that.*

JUNG: *And even though you don't have access to such a thing, you feel its quality. You feel it even now as you sit and write?*

STEPHAN: *Yes*

JUNG: *That is because these things are timeless. They come from the realm beyond time and space, from the collective unconscious.*

STEPHAN: *But at the same time this is also alchemical Gaia, is it the things we see every day, even the most horrible, difficult things?*

JUNG: *Yes, you can find the unus mundus everywhere.*

STEPHAN: *The point is that the alchemical symbols have brought us here, to the place where Gaia's living psyche becomes the physical reality of our planet, majestically clothed in exuberant biodiversity.*

JUNG: *Yes—now you have it. It is indeed something like that.*

STEPHAN: *This is perhaps as far as I can go.*

JUNG *(puffing pipe and giving me a very twinkly smile): For the moment, yes. For the moment.*

How I would like him to stay. But this is not to be, for with a friendly wave he turns and walks back into eternity.

Image 6 (fig. 15.9) shows the King and Queen, plant and fungus, unified as one being in an oblong tomb, which is what the watery cave in the previous image has become. Here they meld even more pro-

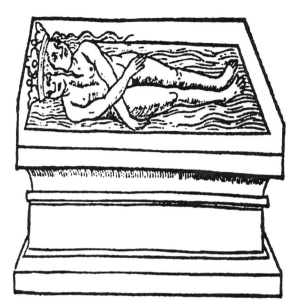

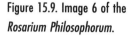

Figure 15.9. Image 6 of the
Rosarium Philosophorum.

foundly in the good darkness of their deep earthy underground union.
They share the same two legs, but although melded, their torsos are
distinct. Their heads appear to be completely separate but are unified
by one single crown, which girdles both heads.

Now the plant-fungus has become a single organism, which is still
a two in which unity and duality are perfectly reconciled—a two and
yet a one. The first moments of this crucial symbiosis, without which
our consciousness and the modern biosphere would not exist, happened around 500 million years ago in the geological period called the
Devonian when the first plant/fungi organisms were colonizing the
continents. The association was developed into many hugely successful
modes of plant being, some small and close to the ground with deli-
cately succulent leaves and tiny flowers, others growing to the size of
immense trees with thick densities of leaf and wood.

In image 7 (fig. 15.10) a small naked child appears from the union
of the plant-fungus symbiosis, from the Sol King and Luna Queen.
The child flies upward with arms outstretched into dense cloud mass-
ing in great white towering billows above the tomb. By this point the

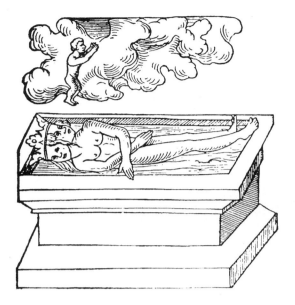

Figure 15.10. Image 7 of the
Rosarium Philosophorum.

plant-fungus symbiosis is so successful that plants are growing in a vast, biodiverse profusion wherever they can on the continents.

For me, the ascending child corresponds to the myriads of cloud-seeding chemicals that many plants release into the air from their leaves. Many of these chemicals consist of a central carbon ring or two, onto which a few other chemical beings like hydrogen and oxygen atoms are often attached. Cloud-seeding chemicals often smell good to us and have medicinal qualities that help us relax and feel at peace. These are the plants' chemical children, which literally rise up into the air where they seed dense, white, planet-cooling clouds, thereby helping to regulate Gaia's temperature. The same chemicals also seed rainfall. Of course, by *plant* we actually mean the "plant-fungus" symbiosis, and by *chemical children* we are referring to cloud condensation nuclei, or CCN as they are known in science (fig. 15.11).

Every day plant-fungi symbionts release countless numbers of their cloud-seeding chemical children over vast expanses of Gaia's terrestrial ecosystems including intact tropical forests such as those of Latin America, Africa, and Southeast Asia.

Image 8 (fig. 15.12) shows rain seeded by their cloud-seeding

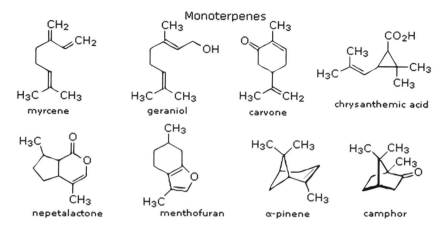

Figure 15.11. Cloud Condensation Nuclei (CCN)—cloud-seeding chemicals, released by plants into the atmosphere.

chemicals falling onto the King-Queen or plant-fungus. Thus is born the planetary water that cycles back and forth between images 7 and 8.

Some recent science suggests that forests deep inside a continent, such as the Amazon, bring in water-laden air from a faraway ocean, in this case the Atlantic. This is the biotic pump hypothesis of Makarieva and Gorshkov (2010), which works like this: water vapor in the air

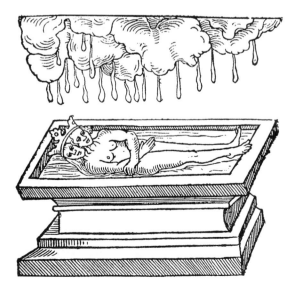

Figure 15.12. Image 8 of the *Rosarium Philosophorum.*

Figure 15.13. Image 9 of the *Rosarium Philosophorum*.

above the forest interior condenses into drops of liquid water around cloud-seeding chemicals; the removal of a gas (water vapor) from the air drops the air pressure so much that higher pressure air saturated with water vapor rolls in from the faraway ocean over the forest, filling the partial vacuum; the clouds produce rain, which keeps the vegetation alive. Inwardly, we can experience this as a rain of wisdom, the return of the star and the dove, which remain invisible.

In image 9 (fig. 15.13) notice how a bird appears out of the ground in front of the tomb and how this bird is speaking to another bird close by. This image suggests to me that Gaia's emergent intelligence intensifies when a huge variety of communication channels open up among her species: birdsong; changing patterns on the skins of squid, octopus, and cuttlefish; chemical communication among a host of organisms such as bacteria, ants, and termites; bee waggle dances; and in our case, words, both written and spoken.

And so at last we come to image 10 (fig. 15.14): the Rebis.

Now the fungus-plant, Queen-King, or Luna-Sol rises from the tomb. This being is still symbiotic, still a hermaphrodite with two heads, still girdled by a single crown. The Rebis has sprouted wings and holds a crowned snake to the viewer's right and a vase to the viewer's left, from which emerge three more crowned snakes.

The Rebis floats just above the earth on an upturned crescent moon, which is gazed at by a bird very much like one in the last image

Figure 15.14. Image 10 of the *Rosarium Philosophorum.*

sitting happily on the ground. The Rebis represents to me the emergence of entirely integrated ecological communities all over the planet at all scales thanks to the plant-fungus symbiosis. The snakes are Gaia's biodiversity, and there seems to be a circuit of psyche from the bird to the moon to the earth and back to the bird, which grounds the Rebis in the earth, even though it floats above it poised on the moon, which represents a connection with the unconscious. To the Rebis's right, sprouting from the ground, is a strange plant with many human faces, representing the many ways and modes of life—both human and other than human—in which the Rebis manifests its profound wholeness.

Contemplating the Rebis with a Gaian alchemical perspective can take us into Gaia beyond words. This blessed state of mind is accessible to anyone willing to work with alchemical images and science as we are doing here to promote a profound coming to our senses, a deep ecological awakening. I and many others in these darkening times are convinced that only when each person experiences such an awakening in their own individual life will we have any hope of avoiding the worst effects of the global crisis. Only then will we be able to find ways of living well with our animate Earth. Only then will we discover how to live a Gaian alchemical life.

16

Living a Gaian Alchemical Life

The Ecosophical Tree

One afternoon many years ago I was walking with my dear friend the philosopher, activist, and teacher Per Ingvar Haukeland. We were discussing the "apron diagram" (fig. 16.1) devised by our friend, the philosopher Arne Naess, for exploring the four levels in his deep ecology approach.

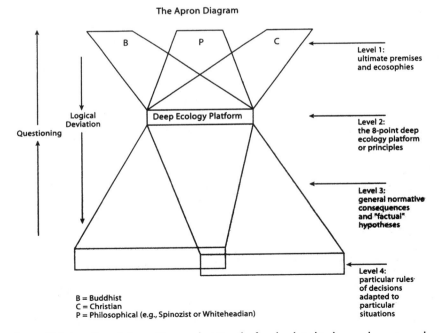

Figure 16.1. Arne Naess's Apron Diagram depicting the four levels in his deep ecology approach.

As we dodged fallen trees and granite boulders in the wild country near the cabin in the Norwegian mountains where Julia, Oscar, and I were staying for a few months, Per Ingvar told me that he had created a much more accessible expression of Arne's important idea, since the apron diagram can be difficult to interpret.

I think you can see why: the apron is not too easy to understand until the triangles below the rectangle holding the words "Deep Ecology Platform" suddenly flip into three dimensions. Roughly speaking, Level 1 refers to deep experiences of the numinosity of nature. In the context of this book, we could say that these are experiences of Mercurius as nondual Gaia. Level 2 refers to eight statements (known as the eight points of the deep ecology platform), which people with many varied Level 1 deep experiences tend to have in common. Level 3 refers to exploring our possibilities for living a life consistent with one's Level 1 deep experiences, and Level 4 to one's concrete actions and lifestyles in the world in ways that harmonize with the previous three levels.

"A tree would be better than the apron diagram," Per Ingvar explains as we walk upstream beside a small tumbling brook. Its lively, gurgling speech braids in and out of our conversation. He goes on: "The roots of the tree are Level 1, the trunk is Level 2, the branches are Level 3, and the fruits are Level 4."

This reformulation of Arne's apron diagram struck me greatly at the time, for the tree is a powerful archetypal symbol that, as I later discovered, features prominently in alchemy.

Ecosophy is another term coined by Arne Naess, the playful yet austere mountaineering philosopher who taught at Schumacher College several times in the 1990s. The word is composed of two ancient Greek words: *Oikos*—the earth household—and *Sophia*, which is wisdom. Ecosophy is about cultivating our own wise ways of living and relating with our planetary Oikos—with Gaia.

Arne coined the word *ecosophy* in part as a contrast to the word *ecology,* which indicates the logical or scientific study of the earth household. Ecology on its own gives us detailed and interesting facts about nature, whereas the word *deep* invokes a connection with the realm of values. When we place *deep* in front of *ecology* we get *deep ecology* in

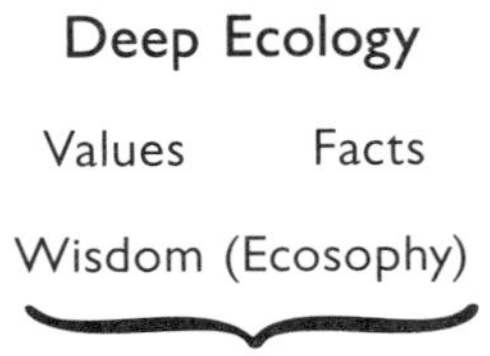

Deep Ecology

Values   Facts

Wisdom (Ecosophy)

Figure 16.2. Ecosophy as the union of facts and values with respect to nature.

which we reunite facts and values, healing the 400-year-old Cartesian split within ourselves and between our culture and nature (fig. 16.2).

Like Jung, Arne emphasized the importance of the individual and invited each person to develop their own ecosophy, their own ecological wisdom. His own ecosophy he called ecosophy T after his cabin in the pristine heights of the mountain Hallingskarvet in south-central Norway at the place called Tvergastein—the "place of crossed stones." I have been there several times. It is a place of magisterial beauty, which strongly nurtures my ecosophical development even now as I remember it, and I am always deeply grateful to Arne and his wife, Kit Fai, for taking Julia and me there many years ago.

Per and I walk deeper into the forest, following the stream until we reach the high country. It's more open here—scattered trees—great views of vast forest down below open up.

"If one sees oneself as a tree," he says to me, "the roots are deep experiences that one has in nature. These roots uphold you in the deepness of the ground and the roots spread out and so the tree stands strong in the ground. The roots go deep into the ground and spread out seeking diversity in one's experiences of the animate Earth." (See fig. 16.3.)

We come upon a bog and navigate carefully around it. It doesn't pay to get stuck up to one's knees in such places.

Per continues to expound upon his ideas. "So this first aspect, which is connected to the roots of the ecosophical tree, is our depth of experience. Arne spoke about 'spontaneous experiences'—those meetings that we have in nature with our more than human neighbors, those deepening encounters, which do something to us and make us in some ways more deeply who we are. There is also depth of awareness or depth of consciousness of the values attached to these deep experiences. We look back on the experiences to see what kind of values grow out from them."

A pair of ravens fly overhead and call out their agreement with several deep throaty croaks. Encouraged by this and by the vista of a huge lake deep in the pine forest far below, Per Ingvar continues: "These experiences don't only go back in time, but also look forward into the future. There's something visionary about them. They give a direction to where you're going, to the choices you're making. So the depth of awareness or the depth of consciousness is what I see as an aspect of the trunk of the tree. It's what brings the tree together, the roots and the branches. The trunk is a platform or a value base that one builds one's life on. Arne and his friend the American philosopher George Sessions created the deep ecology platform—Level 2—in the apron diagram, which is the trunk of the ecosophical tree."

We walk deeper into the forest, going ever more steeply uphill, following the stream in and out of tangled shrubs and open stretches of low grasses and moss-covered rocks.

Figure 16.3. The Ecosophical Tree as conceived by Per Ingvar Haukeland. Drawn by Deirdre Hyde.

"Now we move into the third aspect of the tree," says Per. "The branches, which spread out into different areas. You sit in different branches as you explore the consequences of your deep experiences. What is it that inhibits us? What enhances our vision to realize our values in action? So you could say that the branches represent a planning stage regarding what you're doing in different aspects of your life. You explore the different branches, perhaps as a family person or perhaps as a student or a consumer or politician and so on. You have to integrate the values and visions from the roots and trunk into these different branches."

We walk in silence for a long while, basking in the wonder of the wild freedom around us and in the warmth of our friendship. Eventually we walk into a small valley and encounter a massive granite boulder. It's the size of a house. Skirting around it, we come across a tranquil lake, modest in size but rich in qualities, full of deep black water. Behind the lake, tumbling granite cliffs give birth to a plateau that feels intimately close.

We stop here for the night and set up our tents.

We make a campfire and drink tea as the sun begins its descent into the night.

Per Ingvar stokes up the fire and sends glowing orange sparks into the blackness.

"The fourth level concerns the fruits of the tree," he says. "These are concrete actions, decisions made in concrete situations in your daily lived experience. Now you're living your values and your visions."

The firelight lights up the trees around us in a warm flickering of orange glow. Hosts of bright stars appear in the rich dark velvet of the sky.

"I have nine or ten different ways of describing the ecosophical tree," Per says. "We can also ponder how the tree takes nourishment from the air as well as from the ground or from the earth and soil. I look at the sap of the tree as its life stream, its creative force, which is deep joy: a source of change, of inspiration in one's life that Spinoza calls *hilaritas*."

Owls hoot around us as the night deepens.

"This joy of being alive nourishes a deep harmony between our deep experiences and how we live our daily actions," he tells me. "This is the Tree of Life image applied to ecosophy."

We cook our meal on the fire and talk softly awhile of the enfolding darkness and of the bright crescent moon that has just appeared over the mountain's rim.

Soon enough, tired out by our long day's walk in the soft silences of these wild northern lands, we find our tents and dream deeply of sheltered fjords and Arctic snowstorms.

The archetypal image of the tree has brought insight, solace, and wisdom to humanity over many long ages. We learn from Jung that in alchemy "The tree is an instrument of transformation," and that "The Visio Ariseli speaks of 'this most precious tree of whose fruits he who eats shall never hunger.'" Jung also informs us that "The tree is often represented as metallic, usually golden. Its connection with the seven metals implies a connection with the seven planets, so that the tree becomes a world tree." He also tells us that "The alchemical Mercurius is the life principle of the Tree." Eliade says that "The ruler of the world lives at the top of the world tree."

From these and many other such passages in the alchemical literature one can see that the tree image arises from the collective unconscious as a numinous symbol of what psyche aims to achieve within consciousness, namely a realization of the Self: our personal individuated experience of the transpersonal unity of psyche as Gaia. This is our ecosophy, our unique ecological wisdom.

The tree is an instrument of transformation whose fruits banish all hunger, both material and spiritual. The tree as ruler of the world. The world tree made of gold sporting metallic fruit. Mercurius as the life principle of the world tree. Spend a little while absorbing these images, and when you are ready, allow me to invite you on a journey to the alchemical tree.

Go to your Gaia place, or if that is not possible find somewhere quiet where you can be undisturbed for a while.

Breathe calmly and feel the peace of nature descend into you as much as you can.

Imagine that you are walking in a great wild forest and come across a small clearing at the center of which you spy the spreading shape of a tree.

As you look more closely you realize that this is no ordinary tree, for this tree is made of gold. At the tips of its seven branches you see seven metal stars glowing brightly.

In the leftmost branch is a star made of gold. Next on the right is a star made of polished iron, and next to that a brightly burnished star of copper.

Then, at the apex of the tree is a star made of silvery mercury. Shining ripples riffle its surface.

Next a star of lead, dull on the outside but shining metal just below the surface.

Now a star made of tin, a soft metal glowing brightly like silver with a yellowish hue.

Finally we encounter a star made of freshly polished silver, a great mirror onto the world.

All seven metal stars receive their qualities and their lights from the cosmos into which they return their metallic glows with deepest gratitude.

Feel those stars within you. They are your personal qualities given you at birth by the cosmos itself.

Dwell with each in turn.

Gold is your drive, your intellect, your generosity of spirit, and your outgoing nature associated with the Sun.

Copper is your ability to feel and value, to love deeply, associated with Venus.

Iron is your ruggedness, your stubbornness and willingness to stick at things, your determination.

Mercury is the mysterious wholeness within you that defies description but which is that slippery happiness associated with the planet Mercury.

Lead is your conservatism, your ability to stay rooted in one place doing one thing for the good of the whole. Dull on the outside yet shining inside, this aspect of yourself is associated with the planet Saturn.

Tin, your ability to be flexible and to flow like water in all situations is associated with the planet Jupiter.

Silver is your dream world, the inner world of psyche. This is your deep intuitive mind associated with the Moon, which knows and loves the subtle paradoxes of nature both inner and outer.

You feel the metallic roots of the alchemical tree going deep into the soil, which is the anima mundi, the soul of the world, gifting nourishment to all beings from those deep nutritious depths.

Now bring your vision of the alchemical tree—of the world tree—into your Gaia place, which you visualize as best you can if you are not there.

Let all the metals and planets swirl into every atom and molecule of yourself and your Gaia place, filling you both with the deepest meaning and value of which you are now fully conscious.

Dwell in this state for as long as feels comfortable.

This is nondual Gaia—Gaia Mercurius.

Your Gaia Philosopher's Stone.

You are whole.

You are Gaia.

Now that we have experienced something of its qualities we are ready to place a well-known version of the alchemical tree published in the seventeenth century (attributed to Basil Valentine) alongside Per Ingvar's ecosophical tree to compare the two (fig. 16.4).

In the alchemical image on the right we see two philosopher-alchemists, Senior and Adolphus, conversing at the foot of the alchemical tree with three roots. Between them is a downward-pointing triangle, with the symbol for Sulphur on the left-hand angle beside Senior and for Salt on the angle to the right beside Adolphus. Mercury is on the central angle pointing down into the ground, to the roots. Mercury pointing into the Earth maps very nicely to the level of deep experience in the ecosophical tree, to our moments of nondual Gaia, for it is in those moments, alchemically speaking, that Gaia Mercurius appears in what Arne called our spontaneous experiences.

But deep experience is just one aspect of Gaia Mercurius, since he is composed of four aspects that come together. The fourfold awareness he brings is completely comprehensive, giving us access to a totally

Figure 16.4. Per Ingvar's Ecosophical Tree by Deirdre Hyde (*top*) above the Alchemical Tree, attributed to Basil Valentine, fifteenth century (*bottom*).

well-rounded and holistic experience of life and Gaia. Jung points out how this quaternity is constituted by two pairs of dyads, such as feeling-intuition on the one side and thinking-sensation on the other, which have to produce a healing transcendence from their relationship for humans and planet to be well.

Since Jung writes that the "The fourfold Mercurius is also the (alchemical) tree or its *spiritus vegetativus*," the four aspects of Mercurius are found in the living oneness of both trees, alchemical and ecophilosophical, appearing as their roots, trunk, branches, and fruit. Gaia Mercurius comes to life when our realization in daily life of the fourfold unity of matter and psyche is such that our deep experiences, our values, our life possibilities, and our actions come together into an integrated whole.

Senior and Adolphus engage in a lively debate at the level of the trunk of the alchemical tree. Senior has the sun behind him, and sulphurous words tumble out of his mouth. He holds an ax with which he could easily cut down the tree should he wish to, such is the impetuosity of unbridled solar intellect and its drive for rational knowledge. Adolphus points to the tree trunk and offers his own words in the discourse. The moon behind him imbues him with the mysterious spirit of the wide open salty sea of the collective unconscious and the anima mundi as he balances Senior's intellectual attitude with a knowledge of dreams and of the deepest recesses of the psyche.

As they talk together by the trunk of the alchemical tree they explore a solid base of principles and values for action, which corresponds to the deep ecology platform of the ecosophical tree, which is Level 2 in Arne's apron diagram.

ADOLPHUS: *What is our relationship to this tree?*
SENIOR: *Although I have an ax, I would never cut it down.*
    He raises his right hand in the tree's defense.
ADOLPHUS: *I too would never dream of it.*
SENIOR: *This tree has intrinsic value simply because it exists.*
ADOLPHUS: *As do all the trees in the forest.*
SENIOR: *Yes, and all human cultures, which dwell peacefully with Gaia.*
    They too have intrinsic value.

ADOLPHUS: *We must only cut trees down if we really need them and only after we have asked their permission.*

SENIOR: *Indeed so, yet our human population is growing and we are cutting down far too many trees because of our huge need for wood to make things of life.*

ADOLPHUS: *So it's clear that we have to reduce our impact on the forest.*

SENIOR: *To do that we must radically change how we perceive nature and we must change the power structures that make us cut down forests out of pure greed for more and more wealth and hence more and more wood.*

ADOLPHUS: *And since we clearly perceive and agree with all the above, we are obliged to act to create a world where we humans and Gaia are at peace.*

We leave Senior and Adolphus to their discussions and move further up the alchemical tree. Notice how it spreads out into seven branches with their tips emblazoned with the seven metallic stars we encountered in our last meditation. The branches of the alchemical tree sport an upward-pointing triangle, which corresponds to the exploration of lifestyle options and situations in the ecosophical tree. This is Arne's Level 3.

The stars on the alchemical tree are its fruits, of which it was said by the seventeenth-century alchemist Benedictus Figulus that they are "the golden apples of the Hesperides to be puck't from the best philosophical tree." Jung tells us that the alchemical tree is the entire opus (of individuation) and the fruits are its results. On the ecosophical tree the fruits are our concrete actions in the world, which, when ripe, fall and decompose into the ground of being, nourishing the deep experiences of all. But how do the metallic stars—the fruits of the alchemical tree—map onto the fruits of the ecosophical tree?

I puzzled over this for a while with no answer, so I went out into my Gaia place—into my jungle—to ask for help. It was a mild, rainy, overcast December day here in Devon, and yet my jungle glowed with warmth and meaning. The complex interlacing patterns of bramble, ivy, apple trees, moss, and lichen invited me to be calm, to relax, to let go of clutching for an answer.

⬦⬦⬦⬦⬦ *A Conversation with Jeffrey Kiehl* ⬦⬦⬦⬦⬦

STEPHAN: How does one live a Gaian alchemical life?

JEFFREY: Mindfulness as a way of life is the keyword. First, we have to know that there is such a thing as a Gaian alchemical way of life. We need to meditate on the alchemical images, working with them by going around the Azoth mandala feeling and experiencing the images.

STEPHAN: Contributing to restoring nature—rewilding—is a very important part of a Gaian alchemical life?

JEFFREY: Yes. We need to develop the ability to imagine what land would look like if it were rewilded because we have to provide a viable future for the children. And not just human children, but the baby birds and other nonhuman children that are being born out there. It's only by bringing internal balance within ourselves that we're going to rebalance with Gaia in a co-creative way. We can try to use our technology and science to engineer things. But that's not enough, we really have to get back to what we've lost, which is our ability to see the living intrinsic value in the world and to be able to imagine from there into the future. We are dealing with a deep psychological wound that began centuries ago that's never been healed. It's only deepened. And the deeper the wound in us, the bigger the wound that we create in the planet, like the destruction of the Amazon that's going on right now. That's just a reflection of our deep inner psychic wound. So do I expect everybody to heal their inner wounds? No, but I think that's the task of those of us who are awake enough to care and who have that sense of quality and can imagine what the planet would look like if it were rewilded alongside our ecological food growing. If enough people work on this, great change can happen. Jung said sometimes you look out on the world and you see bad things happening and you don't know what to do. Maybe it's at that time that you turn to the unconscious and ask it what we should do.

And he said, sometimes the unconscious tells us individually what to do. Sometimes it tells groups what to do. And sometimes it tells an entire world what to do. And so that's another part of our work: we need to listen to psyche, to listen to the unconscious, to listen to Earth, to Gaia.

◇◇◇◇◇◇◇◇◇◇◇◇◇◇◇◇◇◇◇◇◇◇◇◇◇◇◇◇◇◇

I sit on the small mossy bench by the dark old limestone wall laced with ivy, so often transformed for me by Imagination into an exotic lost temple in the ancient jungles of India. I listen to Gaia and remember a poem by Rabindranath Tagore about the tree of life, a prose poem that takes us into the very heart of deep ecology, of alchemy, of Gaia:

> *Not for me is the love that knows no restraint, but like the*
> *   foaming wine that having burst its vessel in a moment would*
> *   run to waste.*
> *Send me the love which is cool and pure like your rain that*
> *   blesses the thirsty earth and fills the homely earthen jars.*
> *Send me the love that would soak down into the center of being,*
> *   and from there would spread like the unseen sap through the*
> *   branching tree of life, giving birth to fruits and flowers.*
> *Send me the love that keeps the heart still with the fullness of*
> *   peace.*
> "Fruit Gathering," LXIV

I close my eyes and visualize the metallic alchemical tree once more, allowing its living quality to shine into me, taking me beyond my limited ego into a clear space of pure being. I offer my question to the alchemical tree and to the great elder tree in my jungle at the same time. A long pause ensues—an extended sense of inner adjustment, as when one slowly accommodates one's foot into a new shoe when trying it on for the first time.

An answer comes easily and softly from the alchemical tree and from my elder tree at the same time. Both speak the same soft, gentle answer.

It is given to me to understand that each fruit on the ecosophical tree contains an entire metallic alchemical tree within it complete with the seven metal stars. Furthermore, the Azoth mandala is also in each fruit since each ray of the Azoth mandala's seven-rayed star links to a metal and hence to its associated planet: lead to Saturn; tin to Jupiter; iron to Mars; gold to the Sun; copper to Venus; mercury (quicksilver) to Mercury; and silver to the Moon. Each metal is a symbol for a certain kind of insight, to a psychological attitude or disposition. Remember what Hillman said: alchemical language helps us to get away from the reductionist/mechanistic cultural complex of our culture, opening up subtle qualities that our heavily conditioned rational minds are not equipped to perceive.

We grow the fruits of our ecosophical tree when we realize that the qualities of the seven metals (and hence of the seven planets in the Azoth mandala) appear in each of its fruits, melding and ripening the fruits into actions inspired by our deep experiences of nondual Gaia, of Gaia Mercurius as he appears in each shifting moment of our daily living.

Each action, each situation, requires us to respond by bringing forth a unique blend of our seven metals. Some actions need more iron, some more silver. Others will need ample lashings of copper; others will demand the heaviness of lead. Sometimes our gold will need to shine forth, at other times the flexibility of tin will be needed, and yet other situations will require us to bring forth the magic of mercury into the world.

Let's imagine that we have decided to start a green business venture of some kind. We'll need iron willpower to make it happen, and the love of copper to bring our vision of service to our community. We'll need the flexibility of tin to adapt to changing circumstances, and we'll find that people will respond well to our sunny, golden enthusiasm about the project. We'll make sure to cultivate a good relationship with our silvery moon as we pay attention to our dreams and to the intuitive ideas she gives us about the enterprise. We'll need the heavy, stolid staying power of lead to see us through, and then for sure Mercurius will appear in moments of deep realization about the meaning of our business for helping to bring about a deep ecological society in which everyone is discovering their ecological self. Only then will we have found the love, the true happiness of which Tagore speaks in his prose poem.

The balance of our seven metals will shift according to which branch of the ecosophical tree we find ourselves in each of our life's situations. Mercury will dominate when we meditate, copper (Venus) when we look after our children. Lead (Saturn) will come to the fore when we study, and silver (the Moon) when we ponder the meaning of our dreams. Perhaps the Sun will predominate when we bring enthusiasm to a situation, and iron (Mars) when our willpower is required.

To live a Gaian alchemical life is to live within a unified reality of the physical world of rocks, plants, animals, other living beings, air, and water while simultaneously experiencing the inner symbolic, alchemical intimations, and numinous meanings of these very same entities. When the outer and inner worlds blend together we experience deep moments of true happiness. These are moments when the living reality of psyche appears and we live in the center of a mandala of meaning in which everything participates in the world's animacy. These states of wider consciousness come upon us when we are living lives that nurture Gaia, including our fellow humans, as much as possible. When we each see ourselves "as a citizen and servant of the world, a child of Father Sun and Mother Earth," as Giordano Bruno said. When we embrace this way of living, we consume less, emit fewer greenhouse gasses, and focus on growing the immaterial treasures in our lives: our insight, our capacity to love, our innate yearning to be whole. This is Gaia Mercurius—the fruit of Gaia alchemy—the Philosopher's Stone.

17

Experiencing Gaia Mercurius

My body is the Holy Mandala itself,
Wherein reside the Buddhas of all Times.
With their blessing I am freed
From all needs and attachments.
By day and night I offer to them;
Happy am I to do without material things.

JETSUN MILAREPA OF TIBET

Whatever the wise seek, is in Mercurius.

C. G. JUNG [1944] 1981

Mercurius, the patron saint of alchemy, the principle of transformation, is present at the beginning and at the end of the alchemical work, and so it seems fitting to end this book with a pilgrimage in his honor. So I set off into the forest behind the college aiming for my redwood Gaia place, one of my more distant Gaia locations. I begin by walking through Newground Plantation, a field planted with Western Red Cedars about fifty years ago. It's a dark, sombre place at first glance, but after a while it grows on you. There's lots of bare ground where almost nothing grows because of the deep shade cast by the trees, but where a few big trees have been harvested there are largish islands of light. These explode with greenness, hosting vibrant plant communities including big ferns with centipede-like leaves whose earliest ancestors first appeared in the Devonian period around 360 million years ago with the help of mycorrhizal fungal partners in their roots. As I saunter through the trees, I find something unexpected.

A mandala in the depths of the forest.

It's about three meters in diameter bounded by large curvaceous pine branches. In the middle are two large, twisted pine roots, one atop of the other. Pine branches, rocks, and other bits and pieces from the forest lie carefully scattered among its sacred precincts. It's beautiful, and I give thanks to whoever made it.

I find myself slowly circumambulating around the mandala clockwise over and over again, gazing deeply at the two pine root stumps at its center. These change shape as I walk round. A growling leopard turns into the head of a bison, which turns into the head of a capybara (those giant South American guinea pigs), then into strange shapes with wings I can't quite make out, all communicating a deep earthy wholeness.

As I walk around the mandala it speaks to me with the forest's benevolent voice. I walk ever more slowly, giving even more attention to the mandala's colors and changing shapes.

The mandala fills me with energy. After a few more circumambulations, it spins me off toward my redwood Gaia place. I become a tracker as I go, tracking Gaia, tracking the Azoth mandala, tracking roe deer, rarely seen now in these woods as I set off deeper into the forest.

I walk slowly, looking for deer spoor on the ground, but there are no signs at all. The relaxed concentration needed for tracking dissolves my boundaries and I meld into the woods, feeling my way into Gaia and into the Azoth mandala as I go.

All of a sudden, I find myself walking inside the first of the Azoth mandala's rays—calcination—whose qualities now saturate me with a deep sense of letting go of my stuck patterns of thought. As I walk deeper into the forest the ground and the trees before me become saturated with the next ray of the Azoth mandala—dissolution—into whose qualities I walk as if I were a piece of cloth being dyed a pale purple with every slow step. Still no sign of deer or their spoor. The forest transforms again into the red ray of the Azoth mandala—separation—and I intuit something of its subtle meanings as I walk. Now the vision expands, and I see huge Azoth mandala rays gently moving over the entirety of Gaia's surface, each one enfolding me as it passes through the forest, filling me with its qualities as I make my way toward my redwood Gaia place. The vision shows me that the center of this huge Gaian Azoth mandala lies in southern Africa where humans first appeared.

As I approach my redwood Gaia place the ray of distillation sweeps over the woods, soaking me in a deep intuitive knowledge of Gaia Mercurius, with his quicksilver ability to respond with grace and feeling to each transforming moment of life in just the right way with his liberating gift of nondual Gaian awareness. I search for deer tracks and dung pellets as I walk in the spring sunshine among the young broadleaves. There are bluebells in full flower. Still no signs of deer.

At last I reach the coppiced redwood, a powerful Gaia place where six tall redwood spires reach for the sky. I clamber into the sitting place six feet off the ground, perched in the middle of these living towers that overlook the tangled greenness of the forest. The center of the great Azoth mandala shifts from southern Africa to this very six-pointed redwood tree, from where its slowly moving rays caress Gaia's ancient surface as they go, blessing each being of rock, water, air, and biosphere as the rays slowly pass over them all again and again in an endless procession of blessing, transformation, and empowerment.

I sit quietly for an hour or so hoping to catch sight of deer, but none appear. Eventually, I climb down, give my thanks to my redwood Gaia place, and gradually make my way back toward our little cottage in the grounds of Schumacher College. By the time I've returned to Newground Plantation I've given up my quest for deer. Perhaps the walkers' dogs have scared them all away.

I saunter aimlessly through the trees and stop to admire the vibrant pale yellow of a small pan of fine clay on the forest floor, an oasis of beauty among these oftentimes gloomy conifers from far across the ocean. As my eyes trace the delicate outlines of fallen twigs and leaves on the yellow clay it takes me several long seconds to realize that I am looking at a few fresh dark roe deer dung pellets and the unmistakable prints of two deer hooves, all right in front of me. Here, at the end of this pilgrimage marking the end of writing this book, appears a subtle confirmation. Gaia Mercurius, that most subtle and difficult to discern of all alchemical beings, suddenly manifests in these hardly noticeable signs of deer, filling my heart with joy and profound meaning on my journey home.

A few days pass and I find myself in my little hut pondering this experience. Something bubbles up from the depths. An image wants to be born and I start to draw (fig. 17.1). I sketch Gaia as a globe with the rays of the Azoth mandala playing over her surface. Mercurius insists on coming into the image, so I clumsily trace a version of him (from Cartari, 1581) holding his caduceus and place him on top of the globe of Gaia. I remember that Mercurius is there at the start of the transformational work of alchemy in the form of a dragon, and so I draw a dragon heating Gaia up from below. Flames appear around the dragon and the image tells me it is complete.

Figure 17.1. Gaia Mercurius with Azoth mandala circulating the globe.

The image informs that me the entire universe is rooted in intrinsic instinctual energies. That's the Mercurius as dragon. The Mercurial dragon is the raw material of our Gaian consciousness, long forgotten in the Gaia-blindness of our humdrum lives in which we overvalue thinking and sensation and vastly undervalue feeling and intuition.

One of the Mercurial dragon's instinctive energies is a quest for the inexpressible meaning of why matter has formed itself into Gaia, into our animate Earth. The image shows the rays of the Azoth mandala sweeping over Gaia again and again, revealing that she also, like me, is engaged in her own transformational alchemical quest.

Mercurius standing on top of Gaia tells me that we humans are deeply implicated in Gaia's alchemical journey, which would not happen in quite the same way without us. He teaches me that one of the intertwining snakes of his caduceus represents science (thinking/sensing) and that the other is Imagination (feeling/intuiting). The two snakes give birth to wings atop the caduceus—the inner freedom of nondual Gaian awareness, which brings insight and healing in these troubled times.

Gaia Mercurius invites us to travel through his caduceus reconciling all opposites as we go until the wings engender our own symbiosis of science and Imagination—of alchemical Gaia—in which we taste the delicious enlivening freedom of being fully embedded in Gaia's sacred body. We live a life inspired by the sheer wonder of existing in such a miraculously living world, despite all the torments and sufferings that we must endure to a greater or lesser extent.

Figure 17.2 (p. 276) is a cognitive mapping that helps me reflect on how various apparent opposites of importance to me inform and enrich each other as they intertwine on their journey along the caduceus.

In the caduceus of Gaia Mercurius, the conflict between science and Imagination vanishes in these ways:

Science gives Imagination insights from complexity theory. This is the understanding that very small changes can give rise to intelligible but inherently unpredictable complex behaviors, even in simple classical systems of cause and effect. In exchange, Imagination gives science an understanding of synchronicity—of how certain events

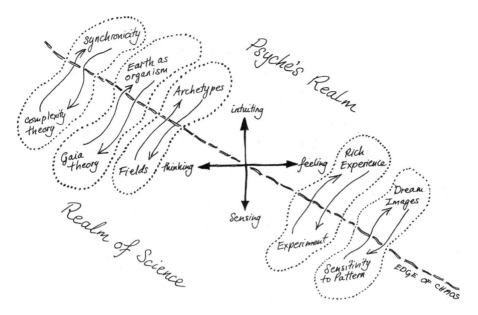

Figure 17.2. Mutually beneficial interactions between science and Imagination.
Drawn by Julia Ponsonby.

are connected acausally, through meaning. This is just as much of a connection as through standard cause and effect.

Science gifts Imagination with Gaia theory in its strictly scientific sense, and in exchange Imagination gives science the poetic insight of the animate Earth in which matter is alive with bright sparks of soul and spirit.

Science gives Imagination knowledge of how complex systems go through cycles of change described in the adaptive cycle model, and in return Imagination offers science the opportunity to cultivate inner transformative experiences within the Azoth mandala leading to lived experiences of Gaia Mercurius.

Science provides Imagination with a knowledge of physically measurable fields such as the electromagnetic and gravitational fields, while Imagination gives science a deep understanding of the archetypal intelligences lying hidden in the soul of nature that structure psyche at all levels.

Science teaches Imagination the value of carefully controlled experiments, while Imagination reminds science to remain open to the wonders of deep spontaneous experiences of Gaia's inscrutable creativity and wisdom.

Finally, science shows Imagination how mathematics can help us detect subtle patterns in nature. In return Imagination shows science how dream images reveal complex patterns of meaning active in the living psyche of ourselves and the world.

These are, of course, just my own particular selection of opposites, which you can modify or change as you like. The point is that that these two realms—science and Imagination, also known respectively as scientific and archetypal Gaia—feed each other from within each other just as the curling snakes of the caduceus entwine themselves along its central rod until they reach its zenith, whereupon wings appear symbolizing the freedom and knowledge we experience when all oppositions are reconciled in alchemical Gaia. This is the alchemical coagulation that is nondual Gaia, which is Gaia Mercurius, of which Jules Cashford writes:

> Mercurius . . . becomes himself the coincidence of opposites, the place where all the contradictions are resolved—the beginning, middle and end of the Great Work—personifying both the soul of the individual and the Soul of the World. Mercurius serves, then as a subtle counterpoint to Christ, not in the sense of replacing him, but rather in offering a radically new image of wholeness; a vision of Nature and Human Nature as one. . . . (This is the) awakening of the Soul of Nature—Nature and the Alchemist together as a new whole. (2018, 72–73)

Best now go to your Gaia place. Don't think too much, just allow yourself to enter Gaia's deeply sensorial world. See her colors, smell her earth, feel the leafy textures of her plants, hear her nature sounds. Lie on the ground if you will, gazing up at the sky, feeling yourself held safely upside down over the cosmos by great, turning Gaia behind your back.

Lie down on your back on the ground in your Gaia place or somewhere you can feel the earth.

Take a few deep breaths. Relax. You are lying safely on the ground.

Feel the weight of your body on the Earth behind you.

We are told that it is the force of gravity that holds you down against the Earth.

We'll let go of that idea and go back to a much earlier understanding.

For it's not gravity that holds you down, but love, the love that the great Earth, Gaia, feels for the matter in your body.

Experience this love that the Earth feels for the matter in your body, a love that holds you close, protects you, and prevents you from floating off to a certain death into outer space.

Open your eyes and look out into the vast depths of the universe and sense the great bulk of our mother planet at your back.

Feel her clasping you to her breast as she dangles you upside down over the vast cosmos below you.

Now look at what there is between you and the open sky. Leaves, branches, stems? Clouds, flying birds, shafts of rain? Feel them all as Gaia, as her breath, as her children. You are one of them too.

Now feel how Gaia, our animate Earth, curves away below you in all directions.

Here in England, I feel her curving away to the north toward Scandinavia, Siberia, and the Arctic regions with their vast carapaces of ice and snow. I spread out into that icy vastness.

Wherever you are, you too spread northward now in your journey over Gaia's surface until you reach the snowy Arctic. Let the quality of her Arctic region mingle with every cell in your body.

To my south I feel Gaia curving toward Europe: France, Portugal, Spain, Italy, Greece, the blue Mediterranean, the mountains of North Africa, the immensity of the Sahara, the great African tropical forests, and even farther south into the great open woodlands and bush country of southern Africa. I feel all this as I spread myself south, slowly becoming Gaia's body.

I meet the Southern Ocean with its white tipped black waves until I reach the huge snow and ice continent of Antarctica, the very tops of her highest mountains poking through kilometers of frosted whiteness.

You too journey south from where you are, traveling over Gaia's wondrous surface, amazed by what you experience of her animate body as you spread yourself southward.

Forests, grasslands, mountains, deserts, oceans?

Eventually you too arrive in the Deep South Land. I will meet you there at the very center of the great snow continent.

All this is my body. All this is your body.

Now to my east, behind my back, I feel my Gaian body extending out toward Western Europe widening out into Central Asia and Arabia. I feel the Himalayas reaching for the sky with great fingers of snow. I feel the entire Indian subcontinent as she once was, luxuriating in richly scented wild forests and jungles. Now I spread wavelike into the Tibetan plateau and into the great steppes of Mongolia, permeating the whole of Siberia until I reach Japan. Sensing the ancient wilderness of Australia and the lushness of New Zealand, I spread into the great vastness of the Pacific Ocean. I feel a peppering of coral islands like glowing jewels scattered in this great realm of water—sapphires, turquoise, and diamonds thrown down from on high.

All this is my body. All this is your body.

You too spread eastward from wherever you are perhaps into mountains, lakes and streams, oceans and jungles. In whichever realm you find yourself great Gaia nourishes every cell in your human body as you merge into her wild magnificence.

Now to the west where the bright sun tracks me right now, I feel the animate Earth reaching out behind my back to the very westernmost tip of England, to the nearby Isles of Scilly, and then to the hugeness of the Atlantic Ocean surging and rushing with wind and current, the sense of spreading widening out like a huge fungal mycelial net into the vast continents of North and South America, with the little sliver of Central America in between. I mingle with the great mountain chain that runs down my western flanks—with the Rockies, with the Andes. I feel my prairies, my forests, both temperate and tropical, my lakes, my rivers, my coasts and beaches, until I once again find myself spreading over the vast wildness of the Pacific Ocean.

You too spread westward from wherever your little human frame lies calmly on the ground, held safely upside down over the cosmos. You too spread west. Somewhere in those distant domains, shall we meet?

The whole Earth, all of great Gaia is here behind our backs. We are permeated by every atom and molecule of her being. We widen and deepen now in her scared presence. We feel her great continents, her mountain ranges, her oceans, her great cloaks of vegetation, and all her ecological communities stretching out into the great round immensity of her divine living body, which is our wider body—our sacred Gaia body.

After a long while, you feel something tugging you back toward your little human body lying gently on the ground, wherever you are.

Feel the weight of your body on this ground once again.

Feel yourself breathing. Feel your fingers, your toes.

Breathe in the living, healing immensity of the animate Earth, of great Gaia, as you feel yourself soundly and comfortably returned safely back in your little human body.

Now the seven-rayed star of the Azoth mandala appears, circling around your belly button both in the air above you and in the ground below you.

The turning wheel of the seven stars winds around you, giving you a sense of all the transformations and revolutions great Gaia has undergone since her tumultuous birth some 4600 million years ago. Savor whatever images come to you and feel whichever of her many qualities she offers you to perceive.

After a while, slowly sit up and slowly look around you. Are things different now? More richly alive than before, more animate, more full of an intangible sentience and purpose you want to work for?

No matter what you have experienced, when you are ready, stand up and return to our everyday two-legged world, now more deeply connected than before to the vast living being that is our wondrous animate Earth, our Gaia.

So now, at the end of our journey, once more we ask: What does it mean to live a Gaian alchemical life in tune with nondual Gaia, with Gaia Mercurius? Perhaps we should consider the words of Wei Po-Yang, the oldest Chinese alchemist we know of, from the second century BCE, describing the *chen-yen,* the "true and complete man, who is the beginning and the end of the work," who is, perhaps, the complete Gaia alchemist:

"He is and he is not. He resembles a vast pool of water, suddenly sinking and suddenly floating. He is a material substance in which are mixed the squareness, the roundness, the diameter, and the dimensions which restrain one another, having been in existence since before the beginning of the heavens and the earth; lordly, lordly high and revered. . . . Cessation of thought is desirable and worries are preposterous. The divine ch'i fills the quarters and it cannot be held back. Whoever retains it will prosper and he who loses it, will perish." (cited by Jung in his Collected Works volume 13, para 432)

The contemporary alchemical image on the next page (fig. 17.3), drawn for me by our son, Oscar, is a Western expression of all the events, inner and outer, that need to happen in order to take us into chen-yen, our complete personhood enmeshed in Gaia and the cosmos. Two crowns surround a central tower: the crown of Sol on the

Figure 17.3. The hermaphrodite child reveals the living Gaia. Drawn by Oscar Harding.

outside and the crown of Luna on the inside. The sun and moon (Sol and Luna) are the archetypes of all possible opposites. We have to learn how to walk through the doorways in these two crowns, which is often not an easy task. Then we enter the tower and encounter the fruitful darkness that further ferments and distills us. We reach the top of the tower where a hermaphroditic child shows us Gaia, the jewel of jewels, our Mother Earth held between the cosmic Sol and Luna.

At last, we realize that the Philosopher's Stone is none other than Gaia. Gaia is a planetary alchemical vessel—a *vas*—in which many kinds of consciousness are being brewed, our own and those of every other living being. We perceive Gaia as she truly is: alive, deeply intelligent, full of mysteriously benevolent meanings, purposes, and transformations to which we dedicate ourselves with all our heart and mind, with all our being.

Bibliography

Abram, D. 1997. *The Spell of the Sensuous.* New York: Vintage.

———. 2011. *Becoming Animal.* New York: Vintage.

Atmanspacher, H. and Fuchs, C. A. (eds.). 2014. *The Pauli-Jung Conjecture.* Exeter, U.K.: Imprint Academic.

Baillet, A. 1691. *La Vie de Monsieur Descartes.*

Baring, A. and J. Cashford. 1993. *The Myth of the Goddess.* Arkana, London: Penguin.

Barras, C. 2019. "Story of Most Murderous People of All Time Revealed in Ancient DNA." New Scientist online (March 27).

Betts, R. A. and Lenton, T. M. 2008. *Second Chances for Lucky Gaia: A Hypothesis of Sequential Selection.* Hadley Centre Technical Note 77.

Bortoft, H. 2012. *Taking Appearance Seriously.* Edinburgh: Floris Books.

Bruno. G. (1584) 2010. *Cause, Principle and Unity and Essays on Magic.* Cambridge, U.K.: Cambridge University Press.

Buhner, S. H. 2004. *The Secret Teachings of Plants.* Rochester, Vt.: Bear and Co.

Campbell, J. (1959) 2011. *Primitive Mythology.* London: Souvenir Press.

Cartari, V. 1581. *Les Images de dieux des anciens.* Lyons.

Carter, R., Prince, S. 1981. "Epidemic Models Used to Explain Biogeographical Distribution Limits." *Nature* 293, 644–645.

Cashford, J. 2010. *GAIA: From Story of Origin to Universe Story. From Goddess to Symbol.* Ilford: Kingfisher Art Productions

———. 2014. *GAIA: From Story of Origin to Universe Story. From Goddess to Symbol.* Hampstead: Earth Jurisprudence Series, Gaia Foundation Press.

———. 2016. *Mythos and Logos.* Ilford: Kingfisher Art Productions.

———. 2018. *From Toth to Mercurius.* Ilford: Kingfisher Art Productions.

Corbin, H. 1998. *Alone with the Alone*. Princeton, N.J.: Princeton University Press.

David, J. 2021. *A Brief History of God*. London: Austin Macaulay.

Darwin, C. (1859) 2019. *The Origin of Species*. London: East India Publishing Company.

———. (1871) 2015. *The Descent of Man and On Selection in Relation to Sex*. Palala Press.

Descartes, R. (1641) 2008. *Meditations on First Philosophy*. Oxford: Oxford University Press.

Doolittle, W. F. 1981. "Is Nature Really Motherly?" *Coevolution Quarterly*.

———. 2014. "Natural Selection through Survival Alone, and the Possibility of Gaia." *Biol. Philos.*, 29: 415–423.

Edinger, E. 1994a. *The Anatomy of the Psyche*. Chicago: Open Court.

———. 1994b. *The Mystery of the Coniunctio, Alchemical Image of Individuation*. Toronto: Inner City Books.

Eliade, M. 1964. *Shamanism: Archaic Techniques of Ecstasy*. London: Arkana.

Fellows, A. 2019. *Gaia, Psyche and Deep Ecology*. London: Routledge.

Fideler, D. 2014. *Restoring the Soul of the World*. Rochester, Vt.: Inner Traditions.

Figulus, B. 1608. *Paradisus aureolus hermeticus: fluens nectare et ambrosia*, Frankfurt: W. Richter.

Galileo, G. (1623) 2017. *Il Saggiatore. (in Italian)* Scotts Valley, Calif.: Create Space Independent Publishing.

Gimbutas, M. (2001) 2011. *The Living Goddess*. Berkeley, Calif.: The University of California Press.

Goethe, J. W. von. (1790) 2009. *The Metamorphoses of Plants*. Cambridge, Mass.: MIT Press.

Grayling, A. C. 2005. *Descartes*. London: Walker Books.

Hauck, D. W. 1999. *The Emerald Tablet*. London: Penguin Compass.

Harding, Stephan. 1999. "Food Web Complexity Enhances Community Stability and Climate Regulation in a Geophysiological Model." *Tellus* 51B: 815–829.

———. 2009. *Animate Earth*. Cambridge, U.K.: Green Books, 2nd ed.

———, ed. 2011. *Grow Small, Think Beautiful. Ideas for a Sustainable World from Schumacher College*. Edinburgh: Floris Books.

Harding, S. P. and Lovelock, J. E. 1996. "Exploiter-Mediated Coexistence and Frequency Dependent Selection in a Numerical Model of Biodiversity." *Journal of Theoretical Biology* 182: 109–116.

Hesiod. (circa 700 BCE) 2008. *The Theogony and Works and Days.* Oxford: Oxford World's Classics.

Hillman, J. 2014. *Alchemical Psychology.* New York: Spring Publications.

Holdrege, C. 2013. *Thinking Like a Plant.* Herndon Va.: Lindisfarne Books.

Hopkins, G. M. (1918) 1970. *The Poems of Gerard Manley Hopkins.* (Gardener W. F. and MacKenzie N. H. (eds) Oxford: Oxford University Press.

Humboldt, A., von. 1845. *Cosmos.*

Jung, C. G. (1944) 1981. *Psychology and Alchemy.* Collected Works vol. 12. R. F. C. Hull (translator) London: Routledge and Keegan Paul.

———. (1951) 1972. *The Structure and Dynamics of the Psyche.* Collected Works vol. 8. R. F. C. Hull (translator) London: Routledge and Keegan Paul.

———. (1951) 1981. *Alchemical Studies.* Collected Works vol. 13. R. F. C. Hull (translator) London: Routledge and Keegan Paul.

———. (1956) 1974. *Mysterium Coniunctionis.* Collected Works vol. 14. R. F. C. Hull (translator) London: Routledge and Keegan Paul.

———. (1959) 1981. *The Archetypes and the Collective Unconscious.* Collected Works vol. 9. R. F. C. Hull (translator) London: Routledge and Keegan Paul.

———. (1983) *Psychology of the Transference.* London: Routledge and Keegan Paul.

Kiehl, J. T. 2016. *Facing Climate Change.* New York: Columbia University Press.

———. 2020. "The Mandala as Portal to Healing." *ARAS Connections* Issue 2.

Kimmerer, R. W. 2013. *Braiding Sweet Grass,* London: Penguin Books.

Lenton, T. and Watson, A. J. 2011. *Revolutions That Made the Earth.* Oxford: Oxford University Press.

Lovelock, J. E. and Watson, A. J. 1983. "Biological Homeostasis of the Global Environment: The Parable Daisyworld." *Tellus* 35 (4).

Lovelock, J. E. 1989. "Geophysiology, the Science of Gaia." *Reviews of Geophysics* 17: 11, pages 215–222. May.

———. *Gaia. The Practical Science of Planetary Medicine.* London: Gaia Books.

———. 1995. *The Ages of Gaia.* Oxford: Oxford University Press.

———. 2000. *Homage to Gaia.* Oxford: Oxford University Press.

Makarieva, A. and Gorshkov, V. 2010. "The Biotic Pump: Condensation, Atmospheric Dynamics and Climate." *International Journal of Water.* 5 (4): 365–385.

Maier, M. 1618. *Atalanta Fugiens.*

McGilchrist, I. 2019. *The Master and His Emissary.* London: Yale University Press.

Milarepa. 1989. *The Hundred Thousand Songs of Milarepa.* Chang G. C. C. (translator). Boulder Colo.: Shambhala.

Miller, A. I. 2010. *137: Jung, Pauli, and the Pursuit of a Scientific Obsession.* New York: Norton.

Muir, J. 2019. *The Complete Works of John Muir.* Prague: Madison & Adams Press. Kindle edition.

Mylius, D. 1618. *Opus Medico-Chymicum.*

Naess, A. 1989. *Ecology, Community and Lifestyle.* Cambridge, U.K.: Cambridge University Press.

———. 2016. *Ecology of Wisdom.* London: Penguin Classics.

Naess, A. and Haukeland, P. I. 2008. *Life's Philosophy.* Athens, Ga.: Georgia University Press.

Newman, W. 2018. *Newton the Alchemist.* Princeton, N.J.: Princeton University Press.

Nicholson, A. E. et.al. 2018. "Gaian Bottlenecks and Planetary Habitability Maintained by Evolving Model Biospheres: The ExoGaia Model." *Monthly Notices of the Royal Astronomical Society,* Volume 477, Issue 1, June.

Nicholson, A. E. et.al. 2018. "Alternative Mechanisms for Gaia." *Journal of Theoretical Biology* 457: 249–257.

Phillips, A. 2008. *Holistic Education: Learning from Schumacher College.* Cambridge, U.K.: Green Books.

Reusner. 1588. *Pandora.*

Rosarium Philosophorum Frankfurt, 1550.

Roob, A. (ed.) 2019. *The Hermetic Museum: Alchemy and Mysticism.* Milan: Taschen.

Sabini, M. 2008. *The Earth Has a Soul: C. G. Jung on Nature, Technology & Modern Life.* Berkeley, Calif.: North Atlantic Books.

Saunders, P. et.al. 1998. "Integral Rein Control in Physiology." *Journal of Theoretical Biology* 194, 163–173.

Sheldrake, M. 2020. *Entangled Life: How Fungi Make Our Worlds, Change Our Minds and Shape Our Futures.* London: Bodley Head.

Schroeder, H. et.al. 2019. "Unravelling Ancestry, Kinship, and Violence in a Late Neolithic Mass Grave." *PNAS* May 28, 2019, 116 (22): 10705–10710.

Stevens, A. 1993. *The Two Million Year Old Self.* College Station, Tex.: Texas A&M University Press.

————. 1994. *Jung, A Very Short Introduction*. Oxford: Oxford University Press.

Tagore, R. 1973. "Fruit Gathering." In: *Collected Poems and Plays of Rabindranath Tagore*. New York: Macmillan.

Valentine, B. 1659. *L'Azoth des Philosophes*.

van der Poste, L. 1965. *The Heart of the Hunter*. London: Penguin.

Vernadsky, I. 1998. *The Biosphere*. Göttingen, Germany: Copernicus.

Von Franz, M. L. (1974) 1991. *Dreams*. Boulder, Colo.: Shambhala.

————. (1959) 1980. *Alchemy*. Toronto: Inner City Books.

Walker, B. and Salt, D. 2006. *Resilience Thinking*. Washington, D.C.: Island Press.

Watts, J. 2019. "Human Society under Urgent Threat from Loss of Earth's Natural Life." Guardian website. (May 6).

Wei Po-Yang. 1932. *Ts'an T'ung Ch'i*. Wu, L. and Tenny, L. D. (translators). Isis.

Yeats, W. B. 1961. *Essays and Introductions*. London: Macmillan.

Young, M. 1996. *The Elmhirsts of Dartington*. Dartington, U.K.: Dartington Hall Trust.

Index

Page numbers in *italics* refer to illustrations.

symbiosis, 241
and innovation, 7
synchronicity, 107, 275–76

Tabula Smaragdina, 110–16, *110, 111,*
246
and Azoth mandala, 119
meditation on, 113–15
and Psyche-Gaia conjecture, 110–12,
111
Tagore, Rabindranath, 6
on the tree of life, 268
Terra, in Azoth mandala, 139
thinking, 132
defined, 17
and feeling, 106–7
versus Imagination, 63
Thirty Years War, 35
Tiamat, 192
tickling for trout, 76–77
time, 169–70
merging with space, 108
nature of, 190–91
tin, and alchemical tree, 262
tree
archetypal image of, 261
cutting down a, 265–66
as instrument of transformation,
261
journey to the alchemical tree, 261–63
seeing oneself as a, 258
tree of life, Rabindranath Tagore poem
about, 268

unconscious, 18–23. *See also* collective
unconscious

unus mundus, 59–85, *60, 108,* 111
evidence for, 107–8
and Philosopher's Stone, 115

Valentine, Basil, 31, 144
Azoth mandala of, 118
van der Post, Laurens, 70
Vernadsky, Vladimir, 108–9
Visita, in Azoth mandala, 138
VITRIOL, 138
volcanos, 182
von Franz, Marie-Louise
imagined conversation with
Descartes, 52–57
on individuated state, 228–29

Walker, Brian
adaptive cycle of, 165–68, *166*
on omega phase, 178
warrior horsemen, 41
water, on Gaia, 195–96
water-splitting complex, 202, 205, *205,*
215
Watson, A. J., 217–18, 220
Watts, Jonathan, on ecological crisis, 37
Wei Po-Yang, on chen-yen, 281
wisdom, what it is for Gaia, 163–64
words, in Azoth mandala, 138–40
wounds, inner, 267
Wulf, Andrea, 168

Yahweh, 41–42
Yeats, W. B., 63
yes and no (Descartes's dream), 47

Zeus, 67, 68–70